"As you read and learn more about Christ, your relationship with Him can be strengthened. What a blessing to better understand, through *Cultivated in Christ*, how the love of God can guide you through love through life."

—**GANEL-LYN CONDIE**, host of *Real Talk CFM* and best-selling author of *The Stewardship Principle: Reframing Your Life*

CULTIVATED *in* CHRIST

SIGNIFICANT GROWTH & REWARDS COME *as we* REACH UPWARD

CULTIVATED *in* CHRIST

SIGNIFICANT GROWTH & REWARDS COME *as we* REACH UPWARD

THOMAS HOLTON

CFI
An imprint of Cedar Fort, Inc.
Springville, Utah

ISBN 13: 978-1-4621-4357-3

Published by CFI, an imprint of Cedar Fort, Inc.
2373 W. 700 S., Suite 100, Springville, UT 84663
Distributed by Cedar Fort, Inc., www.cedarfort.com

Library of Congress Control Number: 2022916000

Cover design by Shawnda T. Craig

Edited and typeset by Valene Wood

Printed in the United States of America

10 9 8 7 6 5 4 3 2 1

Printed on acid-free paper

I dedicate this book with love to my wife Veronica, my son Thomas, my mother Ella, my brothers Michael and Peter, my late mission president Chappy Winstanley, and all my family and friends. I am especially grateful to Veronica and Thomas for providing valuable recommendations, and for their encouragement, support, and ongoing love in the special garden that is family.

I express my sincere gratitude to all at Cedar Fort for their professionalism, optimism, hard work, and energy in bringing this project to fruition.

Other books by Thomas Holton

Alive in Christ

Contents

Introduction

DEAR READER, THIS BOOK IS ABOUT YOU. IT IS ALSO ABOUT THE LORD Jesus Christ. I have come to know that Christ loves you with a deep, abiding love. This love transcends space and time, traverses continents, surmounts obstacles, penetrates hearts, and is at the root of majestic opportunities that lie before you. This book is about what our Lord sees in you with respect to your past, present, and future. He sees you in a remarkable way. He knows that if you were not alive, this universe would be poorer for it. From His vantage point, you are worth His time, His notice, His special attention, His marvelous Atonement. He lives to cultivate your deepest hopes, to bring to fruition your noblest longings, to make possible your greatest joy. This is the Christ I know and love. What follows represents my profound wish that you might sense His marvelous concern and regard for you.

Imagine if certain things that did happen in this world had never occurred, such as:

What if Eve decided not to partake of the fruit or if Adam decided that he would stay in the Garden after Eve already partook of the fruit?

What if Jesus of Nazareth had no interest in the scriptures as a child?

What if Joseph Smith had not gone in prayer to the grove of faith?

These individuals would not have fulfilled their destinies if they had not cultivated their spiritual talents. In addition, the rest of us would have lost out in deeply significant ways. Thankfully, these children of God did incline themselves toward truth and we are blessed in ways that are of earthly and eternal importance.

The foregoing examples serve to illustrate wondrous truths. We each come to this life with a divine nature and destiny. We each come with a purpose. We each come with a spiritual gift and a special talent. That destiny, that purpose, and those gifts will always bless us and others as we come to know, develop, and share them. While the examples I have cited are extraordinary ones, I believe that the principle applies to each person. We do not have to be well known or greatly talented to come to know our mortal and eternal purpose for being. Of course, we will each struggle with challenges before we become masters of the craft of living well. However, with a sense of spiritual purpose and resolve, we can bring to fruition the special spark of divine fire that is uniquely ours. I want to shed light on the great truth that we are each intended for great and glorious things. The Lord's perspective can ignite in us a powerful vision of what we are truly capable of as literal spirit children of the Supreme Being.

What is our Father's love for His Only Begotten Son Jesus Christ? The revelations teach that our Father in heaven loved His Son, "who was in the bosom of the Father" (Doctrine & Covenants 76:25). I have been indelibly impressed with deep and tender feelings by this powerful truth. Christ is an extremely lovable son. In fact, the Father introduces His special Son using the descriptor "beloved" (see Joseph Smith History 1). It is not difficult for me to see that the Father has great affection and regard for His lovely son! The Son likewise loves our Father. The Father is easy to love! This mutual love is beautiful to them. Their love for each other is deep, heartfelt, sincere, lasting, and far-reaching.

When the Savior gave us the two great commandments, He was not preaching a sermon that He did not live. He was sharing His deep thoughts and personal feelings on His binding love for His Father. His love for the Father, and for us, was clearly with all His "heart . . . might, mind, and strength" (Doctrine & Covenants 59:5). This was doctrine that He practiced. This was counsel that He always followed. This was personal knowledge that He possessed. This was unending relational love between two divine eternal beings. This is a true love that blesses them both!

Of course, the Father and the Son also have much love to share with us—their children. Their love extends infinitely. Modern revelation teaches that their love for us has been displayed in real terms—"And the *great* and *wonderful love* made *manifest* by the *Father and the Son* in the coming of the Redeemer into the world" (Doctrine & Covenants 138:3, emphasis added). Hence, the love of the Father and the Son as revealed in the Messiah's coming into this world was both out of the ordinary and evidenced in a specific way. It was shown in covenant action. It was an overarching love with rescuing redemption at its core.

I love the hymn "God Loved Us So He Sent His Son" (*Hymns* no. 187). Think on that instructive doctrine. What did the Father do to show us how deeply He loves us? He sent His eldest Son to the rest of the family! This was His firstborn in the spirit, His well-beloved, His perfectly obedient offspring, His choice and chosen child. This was the Father's precious gift to all the world. This was a surpassingly wonderful gesture, a magnanimous proffer, a token of amazing goodness. This was a treasure beyond all worldly riches. I testify that the Son fulfilled His mission superbly well. He honored the Father with total devotion and complete loyalty. How the Father rejoiced in the goodness of His Son! Their demonstration of holiness is beyond doubt to me. I have felt of their goodness. I have known of their love. I have sensed of their power. Indeed, my cup runneth over!

To be loved by another human is marvelous. When I have felt love from others, it has been like a warm blanket of acceptance. It has inspired my heart. It has touched me deeply. It is so empowering and encouraging; soft and gentle; strong and forceful. What does that tell us about the love of the Father and the Son for each of us? It shows us that this perfect love causes us to be amazed beyond what human love can engender. It is a divine love which is superb. There is no greater love than that possessed by God, for "God *is* love" (1 John 4:8, emphasis added), meaning He is the incarnate and tangible embodiment of true love. The fact that both the Father and Son love us should cause us to ponder. We might reflect on whether we have felt of this affection personally and then consider its meaning and significance. This is love which overwhelms, astonishes, comforts, and embraces me. It causes my soul to soar. It transforms me into someone better. I love my Father in Heaven and love to hear Him speaking to me. I love my Savior and rejoice to feel of His love.

In my first book, *Alive in Christ*, I focused on the overarching goodness of our Lord and Savior. I wrote about the amazing nature of the new bounteous life He offers to each of us. I now focus on what happens to us individually as we accept the offer of the Lord to experience abundance of life through Him. I will paint a picture of what your life (and mine) looks like through the eyes of God and His beloved Son, Jesus Christ. I will discuss in depth how God sees us, so we can see ourselves anew. I will use symbolic representations that are powerful in helping us to see more clearly from the bright viewpoint of their visionary perspectives. I hope that this will prove to be a source of unending inspiration, wonder, amazement, encouragement, and profound comfort to each of us all the days of our lives.

What is this great love that Christ has for us? I believe it is the kind and type of love He witnessed in His Father. It is a mighty love that Jehovah had for us in premortality, continued to have for us in mortality, and still has as a resurrected being. Of course, this love is pure, strong, constant, and powerful (See Moroni 7:48). It is not simply generalized but specific to each person and able to include all people. The Savior said to John the Apostle "John, *my beloved*, what desirest thou?" (Doctrine & Covenants 7:1, emphasis added). The Savior loved John and told him so directly. He was unafraid to love another man and to show him profound brotherly regard. What impact do you think such a declaration had upon John? No doubt it stirred his soul to devotion. This was reciprocated affection!

There are so many examples of this spoken love that our Savior feels for others:

He *"so loved the world that he gave his own life"* (Doctrine & Covenants 34:1–3)

He said to those He chastened—*"I have loved you"* (Doctrine & Covenants 95:1)

He has *"a great love for the children of Jacob"* (Doctrine & Covenants 109:61)

Of Hyrum Smith—"I, *the Lord, love him because of the integrity of his heart*, and because he *loveth that which is right* before me" (Doctrine & Covenants 124:15, emphasis added)

Of George Miller—*"for the love which he has to my testimony I, the Lord, love him"* (Doctrine & Covenants 124:20)

Of Isaac Galland—*"I, the Lord, love him for the work he hath done"* (Doctrine & Covenants 124:78)

These verses evidence the loving character of the Savior. Our Lord loves both those who are well known and those whose names and lives are only known to a modest few. He calls us by name because He knows and remembers our name. He gave His life so that you and I might know how He values us. This display of love is to all humanity one by one. He chastens those He loves, so when we feel chastened, we can remember that such correction comes from a loving God. He loves with a great love the scattered covenant people and seeks to bring them home to Him. He loves those who love doing the right thing because it is right! He loves those who love to bear testimony of Him. He loves those who are invested in His work. Do you think you are excluded from that list of people He loves? Surely not. His love includes you and everyone you know. It includes all. It includes those who do not yet love themselves.

The day will come, if we are faithful to Him, when we will recount our thankfulness to Him for His perfect love. We will mention His *"goodness"* and *"loving kindness, forever and ever."* Indeed, in His loving pity, He saves, redeems, bears, and carries us (Doctrine & Covenants 133:52–53). What will we feel and say on that day? We will openly talk about His regard, and His eternal mercy. We will remember that He walked the thorny path with us; that He is intimately acquainted with our sorrows, heartbreak, and pain. We will talk about when He visited, comforted, listened to, acknowledged, and strengthened us. We will speak about how we felt of His charity and knew of His concern. We will convey that we sensed His empathy—even when no one else knew what we felt, He did. We will testify that He lifted us from being distraught, that He supported us in our darkest hours and that we felt His bolstering influence when we were faint and weary on the way.

1

Beckoned by Our Loving Lord

I AM DEEPLY GRATEFUL THAT OUR MERCIFUL LORD INVITES US WITH deep longing to come to Him so that we might eat "the *fruit of the tree of life*" and "*eat and drink* of the *bread and the waters of life* freely" (Alma 5:33–34, emphasis added). God is redemptively reaching out to each one of us. He is pleading with us with outstretched arms to repent and be made new. Our Savior is offering us blessings beyond compare. He wants to give us living bread, living water, and eternal joys. This promise goes to all willing to receive His word. When Lehi related his visionary dream of the tree of life, he said he saw *"a man, and he was dressed in a white robe"* who *"bade me follow him"* (1 Nephi 8:5–6). This heavenly messenger interacts like our Savior!

Lehi accepted this invitation to follow. However, this led him to an unknown place and through dark territory. After Lehi traveled for *"many hours in darkness,"* he prayed to God according to the *"multitude of his tender mercies"* (1 Nephi 8:8). God answered this sincere request affirmatively. He blessed Lehi not only with comfort and light, but also tremendous happiness, love, and joy for him and his loved ones. The fruit of the tree was *"desirable to make one happy," "most sweet," "exceedingly white,"* and the eating of it filled Lehi with *"exceedingly great joy"* (1 Nephi 8:10–12).

When Lehi experienced this rich outpouring of joy from God, he eagerly sought for his wife and children to receive the same blessings.

Notice that Lehi had to intentionally search for his family (1 Nephi 8:13–17). Sariah, Sam, and Nephi were in a state of confusion. They did not know which way to go and needed guidance. Seeing their need, Lehi motioned to them. He signalled to them to catch their attention. He spoke out loud and instructed them to come to him and partake of joy at the tree of joy. They followed his word and were blessed with joy. Lehi was a beckoning prophet, an inviting servant, a messenger of mercy. As he had been granted light and love, he offered the same opportunity to his family. He encouraged others to come to the source of salvation. He also wanted Laman and Lemuel to come to the tree. He searched for and saw them, and invited them to come, but they would not.

After Lehi awoke from his dream, he did not forget the lessons he learned. His love was deepened, his concern awakened, and his understanding broadened. Lehi was worried for his children. He implored them to seek the Lord of life! (1 Nephi 8:36–38). I love this because I know what it is to feel tender love and regard for a child. He showed loving interest in Laman and Lemuel and wanted them to discover divine mercy. He therefore preached and prophesied to them. His teaching was motivated by true concern! Rather than accepting his dream as the final word, he determined to continue to try to reach them. Impressively, he bade them to be obedient. He put into practice what he saw himself previously doing in his dream! We can do likewise. When the Lord reveals the future to us in inspiring ways, we can turn that inspired direction into reality. We can act in love toward those our concern reaches. Our feelings and faith may move them to come to God. This is especially pertinent when our loved ones are involved.

The Meaning of the Tree of Life

Nephi prayed to see the interpretation of his Father's vision and saw a similar vision of his own! He also was guided by heavenly messengers. He asked an angel what the interpretation of the tree of life was. Then the angel showed him a vision of the mortal mother of the Son of God and the birth of the Savior into the world (1 Nephi 11:18–23). I approach these beautiful concepts reverently. Notice that the tree of life signifies the love of God. This love does not remain within the heart of God only. Rather it sheds itself far outward into the hearts of God's children on earth. It is key to note that this divine love is manifest in a very specific way. It is revealed through the condescension of the Father to bring a very special child into the world. It is shown in Jehovah's willingness to be born as the Son of the Highest on a fallen temporal earth, to a mortal woman. It is known by a woman who is lifted by the power of the Holy Ghost to experience sublime and sacred destiny. A holy human virgin becomes the bearing vessel for God's tangible gift to the entire world.

This tree of life is therefore a representation of the light-filled love of both the Father and the Son as revealed in the coming of the holy Son into this world to save all from sin and death. This active and evidenced love is the most wanted of all things and the most joyful when experienced. Thus, the love of God lodges within our souls through the infinite and eternal Atonement of Christ. It finds its most profound and ultimate fulfilment in eternal life—as the children of men are raised to dwell everlastingly in the literal love-filled presence of God. This is deep-seated, majestic, and transformative love that must be felt personally to be comprehended.

In speaking of the birth of our Lord, consider this beautiful Christmas Carol, based on Isaiah 11:1–10:

Lo, how a rose e'er blooming,
From tender stem hath sprung.
Of Jesse's lineage coming,
As men of old have sung;
It came, a flow'ret bright,
Amid the cold of winter,
When half spent was the night.

Isaiah 'twas foretold it,
The Rose I have in mind,
With Mary we behold it,
The virgin mother kind;
To show God's love aright,
She bore to men a Savior,
When half spent was the night.

O Flower, whose fragrance tender
With sweetness fills the air,
Dispel with glorious splendour
The darkness everywhere;
True man, yet very God,
From Sin and death now save us,
And share our every load.

"Lo, How a Rose E'er Blooming" was written as a translation of the German words into English by Doctor Theodore Baker in 1894.

The message is that Christ is the rose that blooms from the stem of Jesse. This righteous Rose was born on a cold, dark night to show that God's love is a warm light in the winter of our souls. As roses have thorns, so His ministry would be both painful and beautiful. This flower would bring to the world a sweet tenderness. This dual person, being both man and God, would shine His light upon all humanity. He would rescue all from the otherwise insurmountable barriers of sin and death between us and God. What a tender telling in words of the visionary prophecy of Isaiah about the mortal birth of the Messiah!

I am grateful to know that the rod of iron—the word of God—leads to the tree. Hence:

The word of God leads us to the life of God.
The law of God leads us to the love of God.
The prophet of God points us to the Son of God.
The message of God brings us to the fruitful blessings of God.
The scriptures of God draw us to the family of God.
The messenger of God (the Holy Ghost) guides us to the literal presence of the Almighty God and His perfect Son.

In contrast to this, the mockers in the great and spacious building, the filthy waters, the mists of darkness, the strange roads—all these lead us away from the living love of God to a condition of spiritual death. Disobedience to the voice of God takes us away from all the things that should be the most valuable to us—life, love, blessings, family, God, and His Son. Thankfully, the path to the tree of life leads all those who pursue it to the same destination. It is a symbol of the covenant path which always leads to the Lord of Life!

Nephi teaches us that the Book of Mormon would *"make known to all kindreds, tongues, and people, that the Lamb of God is the Son of the Eternal Father"* (1 Nephi 13:40). Thus, it is made known to all the world—to all the lost and dispersed children of God—that Christ is truly the Lamb of the Father, the Son of the Almighty, the seed of the Highest. It is He that brings men back from the brink. He gathers them into the covenant of the eternal family. We are rescued from death through the Lamb slain in our place. In His death, we find life.

Nephi further tells us that the Holy Spirit makes Gentiles beautiful by bringing them into the covenant (1 Nephi 13:15). As the fruit of the tree of life is beautiful, so persons touched by God's influence come to radiate light, goodness, and loveliness. There is a renewing effect that comes upon those who enter an abiding covenant relationship with God. The Gentiles would prosper in the promised land through faithfulness to God's covenant. To prosper in a land of inheritance is to enter the great promised land of Zion on earth—and the eternal promised land of celestial heaven in the eternities. That is a land of promise that we never have to leave!

Nor is it just the Gentiles that are to be brought to salvation. As the house was Israel was like an olive tree, so the family of Lehi was a branch broken from that tree (1 Nephi 15:12). Nephi observed that his father Lehi spoke of the seed of the family of Israel. He specifically pointed to the covenantal promises to Father Abraham relating to his children blessing the entire world with the gospel in the last days being fulfilled (1 Nephi 15:18). Hence, the seed of Manasseh was to be remembered and restored to covenant Israel in the latter days. The broken off branch was to be reconnected to the living olive tree. Indeed, the house of Israel—the children of Jacob—would offer covenant salvation to every family that would ever live on this earth. The house (tree or family) of Israel, was to be unified in righteous covenant connection once again. This was to happen through the covenant redemption performed by Christ in a garden of olive trees and on the cross (tree) of calvary. This everlasting covenant was to be made newly available in the last days and brought to full fruition. It would not be broken, wasted, destroyed, or left incomplete. The tree was not to be one of death or dissolution. Rather, it was to be a living tree. Nephi explained to his brothers that the tree of Lehi's dream was a "representation of the tree of life" (1 Nephi 15:21–22). Family life originates with God!

After explaining these mighty things to his brothers and to us, Nephi explains that he was deeply interested in the salvation of others. He was a loving beckoner, an articulate inviter, a consistent preacher. This he did with great conscientiousness and capacity—"with all the energies of my soul, and with all the faculty which I possessed" (1 Nephi 15:25, emphasis added).

Nephi explained that the fruit of the tree represented eternal life and was "most precious and most desirable above all other fruits; yea, and it is the greatest of all the gifts of God" (1 Nephi 15:36, emphasis added). The tree of life is the great symbol of the Father and the Son. It is the tree of love. It is the unified family of God in time and eternity. To experience this divine eternal family love and life is the greatest blessing we can ever aspire to. We should want nothing more. There is no greater treasure in time and eternity than to be part of the exalted intergenerational family of God.

We can therefore escape all evil only through divine goodness and loving kindness. The loving joy of God protects us from self-imposed tragedy. There is a marked difference between partaking of the exceedingly great joy that follows obedience (1 Nephi 8:12) and the spiritual rebellion which will cause us to be lost (1 Nephi 8:23, 32), ashamed (1 Nephi 8:27), fallen away (1 Nephi 8:28, 34), drowned (1 Nephi 8:32), to lose the opportunity to partake of the fruit (1 Nephi 8:35), and be cast off from the presence of the Lord (1 Nephi 8:36).

This message is elsewhere in scripture. The righteous who seek salvation in the Savior are like unto "a tree planted by the rivers of water, that bringeth forth his fruit in his season; his leaf also shall not wither" (Psalms 1:3). Also, I love the Messianic Psalm of King David:

> THE LORD *is my shepherd*; I shall not want.
>
> *He maketh me* to lie down in green pastures: he *leadeth me* beside the still waters.
>
> He *restoreth my soul*: he *leadeth me* in the paths of righteousness for his name's sake.

> Yea, though I walk through the valley of the shadow of death, I will fear no evil: for *thou art with me*; thy rod and thy staff they *comfort me*.
>
> Thou *preparest a table* before me in the presence of mine enemies: *thou anointest my head* with oil; my cup runneth over.
>
> Surely *goodness and mercy shall follow me* all the days of my life: and I will dwell in the *house* of the Lord for ever. (Psalms 23:1–6, emphasis added)

To me, these verses reflect the vision of the tree of life. I imagine in my mind's eye that David is a traveler in that vision setting. It is as if Christ is standing beside the tree of life, inviting David to come to the tree. David is familiar with the green grasslands of nourishment and the still waters of peace, where he knows refreshment and renewal. He has walked on the covenant path. However, he also knows the lowlands of dark shadows, the mist of darkness. He knows what it is to have enemies who mock him from the great and spacious building. He knows fear, danger, and dread. He also knows what it is to have the Lord lead him and be with him. He has experienced the comfort of holding to the rod of the word of God and the power of God's mighty assistance. He knows firsthand of the food and water that come from a divine source. He also rejoices in the good mercy of God to him. Indeed, he talks of the oil of anointing and the house of ordinances and covenants. This clearly refers to the House of Holiness—the temple of our God.

I love the reality that God's accompaniment is displayed in terms of natural abundance from the throne of Grace. I regard this testimony from David as being like that given by Lehi and Nephi. We are all in this mortal mist of darkness sometimes. We are journeying through a treacherous lone and dreary world, with wolves at our heels. There is darkness and temptation around us. There are snares and pitfalls before us. However, God has foreseen our difficulty and has prepared a course for us to follow. He has given many signs of His refreshing, guiding, warning, and supporting hand along the way. Eventually, if we follow the path of uprightness, we will be able to come out of this trail of tears into a far better land of promise.

God discerns our difficulty and sees us as someone worth helping and saving. The purpose of this sojourn is not for God to trick us or derail us—it is to teach us by experience of the profound difference between good and evil, so that we may choose the good. This good is God's greatest good.

2

A Good Beginning

Let us now consider the inspiring encounter between the premortal Jehovah and the prophet Moses (Moses 1). This is an illuminating revelation because it helps us to see both God and His servant in their true light. God calls Moses by name. God loves conducting personal one-to-one interviews with His children! He tells him the beautiful truth that he is of divine parentage and lineage. Speaking in the stead of the Father, Jehovah is referring to Moses as a spirit son of God. Moses is also told he is in the similitude—meaning image and likeness—of the Only Begotten. That is to say that Moses and Jehovah are similar. This is powerful because it shows that men can be like God! Moses is like unto the Messiah. Moses has a measure of grace and truth. God calls him a son of God living in a mortal world. God paints a picture for him by showing this son a special and remarkable vision. Moses gets to see this world, this earth, from the divine vantage point. God reveals His children to Moses. This is spectacularly new and impressive to the prophet. This revelation is wonderfully awe inspiring. God is in the business of surprising us! Moses was transfixed on what he was experiencing because this was a divine engagement of epic proportions.

God revealed to Moses that he was known to, and seen by, Him. His true nature and identity were apparent to God. His purpose and mission were part of a divine design! Moses also gets to see what God focuses on—His beloved Son, and all the other spirit children created by God, pertaining to this earth. God is an attention-paying being. He sees and knows His children. This was a pivotal revelation to Moses, as he was to be a type of the Messiah who would yet deliver all people. Moses was to teach the Israelites that salvation comes through the blood of the Lamb (Exodus 12:5–7). He was to set the people free from Egyptian bondage. Moses would provide a model for living for millions of people as the great lawgiver of Israel. So much of our legal and moral inheritance is based on the Ten Commandments. As a chosen son of Levi, Moses was of the seed of Abraham. He brought his people out of Egypt (the world) toward the promised land of Canaan. This was a necessary part of God's design in bringing His people to a holy place on the earth (a great symbol of the ultimate Holy Place in heaven). As he delivered Israel from the bondage of Egypt, so Christ would deliver those who looked to Him, from temporal and spiritual death (Alma 33:19–20, Helaman 8:14–15).

God sees the divinity within us, as He placed it there! He knows our capacity for goodness and our mission of greatness. He notices when we strive to develop further. Restored doctrine teaches two connected ideas in this respect. Firstly, God is good (2 Nephi 9:10). Secondly, you, as a child of God, can have great desires for goodness (Alma 41:3–5).

The Goodness of Our God

We can see in holy writ that God is good (Psalm 145:5–7) and that the aim of human discipleship is eventually for us to become as good as God is (3 Nephi 12:48). The goodness of God is described as immediate (Mosiah 25:10), supreme (Alma 12:32), exceeding (Alma 60:11), great (3 Nephi 4:33), and infinite (Helaman 12:1, Moroni 8:3). Through Him we can partake of much good (2 Nephi 3:24) and every good (Moroni 7:20–22, 25, 28). The goodness of God is bound up with His nature, character, and identity (2 Nephi 9:8–26). Also, it is a goodness aimed at blessing others. In fact, His great goodness is directed toward you. Yes, you, the reader of this book. You, personally. He is good to you. He is good for you. He is good with you. His goodness is within you!

God Sees Goodness in You

God's purpose and plan is to see goodness in you. He also aims to enlarge and increase your goodness, far beyond what you presently envision. He sees great potential in you (Doctrine & Covenants 76:5–10). He knows there are hidden treasures in you. He has detected your specialness, observed your uniqueness, seen your capacity, and witnessed your ability. He is completely aware of your life, background, opportunities, difficulties, challenges, circumstances, and possibilities. In truth, He can see elements of His grand goodness in you. He is cognisant of your divine nature and your spectacular capability for truth and beauty. This is a great joy to Him. He rejoices in your goodness and seeks to magnify your virtues, expand your horizons, elevate your vision, and bring to fruition your greatest aspirations (1 Corinthians 2:9).

We know that these things are true by the great revelations to the seer Abraham restored through the Prophet Joseph Smith. We are told that God "saw" that the noble and great spirits were "good" (Abraham 3:23). Think of that! Even before we were born into this mortal world, we possessed the seeds of divine greatness within us. We were good. And that goodness was seen by the Supreme Being Himself. *He saw goodness in us!* Ponder the significance of that. He saw a measure of His great goodness—in embryo—within us. Now, that speaks volumes about our divine nature and potential. If God Himself views us as good, then surely, we are good! A perspective like that can tremendously boost our sense of confidence in ourselves. This does not cause us to be arrogant, but deeply humble and sincerely grateful.

This vantage point is not limited to pre-earth life, but it applies to mortality also. Nor is it limited to only prophets and apostles. It is the divine birthright of all who accept the plan of the Father and the appointment of Jehovah as the Great Mediator of all (Abraham 3: 26, Alma 13). We carry that goodness within us to this life. How important it is that we perceive this goodness within us and do all we can to cultivate it to greater heights in this mortal sphere. In this frail world, God's goodness manifest through His children is desperately needed!

Indeed, we are further instructed that God personally conversed with the prophet Abraham in mortality and displayed in loving terms the wonderful gifts of a generous Father to a cared for child. He called him "My son" and "he *put his hand upon mine eyes*, and I *saw* those things which his hands had made" (Abraham 3:11–12, emphasis added). This is a beautiful revelation because it teaches us that God is personally invested in our growth and development. His touch, His words, His kindness, His appreciation, and His desire to bless were all manifest to Abraham in a way that could never be forgotten. In addition, God showed Abraham marvelous works and wonders which astonished and educated him. He could not even have imagined these things unless his eyes had been opened to see spiritual truth in a whole new way. It is likewise with us. We can come to see with new eyes and hear with new ears. We have capacity to open our hearts and catch the great vision of our stunning nature and potential. We are to be taught and trained in the truths of eternity. We are to be given the gifts that surpass all mortal understanding. This is to happen to each one of us, as we become willing and able to see with the eye of faith.

One Unique Person

It is common to hear references to self-esteem, self-worth, self-development, and self-fulfilment in society. I have listened with intense interest to those who advocate self-help programs or techniques of diverse kinds in helping individuals to achieve inner peace and outward success. While I have benefited greatly from learning about these ideas, the restored gospel, in my view, is uniquely qualified to teach us about self-awareness, self-knowledge, self-actualization, and self-strengthening in deep and lasting ways. The impactful messages of revealed truth have given me unsurpassed insights into my own soul. It is important to see divinity within ourselves as the foundation of our being.

Revealed truth tells us of our unique value. For example, in considering the great worth of a single soul, imagine if Lehi, Nephi, etc. had never been born into this world. Imagine if the Prophet Joseph Smith, Mary the mother of Jesus (Alma 7:10), or indeed Jesus Christ Himself (Alma 7:7) had never taken mortal form. All of us would be impoverished now and eternally by the absence of these spiritual luminaries. Real people accomplish amazing things with the help of God! (Mosiah 16:6–9). The important work accomplished by saints throughout the ages has contributed powerful legacies of faith and redemption to all. The spiritual richness of their individual lives has blessed all of us (2 Nephi 4:15–35). While Joseph Smith was blessed by the nurturing messages revealed to him, these also buttressed him with needed strength to bless others on an ongoing basis. We are greatly blessed by his revelatory teachings even though we never met him in person. Consequently, we do not live only for ourselves, we also live to benefit others!

Self-worth is essentially the value we place upon ourselves. The restored gospel helps us to think divinely about ourselves and enhances self-worth in numerous vital ways. Our self-perception is very important on our spiritual journey through the mortal world because it can either heal or harm us. We may often base our view of ourselves on temporary factors such as our looks, financial status, employment status, nationality, accent, popularity, health, church callings, and even trials we are passing through. However, from scripture we learn that we can see ourselves from the eternal perspective of our character, divine inheritance, faith, testimony, knowledge, and family relationships. We are shown how to base our view of ourselves on solid, everlasting principles of truth. We can thereby have an optimistic and healthy attitude about ourselves forevermore (Alma 7:25–27). As we learn pivotal truths, we make ourselves and every situation we encounter better.

Sacred scripture gives very strong answers to our most important private questions and robust solutions to our most troubling personal challenges. These revolve around our nature and purpose. The everlasting gospel helps us to realize our most beautiful personal dreams and deeply cherished beliefs. The promises of God to us personally are sure as we come to live gospel principles. The gospel is true for you and me in very immediate ways. The Holy Spirit inspires us to be faithful and loyal to God. He teaches us with lifting power about the eternal worth of true doctrine and our own souls (2 Nephi 32:1–3; 33:1).

The combined effect of these elevating truths upon our souls is that we perform good works in our especially talented way. We also accomplish our assigned mission on this earth. And the people whose lives we touch for good will also spread truth and light out into the world. This is no small matter, especially in these turbulent times when there is much confusion about who we really are. To build a strong self-image we need to build our lives on the foundational truths that God has majestically presented to us clearly, regularly, and emphatically. We can nullify pessimism in our lives by promoting revelation-based hope. We can improve our personal strength one small step at a time, one decisive breakthrough at a time, and one courageous determination at a time.

SEEING YOUR SOUL

I believe that spirituality is the most crucial factor in ennobling our view of ourselves. To be spiritually minded is to be able to see who we really are through all the mists of darkness in this fallen world. We can dispel doubt about our personal value through the inspired education that comes in God's word. We need to see our own soul.

Our Father in Heaven is a being who knows what He is doing because He has already achieved the perfect state we are aiming for. God is the ultimate master of self-awareness and self-control. He loves the beauty of holiness. He is free to live, love, and be loved because He knows His own divine nature. He is a being of majestic benevolence. Our spiritual, moral, and ethical standards derive from our doctrinal understanding of the magnificent nature of God. Our basic understanding of the meaning and deepest purposes of life stem from the reality that God is a being of eternal fullness and He shows us the way to Him if we want to be led. We can know that divine directives bless both our eternal spirits and our eternal (temporal and resurrected) bodies. There are no vain or useless commandments from God (2 Nephi 26:24).

I have pondered much on the teaching that we are the children of God, created in His divine image. This is stunning doctrine! It conveys the idea that we are literally the spirit children of the Supreme Being. We are therefore endowed with capacities that are divine in nature. Our ability to reason, choose, love, serve, plan, forgive, create, and endure are just some of the attributes that mirror God's marvelous greatness. We are designed with intelligence, potential, gifts, and capabilities that reflect His ultimate light, His perfect knowledge,

His amazing love, and His stunning power (see parable of the talents, Matthew 24:14–30). There is a spark of marvelous majesty in us.

Our mortal bodies are created in the form and likeness of the Almighty. This is a powerful insight. We look like God. We are therefore tangible evidence that a personal God lives. We display a portion of His grandeur. We are living embodiments of His reality. Our mortal body is a testimony of God. It is a temple of divinity. In this life, we can also be spiritually born again. We can become sons and daughters of Jesus Christ through holy ordinances and sacred covenants (see Mosiah 5). Thus, we become partakers of the divine nature and obtain the mind of Christ while still living in mortality. This is significant. We receive the image of Christ in our countenance (Alma 5). This is further evidence of God's present living reality. Being born again to a newness of life is real. I know because it has been happening to me. In the eternities, we will take upon us a glorious body through resurrection, if we choose righteousness as the essential pattern of our lives in mortality. This is literal and eternal (see Alma 40–42). This sublime gift will make us more fully like the God we worship.

The simple truth is that every beautiful idea, every kind tendency, every wonderful word, every act of courage, and all good things in life bear testimony of the living reality of the Fatherhood of God. In profound reality, we are His offspring, His treasures, His loved ones. He is feeling after us, watching over us, guiding us, and preparing us for a glory beyond description. Every wonder that causes us to bow in humility before His tremendous character is evidence that God is at work in this world. Lovely art, heavenly music, and moving literature inspire us to look to Him as the perfect creator.

Let us remember who we truly are, whose we are, and who we can become. We are children of glory, sons and daughters of destiny, and inheritors of a precious promise that God will watch over us in sunshine and rain. We sometimes need to look in the mirror, open our eyes, open our hearts, come to ourselves, and see the deep magnificence of these sobering things. We are children in God's image with the opportunity to become all that He designs for us to become—fully mature, grown adults with everlasting perfection within us.

We are each like God in appearance and characteristics and are therefore far more than mere animals (Mosiah 27:25, Alma 18:34;

42:23). These fundamental doctrines provide inspirational meaning in our lives. These stunningly beautiful universal truths can be fixed in our minds and rooted in our hearts always. They have a tremendously empowering effect upon us in shaping the way we see everything in this world.

We are personally special to God as we are valued for who we are as unique children (2 Nephi 33:3). Each soul is catered for comprehensively and purposefully as part of His logistically staggering and deeply personal plan (Alma 39:17). Thus, we each have God given gender, talents, gifts, roles, and opportunities. The love of God for us is perfect and everlasting. We can love Him too (see 1 Nephi 8; 11). To know that God loves us can fill us with kind regard for ourselves and others. Imagine what would happen in this world if everyone had this divine love for both themselves and others—we would have a Zion on earth, a new paradise, a second Eden. Scripture shows that we can build heaven on earth and gives us a hopeful glimpse of that possibility (3 Nephi 11–18).

My journey in the religious life has allowed me to feel spiritual closeness to God. I have received experiential knowledge and power to help me throughout my entire life. I am forcibly struck by the gracious nature of God and overwhelmed by what He does for me and all His children. The gift of sacred truth is phenomenally life changing in that it moves me to grow beyond worldly conditioning. I am touched, moved, and comforted. This gives me assurance, resolve, and determination to move forward. The wondrous possibilities offered to each of us are far beyond what we could ever envisage for ourselves. God believes we are worth all His time and effort. The restored gospel shows us a pathway to a life filled with spiritual riches.

As we labor in the work of God, we come to know our true divine selves—the everlasting part of us. All faithful priesthood holders and saints were, are, and will always be like the Son of God in their general appearance (Ether 3), countenance (Alma 5), behavior (3 Nephi 12–18), and ministry (Alma 13). Sensing this allows us to then know a warm closeness to God. It is through the priesthood ordinances, covenants, and blessings that we gain access to the full blessings of the Atonement. This journey gives fully rich meaning to the concept of the worth of a soul, as we come to sense that we are the treasures that belong to God (Mosiah 18). When we willingly accept revelatory doctrinal principles, we make steady and certain progress forward and that tastes good to our souls (Alma 32).

A Great Worth

Worth is a concept with various meanings. Some define worth in purely economic terms, such as in the financial worth of a piece of art, whereas others may see it primarily aesthetically, such as the beauty of a sculpture. Some may see it in educational terms—such as the insights contained in a composition of majestic literature, others the use to which something can be put—such as a piece of jewelry at a dinner party. Music can be valued for its emotional impact on us even if we know little or nothing about who created it or how. Whether we are looking at something in terms of intrinsic worth or instrumental worth makes a difference to how we perceive it. A car is of little use without gasoline to run it if our interest is in using it for travel purposes. A piece of art can be appreciated visually but has little value if we are hungry for food. Music is wonderful for listening to but cannot build our physical muscles. The worth of temporal objects is limited as they can be stolen, lost, become redundant, or be broken. The worth of so many things can alter over time if we view them from worldly perspectives only—looks fade, status is temporary, fame disappears, prominence lessens, achievements are forgotten, talents diminish, and abilities reduce.

However, divine worth is a different matter. We have a wonderful worth from the divine perspective of God—"Remember the worth of souls is *great in the sight of God*" (Doctrine & Covenants 18:10, emphasis added). I am struck by God's perspective! He sees our worth as significant from His point of view. That is remarkable. If a mortal being regards someone's worth as great, then that may well be impressive. However, if the Supreme Being regards someone's worth as great, that is a far better and surer guide to their worth. How precious therefore is each individual soul! We are known, loved, and valued one by one. We are seen as personally important to the Supreme Being. This gives us each a personal purpose, an eternal value, and a deep sense of meaning.

In our world, where value often seems to revolve around status, beauty, wealth, education, strength, popularity, notoriety, etc., it is exceedingly easy to feel that we cannot possibly amount to much. On the worldly scale of measurement, where comparisons with others are the order of the day, it is entirely understandable that we may view ourselves to be worth little or nothing. Others may have low opinions of us. How this reality contrasts with the view that the restored gospel of God offers us! We are starkly and consistently reminded that our worth, value, and importance transcends such temporary and relatively insignificant descriptors such as wealth, etc. Transitory fads and fashions are as a dark shadow compared to the revealed light of eternal truth.

Consider the plain and profound meaning of this one verse in terms of the great worth we have to God (Doctrine & Covenants 18:10). It is laced with edifying doctrine:

The first word "remember," is a very significant word to the Lord. He wants us to remember what really matters. For example, the sacrament prayers speak of remembering Christ, His death and sacrifice for us (Doctrine & Covenants 20:77–79). We are to always remember Him. Alma teaches us to remember the mighty power of the Savior in delivering captive souls from the chains of hell (Alma 5). We are prone to forget our own worth and that of others—hence the Lord specifically asks us to remember our worth. We are to reflect, ruminate, and dwell on it so that we might lodge it permanently into our lives. Otherwise, we are liable to forget and become distracted from our identity and destiny. If the Lord asks us to remember something, it must be because the risk in forgetting it is indeed grave.

What of the word "worth"? I think of value, preciousness, importance, dignity, and respect. We matter to God—we are His jewels, His very work and glory (Moses 1:39).

What of the word "souls"? I am reminded that soul is defined as body and spirit combined (Doctrine & Covenants 93). The physical, mortal body is important to God. The word of wisdom is a wise doctrine regarding the treatment and use of the mortal body, which is designated as a temple of God

(Section 89). We are all spirit sons or daughters of God—children of God for whom He has divine, perfect, everlasting love. The redemption of the soul is therefore found in both forgiveness of sin and resurrection of the body. The soul as combined spirit and body is eternally precious to God and should be to us also. I also reflect on the idea that if one soul is precious to God, then many souls are very precious to God. God is interested in each and every soul. He is concerned about all souls.

What of the word "great"? I believe it means significant, important, and material.

What of "sight"? It refers to view, perspective, opinion, regard, vision, or knowledge. His vantage point is certainly one deserving acknowledgment and merit.

What of "God"? He is our goodly and generous Father. He is the Supreme Being, our ultimate benefactor, the perfect soul.

It is evident that in the opinion of the greatest being in the universe, we, as individuals, are deeply significant and eternally important. How stunning is that? How poignantly remarkable! It is awe-inducing to me. I am shocked, inspired, and comforted by it. This is a simple yet deep doctrine that is profound in its ramifications and soul soothing in its implications. It has the power to transform our view of ourselves and to lift us to a higher place. Oh, how wonderful is the quality, longevity, and impact of God's divine love in our lives!

Think of the other key themes in this section:

The Savior suffered pain and death willingly for a pure purpose—to provide repentance and resurrection so that all people would come to Him willingly (Doctrine and Covenants 18:11–12).

His joy is great when we repent—our change, improvement and development give Him happiness and purpose (verse 13).

We can cry repentance to others. I believe this is an emotional and spiritual reality—like Nephi whose eyes watered his pillow by night for his people (2 Nephi 33:2–4), or like Alma who sang the song of redeeming love to others (Alma 5). We can have a genuine concern for the well-being and salvation of our families, friends, and enemies.

> To work all our life and bring one soul—or many souls—to God will bring lasting joy to them and us! This eternal joy is worth any and every personal price we might pay in so doing. The spending of our precious time, talents, and resources in saving even one soul is a very successful endeavor.

It is abundantly clear that each person is precious and uniquely important. Each person is capable of magnificent feelings, great thoughts, deep experiences, and meaningful contributions. Each soul can catch the vision of this personal worth and turn their life to great purposes. Each can achieve true greatness. The most important type of greatness is moral and spiritual greatness. True greatness is defined by the degree to which our lives come to reflect the teachings and example of our Savior.

Although we are the spirit children of God, we know that all children eventually grow up. They become more than what they once were. This is how we become more than we presently are. In the beginning, we were made in God's perfect image. However, we did not stop there. We grew more into His likeness through learning and development even in the premortal world. In this mortal life, we need to be remade—again and again—in His image and likeness. We are eternal in nature and purpose, so post-mortality is a further opportunity for us to learn important lessons. We need not define ourselves by limiting worldly standards and viewpoints, but rather by powerful revealed truths. We are truly capable of marvelous things when we deeply embed this transcendent knowledge in our minds and hearts.

3

The Garden of the Lord

I LOVED HEARING THE FINAL REMARKS OF ELDER BRUCE R. McConkie in the April Conference of 1985. One of the concepts from that message that has always resonated with me is the idea of the gardens of God—"As we read, ponder, and pray, there will come into our minds a view of the three gardens of God—the Garden of Eden, the Garden of Gethsemane, and the Garden of the Empty Tomb where Jesus appeared to Mary Magdalene" (Bruce R. McConkie, "The Purifying Power of Gethsemane," April 1985 General Conference).

While I did not fully perceive the spiritual significance of this idea as a twelve-year-old young man, I have a much deeper appreciation of this as I have grown in understanding. I have sensed that great things in the plan of God happen in garden settings. The reality that the fall of Adam/Eve and the Atonement and Resurrection of our Lord occurred in garden settings yields great dividends as we carefully reflect on it. In many ways my growing comprehension of this great truth laid the foundation for this book. I am profoundly grateful to Elder McConkie for opening my mind and heart to the stunning truths that accompany this spiritual recognition. I have expanded the ideas presented to my view during that talk and in various other gospel settings since then to bring to light many rich insights I have been blessed to discern around the idea of spiritual events—of both universal, family, and personal importance—taking place in garden settings.

The entire earth is the Garden of the Lord. He is *"God over all the earth"* (1 Nephi 11:6). There is no part of it that does not belong to Him. There is no portion of it that does not serve an important purpose in His plan. He knows all the parts of His Garden. His plan includes provision for this earth and all the forms of life upon it. His earth is truly a garden of glory.

THE EARTH AS WITNESS

Alma teaches us that the scriptures, earth, mountains, valleys, seas, deserts, etc., and indeed the ordered motion of all planetary bodies *"do witness that there is a Supreme Creator"* (Alma 30:44). In this sense, the material world bears record that God is the ultimate architect of the structured world and universe around us. The earth therefore gives testimony to spiritual truth. In addition, the written word of God reflects the divine design of this world we all experience. As we consider this witness of the world, we see that nature accords with the will of God in showing us features of His identity and plan. God is a being of order, structure, pattern, and evidence! He has revealed Himself in the design of material things.

I have reflected often and deeply on the frequent and poignant use of symbolism in the scriptures. Much scriptural symbolism teaches us that God's handiwork is to be seen, heard, felt, sensed, and known. For example, we have the brother of Jared asking the Lord to touch the stones that they might *"shine forth in darkness"* (Ether 3:4). The brother of Jared was right on target. He was pleading with a powerful God who loves to benefit His children. These sixteen stones, molten out of a rock, were to be touched by Jesus Christ so that they could serve a special purpose. His divine power would enable them to be illuminated in such a way that they could be a light in a dark time to the people of God. The Jaredites were to travel from the old world to the new in wooden vessels. This would be a treacherous journey. They would face winds, waves, whales, and worries. They would encounter difficulties such as sickness, hunger, and fear.

However, God would not leave them comfortless. He had prepared means in the form of vessels, stones, and instructions for them. They would know the source of their power and the sureness of their mission. They would be directed, guided, led, and protected. I especially love the imagery of stones of light which would be a miracle for them. These lights would allow them to see one another even though they were surrounded by darkness. They could see the light! They could feel the love of God! They would feel watched over and safeguarded.

It is evident that Christ is the sure rock of our salvation. He is the rock of light that shows us which way to go amidst the darkness of a fallen world. These stones of light were a visible reminder to these venturing and obedient souls that Christ is the living Rock of Ages that showed them the way to the promised salvation they longed for. As for them, so for us in this day. Christ is the ever-guiding, never-failing Rock of Light. He is powerful in overcoming any darkness. He is sure, steady, and steadfast. Let us always look to Him as the certain rock of all righteousness and He will lead us through dark waters to the eternal country we seek for.

Consider the following in terms of how the earth itself and the materials thereon evidence the nature and purposes of God:

The Earth

The earth is a beautiful participant in the creative life. Soil is associated with our mortal bodies. Man was formed from the dust of the earth (Mosiah 2:25). Dust combined with intelligence gives life! The earth gives us sights to appreciate, sounds to cherish, wonders to amaze, and lessons to teach us. The earth has swallowed up wickedness, hidden weapons of war, defied wicked armies, and provided abundantly to the humble. The earth groaned when Christ died. The earth houses, warms, shelters, feeds, cleanses, and sustains the children of God. The earth obeys God. It is fruitful. This is a world of divine blessings! I see the earth as a gift from God which testifies of Him.

Seeds

Seeds are associated with potential. Trees represent knowledge and life. Groves indicate places of sacred or profane happenings. That which gives life and grows is of God. That which destroys and dies is of some other source.

Water

Water is associated with rituals giving newness of life, such as the washing of feet by the Lord. No wonder that scripture speaks of Living Water—given the waters of birth, waters of baptism, sacrament water, and water used to clean dirt and illnesses away.

In baptism we are submerged in warm water (usually!). Water plus heat equals hot water. What does hot water do? It removes stains from clothing, cutlery, etc. It is a cleansing agent. Hence, warm water plus spiritual fire (Holy Ghost) cleanses us from sin.

We swallow water in the sacrament, and it becomes part of us.

We are washed with water in the temple, and it cleans us.

Oceans have carried the faithful to promised lands. Lakes have been waters of baptism for the humble. Rivers and Seas have parted to let the righteous walk through. Water facilitated the Savior when He walked upon it. It sustained His body and did not sink or drown Him! Fountains of water have been sources of strength and renewal.

Fire

Fire is associated with purifying power. It can burn and destroy but can also warm, cook, and fortify. Jeremiah compared the Spirit to a burning fire within him (Jeremiah 20:9). While the baptism of the mortal body is accomplished with water, the baptism of the eternal spirit requires the Holy Ghost (baptism of fire). What does the baptism of fire do? It cleans spiritual stains from souls!

Wind

The wind is like the Holy Ghost in that we see its effects but not its comings and goings. The Holy Ghost encourages us, but winds of opposition can knock us off course. We need to know how to deal with the winds of change. It is vital for us to learn to discern spiritual promptings to move forward.

Rock

Rock is solid and likewise the gospel of Christ is rock solid. Hence, we are to be established upon the Rock of our Redeemer. Christ is the Stone of Israel. The Rock of Revelation is the solid foundation of Christ upon which we must build to survive all spiritual storms. Seer stones and white stones are used to obtain revelations (Doctrine & Covenants 130:11).

Sand—the Lord promises children as numerous as the sand on the seashore to the faithful.

Sea of glass—glass is transparent and so should our lives be to God because in righteousness we are unafraid to be seen.

Wheat/Bread

Manna from heaven nourished God's covenant people. Bread was multiplied to feed hungry listeners. Christ is the Bread from Heaven, the giver of Eternal Life. Tares are not fruitful, but wheat is good for life.

Fish

Fish was given miraculously. The disciples were to be fishers of men.

Fruit

Associated with that which is natural, delicious, nutritious, sustaining, and appealing. It indicates gospel peace and joy. It represents God's marvelous opportunities, blessings, and rewards.

Mountains & Valleys

Mountains have operated as temples (Doctrine & Covenants 128:23; 133:13). Mountaintops represent God's presence. Mountains invite us to look upward, become fitter both physically and spiritually, take on challenges and stretch us to our limits. They look beautiful. Mountains have moved for the righteous. They are associated with times of difficulty and triumph.

Valleys represent the low times of life through which we all must travel if we are to then ascend to a higher place. Also, valleys give us needed respite and rest.

High and lows in spiritual terms are real for everyone.

Olive Oil

Oil was used in the consecration of kings. It was used in temple ceremonies, to spiritually set people apart from the world and to divinely endow people. Oil is used in anointing the sick. Oil was made abundant to feed a starving widow who put faith in God first.

The Garden of Creation

This earth is the Garden of God. This is where Eden was. The creation itself came to fruition in a garden context. It involved living things, in a somewhat idyllic setting. This world was created, owned, and cultivated by God. When I think of that I ponder how blessed we truly are to sojourn in this place of wonder and beauty. Think of the many glories and delights of this beautiful garden from lakes to grasslands to jungles to deserts. In thousands of ways we are blessed to see that this world is prepared to be a place of tremendous learning and a gift to each one of us—if only we have eyes to see, ears to hear, hearts to understand and minds to comprehend it (Mosiah 2:9). We learn many things in a lifetime—motion, skills, talents, facts, memories, sights, sounds, relationships, education, careers, fun, knowledge, callings, etc. It is a privilege to reside on this planet for even a short season. Our Father in Heaven is a creative being who has designed and constructed a goodly garden full of opportunity (Alma 30:44). This living Garden of God provides abundant evidence that the gospel of God is a living, thriving, growing, renewing one!

God rules and reigns over this earth. It is His world, a place of His glory and destiny. He presides over the oceans, seas, and lakes. He governs the sun, moon, and stars. His divine architecture includes mountains, valleys, and trees. He delights in rocks, sand, flowers, and grass. He prepares seeds, grains, and fruit for taste and nutrition. He rejoices in life, cultivates growth, and loves the diversity of creation. His gladness is manifest in lovely colors, remarkable shapes, glorious art, mathematical principles, expressive words, diverse languages, stunning scientific laws, personalized patterns, cultures of excellence, and beautiful types of music. He is the great creator, designer, composer, writer, musician, builder, teacher, engineer, scientist, administrator, doctor, lawyer, and sculptor. He is the greatest intelligence in the Universe and everything He orchestrates brings the greatest possible reality into being.

The Lord created the earth for His children to live on (1 Nephi 17:36). This world is truly the Garden of the Lord (Alma 26:37). In the words of the hymn "Love at Home" we are told that "All the earth's a garden sweet" (*Hymns,* no. 294). Imagine metaphorically that you are a seed planted in the garden of the Lord. Each of us is a small but valuable seed. We can grow from a tiny seed to a mighty tree in God's Garden. We are all capable of becoming a good seed. This garden is like a school and each of us is in class. Each classroom of experience is a part of the living and growing garden of the Lord. In like manner, this mortal life is a school of growth. It is a potentially wonderful learning and growing experience for each one of us.

As we reorient our thinking, acting and being toward growth by flooding our lives with the marvelous messages of the revealed word, we come to perceive this divine reality in a touching way. The precepts of revealed truth then lodge within us forever. Using these sublime doctrines that we learn in each living classroom of the Lord—especially our homes, church buildings, and temples—we will be protected against the deadly dangers inherent in the garden. We will grow to the full stature of our potential as seeds—children—students—of God. I will highlight some spiritual truths that can facilitate our genuine growth during this brief but crucially important mortal experience. I hope each of us will sense the great principles that can help us in our personal ascent to eternal glory. As we do so, we will come to experience the personal perspective of Christ in a remarkable new way.

In this special Garden, our first parents Adam and Eve were placed. This was a paradise, a place of beauty and life. Each tree grown naturally in the garden "became a living soul" and was "good for food" (Moses 3:8–10,15). Think of that! The trees in the garden were living souls! Not identical to the children of God, of course, but living souls nonetheless—combining tangible element and spirit intelligence in a coherent unity. These trees were pleasant to the eyes. They could be seen as evidence of divine handiwork. They were good for providing fruit for food! They were not yet subject to temporal death. The trees were obedient to the divine role given them and were prepared to benefit man. This was a plan with a purpose, a garden with a holy end in its existence. The very existence of the garden was proof that God had a design for all His creations! At the very center of that garden, both the tree of life and the tree of knowledge of good and evil stood—that indicates their core roles in the reasoning of the Almighty. He planned for us to learn how to live forever in the context of learning first how to distinguish between good and evil for ourselves.

From Eden, a river of water sprang and watered the garden of the Lord in the beginning. This river of life gave bounty to all. God used the water of life to bring nourishment and life to all the world. He is the source of watering, the fountain of refreshment, and the giver of abundance. Although the tree of life existed in the Garden of Eden, Adam and Eve were not ready to partake of that fruit. They had truths to learn, experiences to acquire, and qualities to develop before they could really qualify for the kind and duration of life that God had in mind for them. The garden was a temporary home. A new world awaited. While it would be a fallen world and a place of trials and tears, it would be a place to learn by personal experience in a way that would shape them in marvelous, profound, and lasting ways. Mortality was to be a world of opportunity somewhat unlike anything they had known before. It was to be an adventure toward divinity. The fall to mortality was activated by a deliberate choice. It occurred in a garden context. Spiritually pivotal things in the plan of God happen in a garden setting! This is significant to me. Let us consider some of these Gardens and the great events that take place in them.

The Garden of the Mortal Earth

God has given us the *"fulness of the earth,"* the *"good things"* of the earth, for our benefit and use. He is pleased when we use these things wisely to *"strengthen the body and to enliven the soul"* (Doctrine and Covenants 59:16–20). That which "cometh of the earth" is ordained for our abundant use (Doctrine and Covenants 49:19). This tangible earth is a great benefactor to us. This garden earth is a treasure trove of gladness. It makes possible our sights, sounds, touch, taste, and smell. It allows for a profound depth of temporal and spiritual experience. Think of the things we learn while tabernacled with this mortal clay, which otherwise we could not have known. In this lifetime we learn about good and evil; pleasure and pain; joy and misery; health and sickness; life and death. This earth is more beautiful than any man-made structure can be—it is living, colorful, active, majestic, attractive, energetic, productive, calming, exciting, and thrilling. It is also dangerous, erratic, unpredictable, and scary. We are deeply instructed, informed, and improved by our special experiences on this mortal earth. As we see through God's eyes, we awake to fresh vision, new enthusiasm, and refined power to live according to godly ways. This is a rare opportunity and rich privilege which needs to be respected.

This "dirt" our mortal bodies are made from is remarkable. That God can combine simple elements in such a way as to provide for complex life is wonderful. Our mortality is truly a limited-edition experience. We have never been mortal before and we will never be mortal again. This is certainly a unique "once in an eternity" experience. It is therefore deeply valuable to us.

The Savior appreciates that we are here to gain experience and education. He values our mortal time of testing and growth because it is needed for our development. He allows us to use our agency to create new opportunities for ourselves and others. While He has personally encountered our sorrows, it is also true that He knows our joys, successes, laughter, wonder, and rejoicings. With the bitter there also comes much of sweetness.

God knows our wanderings through tribulation. However, He also provides opportunities for us to partake of nourishment while on our difficult journeys. Consider the eight years spent by Lehi's family in the wilderness. Then the Lord brought them to a prepared place of bounty, which had *"much fruit and also wild honey"* and *"many waters."* No wonder they then *"exceedingly rejoiced"* (1 Nephi 17:4–6). I love the fact that the Lord prepared water, fruit, and honey to sustain Lehi and his family in their time of desperate need. He wanted them to live. He wanted them to have hope. He desired for them to sense the bounty of His beautiful blessings. His provisions gave them encouragement to go on. I believe there are so many wonderful things in this world that are divinely prepared to sustain us along the challenging trek toward eternal life. This earth is a testing ground, but it is simultaneously a place of provision, a garden of gladness, and a location of tremendous beauty and peace. We often simply need to recognize and remember God's graciousness to us.

The Garden of Enoch's Zion

Enoch's city became a place of consummate righteousness. It was a community of faith and faithfulness, a haven of purity and power. It was then taken up to a heavenly place. It is useful to note that Zion was endorsed by the Lord as His eternal abode. I understand this to mean that the Savior acknowledged this entire city as a society of people who lived by His standards. He felt comfortable there and sealed the people to Him everlastingly.

The Garden of the Cleansed Earth

Consider the special and chosen land where the brother of Jared and later the Nephites lived. We know that after the "waters had receded from off the face of this land it became a choice land above all other lands." It would be the heavenly New Jerusalem, "the holy sanctuary of the Lord" (Ether 13:2–3). Lands can be washed new and clean!

Noah, who was the father of all living then, was the leading patriarch on this newly baptized earth. It is critical to note that this earth was now cleansed from all the iniquity previously upon it. This was a new start, a second beginning. This was a core experience in the redemption of the earth from the fall of Adam and Eve. This was a preparatory step in the salvation of the earth. The entire earth needed to be immersed in water as a sign and symbol of the death, burial, and resurrection of Christ. God gave the earth another opportunity for righteousness. This was a rebirth of the world. Interestingly, we are made of dirt—which is obedient to the word of God (Mosiah 2). This dirt comes from the baptized, reborn earth (washed in the flood waters at the time of Noah). In other words, our mortal bodies are composed of elements that have already been renewed by the cleansing waters God sent forth to retrieve the earth from corruption and violence. In this sense, our tabernacles are in a great position to overcome the fallen tendency toward immorality and anger. Think of that uplifting thought when you are confronted by troubles.

However, this is not all. There is much more to come for this earth garden which will be impressive to the highest degree. I will return to this idea later in this book. This earth will soon experience a further rebirth of magnificent proportions. This will be done by the redemptive power of Jesus the Christ which relates directly to His divine creation of this beautiful blue planet.

4

Gardens of Reconciliation

We know that our Lord suffered both pain and death in this world. As His pain for our sins was sore, so His rejoicing at our repentance is sublime! His pain draws us to Him and His resurrection brings us to Him!" (Doctrine & Covenants 18:11–13). His suffering was not in vain. It served the purpose of allowing us to repent and to come unto Him. The Messiah came into the world of the living so that He might teach us how to live and how to die. He made possible our immortality and eternal life (Moses 1:39). His purpose was to bring us home, to rescue us, to save us from ourselves and to exalt us to glory. This redemption was intended to be for everyone who wanted it.

Even before He came, His purpose in coming was made known. The reach of His message, labor, and reconciliation was understood by many long before social media arrived! It was announced that all the world should repent because the Son of God would come to earth in shining glory, in the might, majesty, power, and dominion of Him who was "the King of all the earth; and also the King of heaven" (Alma 5:50). Christ was to be the reconciler between fallen humanity and the Eternal Father. He would bridge the otherwise impassable gulf that we might cross safely to God. He would abolish the chasm between us and eternal happiness and progress. That we were separated from God was clear. We needed a repairer of the breach, a restorer of possibility, a Mediator between time and eternity. This would come in the form of the reconciling At-One-Ment, which only a God who was both human and divine could provide.

The Atonement of our Lord was not required by the Law of Justice based on any wrongs He had committed, so it had to be done by means of voluntary activation if it was to be done at all. What choice did He make? How did He activate the process of reconciliation? I find it fascinating that the process essentially commenced in a garden setting—a garden of olive trees. The setting is important, the context matters. The revelations of our day give us some insight into this remarkable event.

We know that the sufferings of the Savior were worse than we can fathom. Indeed, His was the terrible pain that only our great God could endure (Doctrine & Covenants 19:15–19). It is evident that we do not have the kind of empathy for the Savior that He has for us. We cannot possibly comprehend the depth and extent of His sufferings. However bad we think it was, it was worse than that! It was in fact more sore, exquisite, and hard to bear than we can or do know. For the Savior to use those indicative descriptors surely means it was phenomenally difficult for Him to endure. We do not understand His pain. However, He understands ours! He knows the pain of our friends and our enemies, the sorrows of our parents and our children, the woes of our closest associates and our most distant strangers.

One purpose of His suffering was so that we do not have to suffer needlessly—this clearly refers to avoidable suffering which arises due to our own poor choices. He suffered as a God! The Atonement of Christ involved Godly suffering which no individual human being could endure, nor could humanity collectively survive such an ordeal. He suffered both in His body and His everlasting spirit. This is suffering of every kind, type, and degree. The bitterness of His pain did not stop Him from doing the divine will. He fulfilled His Father's glory and brought to fruition our latent potential for divinity, which otherwise would have remained unrealized.

The process of extracting His lifesaving blood came only under pressure of considerable proportions. What more appropriate place to indicate this symbolism than in a garden of olive trees, with the culmination happening while he was fastened solidly to a tree (the Cross of Crucifixion)? As olives, or grapes, are squeezed or trodden under foot, so the Messiah was pressed by means of the burdens of a broken world, so that new life, light, shelter, warmth, sustenance, and healing could come to the children of men. Being in such an environmental setting of growth, life, and connection such as a grove of olive trees would provide, I believe that this was conducive to maintaining the understanding and resolve He needed to carry through to conclusion the plan of the Father whereby each of us could find eternal growth, life, and connection.

Garden of Grief

We know that a child was born to this world who would also be called the Everlasting Father (2 Nephi 19:6). How can a baby be born into the world and simultaneously be called a Father? Babies are not yet fathers—they are only sons or daughters. However, this is a prophetic declaration of divine purpose and capability. Our beloved Savior was born into this world as an infant, but was, and would be, the Everlasting Father—the spiritual father of all who would be born again through Him. We later learn that this child—this Messiah—would grow to maturity and save from sin and death all who believed in Him.

I love the truths shared by the prophet Isaiah about Christ saving His "seed." He would grow up as a "*tender plant,* and as a *root out of dry ground*" (Mosiah 14:2, emphasis added). It is not likely that a tender plant could ever amount to much. In like manner, Christ would have difficult starting circumstances, and many would have a negative perception of Him (Mosiah 14:3–10):

He would be despised and rejected.
He would know sorrow and grief.
We would hide from Him and value Him lowly.
He would be burdened with our grief, carry our sorrow, and bear our iniquity.
We would regard Him as smitten of God.
He would be hurt on account of our wrongdoing.
His punishment would bring us healing and peace.
His covenant faithfulness would bring us back from wandering and selfishness.
He would be silent amidst His unlawful oppression.

Isaiah asks, *"who shall declare his generation?"* (Mosiah 14:8). In other words, do we comprehend His lineage as the Only Begotten Son of God? Isaiah teaches that "when thou shalt make *his soul an offering for sin* he shall *see his seed*" (Mosiah 14:1–10, emphasis added). Hence, in His sacrifice He would behold (see) those He would give new life to. Oftentimes, we as children have resentments toward our well-intentioned parents. In like manner, Christ would be perceived incorrectly by many, even some who would be numbered among His spiritual offspring. Therefore, His "seed" would be those He had spiritually begotten through His infinite Atonement. He would be their Father in the sense of giving them a new and eternal spiritual life. Jesus Christ would become the Everlasting Father of all those ransomed through His Godly powers! Thus, those who believe in our Lord are seeds in the Garden of the Lord.

All seeds beget after their own kind. They produce after their own likeness. This means that, doctrinally speaking, Christ as Father gives spiritual rebirth to children who are of the same kind and type as Himself. He sees His seed—in other words, those who are born again after His kind, likeness, image, and type. We are not seeds of a different kind to Christ after we are born again through His name! We become seeds like unto Him. Our identity, nature and destiny take on a new meaning and potential. We therefore all become capable of being a similar type of seed and tree as He is—one of great fruitfulness. Herein lies a great and marvelous secret, a mystery hidden from the world. It is therefore completely true to say that Christ sees something in us we do not see in ourselves—the literal seeds of true eternal greatness.

I am deeply moved by the true message of Easter. Christ is the lamb without blemish, slain from *before* the foundation of the world. His *offering* was that of a perfectly pure, righteous, holy soul—given in our stead. He gave Himself. He gave His innocence, goodness, love, and power so that we might be reconciled to God and obtain eternal glory if we come to Him with full purpose of heart. He was fully submissive to this divine sacrifice—He did it without resentment or contempt for us. He did not scream injustice or shout about unfairness, although His suffering was clearly unjust. He acted in holy love to ransom our souls. His will was "*swallowed up* in the will of the

Father" (Mosiah 15:7, emphasis added). He had nothing left to give because He gave all that He had.

Let us consider the woman taken in adultery. Why did Christ not condemn her—even though she was clearly guilty and punishable under the Mosaic Law? I believe part of the reason is that He knew He would pay the price for her sin on conditions of repentance. He understood the guilt and shame she felt—or perhaps would yet feel. He saw no virtue in stoning her because He would yet pay her debt to Justice, and she would come to accept Him. What use would it be to kill her? He would be killed so that she could find life. His perfect Atonement would see to that. By extending love she would be far more likely to change her behavior and her heart. It was not just that He had no desire to stone her. He wanted to save her. The pharisees did not share this perspective. By taking the approach He did so openly, the Savior was in essence inviting all others to seek repentance and find forgiveness from sin, including the Pharisees. His example is a lesson to us all.

Garden of Crucifixion

It is my heartfelt conviction that the bitterness Christ experienced in the Garden of Gethsemane and on the Cross of Calvary was endured by Him because He kept firmly in His mind and heart what it was all for. It was to bring salvation to His children (His seed). That motivated Him deeply as He endured the agony. That encouraged Him onwards. That lifted Him to press forward during crushing pain. It was a sweet thought, a happy idea, a loving notion—the concept that His children would thereby be saved from endless suffering and brought to a point of eternal opportunity. What parent would not be spurred on to face terrible bitterness so that their children could see such a magnificent and everlasting outcome? This was what happened in the bittersweet place Golgotha (Calvary). He was nailed to a tree of death so that He could bring us to the tree of life. He was pierced through so that we might be made whole. He was raised in agony so that we might be lifted upwards in glory. This was the cross of the Christ—none other could face this ordeal, triumph over this trial, and turn this travesty into majesty. He was humiliated so that we could face God with a clean conscience on the day of our judgment. He was the Lamb of offering, whose sacrifice was without guile, whose love was without duplicity, whose kindness can never be conquered. This He evidenced upon the cross of condemnation.

Ironically, olives often taste bitter and yet are nutritionally good for us. In like manner, the bitterness of the Savior's suffering blesses us if we accept Him. His bitter death becomes our means of obtaining the sweetest possible life of all. My appreciation for this reality has expanded and deepened over the years. This gives me great resolve to love myself as Christ has so generously loved me.

His Suffering Draws You to Him

I have come to a greater depth of awareness of how Christ knows the challenges each person faces that are unique to them. There are experiences that I have had that others do not understand exactly from my vantage point, just like I do not understand all their experiences in the way they do. However, I appreciate that the Savior can minister to each person specifically, as He knows what they think and feel about each challenge. His ministering is therefore both universal in reaching everyone and personal in that it caters perfectly for the individual. It is comforting to know that the Savior is perfectly able to succor each soul.

I feel greatly assured that Christ had us in mind—individually and personally—as He was put through the incomparable agony, angst, anxiety, and anguish of the Atonement. This unique experience started in Gethsemane and lasted until His final moments on the cross. His terrible sufferings involved body, mind, heart, and spirit. Only by the power of the Spirit, as we reflect on the prophetic word, can we catch a glimpse of the awfulness of what happened during that time. I know that the Anointed One overcame every evil, pain, and affliction that confronted Him. Afterwards, His joy revealed itself in fulness. The Son of God became victorious over sin, death, hell, and the devil. How grateful I am to know this transcendent truth. My love for the Lamb without blemish is beyond words. This redemptive reaching He had toward us was manifest in Him descending into the deepest darkness so that He could lift us to the greatest height. His suffering has drawn me to Him with tender regard and a love that can never be vanquished.

Garden of the Broken Stone

In the garden of the broken stone Christ came forth in a newness of life. This was a literal bodily resurrection. The tomb of death gave way to the garden of new beginnings for the Holy One and for all humanity. A weeping Mary supposed the man she saw *"to be the gardener"* (John 20:15). Mary did not recognize her Lord initially. She thought He was just the gardener who may have moved her Lord's dead body to another location. He was the Gardener! Just not the one she thought He was. This was His Garden of Resurrection. He was the first fruits of them that slept. He was the one who would bring new life to the sleeping dead. He was the ultimate Gardener, tending the fruits of the Garden of God!

Garden of Light

We have, in the life of the young Joseph Smith, an essential lesson about spiritual truth seeking. He was not content to abdicate personal responsibility by allowing other voices—even strong and persuasive ones—to decide his eternal fate. Rather, he accepted accountability for his quest of discovery. This adventure involved his serious consideration of important questions—such as which church was true and which he should join, how he could be forgiven of his sins, and which interpretation of biblical passages was correct given the many diverse and conflicting ones swirling around him.

It became apparent to him that the war of words and tumult of opinions could not possibly yield definitive answers or the peace he sought. Rather than choose incorrectly or leave his decision-making capacity in the hands of others, he determined that he would seek divine guidance directly. He stated the matter thus—"I at length came to the determination to 'ask of God,'" (Joseph Smith—History 1:13). Joseph realized that he only had two viable options. The first was to remain in dark confusion. The second was to plead with God for light and understanding. He opted for the second path. "I retired to the *woods* to make the attempt. It was on *the morning of a beautiful, clear day, early in the spring*" (Joseph Smith—History 1:14, emphasis added). He had faith that God was in the business of giving honest and direct guidance to sincerely seeking souls. This comprehension came to him through genuine pondering and revelatory insight.

So it is with us. In our day and time, we live in a vortex of contention and dissension. This is especially true of spiritual/religious ideas. We simply cannot discover the truth by referring only or mainly to the claims of other mortals. Nor can written texts be sufficient to guide us as they are subject to so much contradictory and divisive interpretation. The Son of God returned to the earth in glory long after His resurrection from the dead. He came to reconcile man with God, to overcome the long night of apostasy, to flood the world with light, to repair the breach that had developed between humanity and the Father. He came to a grove of light, a wood of splendid wonder. He came to answer a prayer, to fulfil prophecy, to keep a covenant, and to save a dark world. Our great need is to "ask of God in faith." As we kneel in humble prayer and seek clear direction, having studied the issues in our minds and heart beforehand, we will find divine answers which soothe our souls with clarity and peace. May we find, as young Joseph did, that God is the great living source of all truth, now and always.

There are few events in the history of the world that can compare with the first vision of Joseph Smith. It is of great moment that this happened in a woodland setting, in a forest if you will. I do not believe that this was a meaningless coincidence. The remarkable theophany of the Restoration happened in a garden setting! It is no surprise that Joseph had to humble himself in a place set apart from the world, so that he might open the heavens and receive forgiveness and reconciliation with God. Joseph was restored to the presence of God. He was united with his divine destiny. What a great type, symbol, and representation this is! Joseph was a good seed in the literal garden of God. It is significant that the name "Joseph" is of Hebrew origin and means essentially "Jehovah increases" (nameberry.com/babyname/Joseph/boy). How perfect that is given that through Joseph light and knowledge of God was phenomenally increased in all the world, false doctrines were corrected, great joy has come to millions through the restoration, and his name is regarded for both good and evil in every nation (Joseph Smith—History 1:33).

I have pondered much on the beloved Hymn number 26, "Joseph Smith's First Prayer." This prayer in song shows that heaven and earth combined in unified voice to bear testimony of the truth of this wondrous experience. Both the physical and the spiritual were aligned. The light of the sun and the light of the Father and Son were all witnesses that day. The sounds of animals, the beauty of the surroundings, and the importance of what was happening became a chorus of sensory manifestations. The prophet Joseph saw, heard, felt, and knew beautiful things that day. The testimony of many other people has also given voice to their heaven-sent witness that this sublime event brought added light and faith in God to the world.

I am deeply grateful to say that my testimony of the latter-day seer Joseph has remained with me since childhood and has grown significantly over the years. It has allowed me to withstand the many times I have heard people criticize and malign the Prophet. I have felt to defend Joseph, his story, and teachings against reviling. For example, when I was a full-time missionary in England, I had many opportunities to teach and testify of the first vision. On every occasion, I felt the Spirit bearing strong witness to the sacred truth of this account. I loved to share this story and I rejoiced to bear testimony of it. It brought me great joy to do so! Why did the Lord give me and my companions (and our friends!) such precious testimonial experiences at a young age? I think the answer is really very simple. Revelation begets more revelation. Truth inspires more truth. When we experience a true spiritual witness, we want to feel it again and again. We also desire to share it with others. We have a Father in Heaven who loves to teach, bless, guide, and share with us. That was what He was doing for me in my youth (and is still doing today in my late 40s!).

God showed me His revealed truth in a personal way and uplifted my life forever. When I reflect on this, it makes perfect sense. Our good and generous God lives to help His children. The message of God calling Joseph Smith resonates with me because it is the perfect pattern of how God works. He calls on each of us—one by one—and touches us in both a quiet and magnanimous manner. I have learned that as each of us truly seeks God, we will find Him. That communion is joyous to our souls—and to His. My testimony of the Prophet Joseph has continually strengthened me to build my growing faith on the rock of revelation and thus has permitted me to survive spiritual storms of all kinds.

As I have come to see the "Seer," I realize that Joseph was a radical revelator. His life and ministry represent an entirely different (and improved) way of seeing spirituality and religion. It is intended to surprise us, wake us up, take us out of traditional comfort zones and change our lives in meaningful ways. When something becomes mainstream, we tend to overlook its significance and take it for granted. However, I believe that as we come to see the first vision as distinctly magnificent, it alters the way we see God. We discern that He is truly a personal being—a concerned Father. This substantially revises, enhances, and magnifies the whole meaning of life. It has done so for me in multifaceted ways.

This shows that God is a perfected living personage who cares for each of us and actively intervenes in our lives in important ways. He seeks to be close to us, to answer our important questions, to guide our destinies, and to assist us on vital issues. This is poignant beyond description. Considering how desperately each of us needs this loving personal influence—especially in a world markedly distant from spiritual values—there has never been a more important time or a greater need to encourage the world to ask of God in personal prayer. As I have reflected deeply, I have come to understand the first vision as a morning of light with a message of love for the entire world. The Prophet Joseph Smith is a window to the soul of God the Father, God the Son, and God the Holy Ghost. He is the great revelator of the living Christ for this dispensation. The jigsaw-like picture we see grows line upon line until we receive a fulness of truth and light.

It was a lovely morning for discovering the true nature of God! It is the perfect pattern for how a true Prophet of God is called. Think of the process:

The preparation for the event.

Joseph was a pure, good, honest seeker of divine truth. He was not satisfied with what men wanted him to believe, or just finding his own way through life. Rather, he wanted to know the right thing, the correct way, the will of God. He studied the matter in his mind, he pondered in his heart, he visited churches, and he listened to ministers. He discussed the matter with others. He also read the holy scriptures and was moved upon by the Holy Spirit to ask of God. The impression was so clear that it was unmistakable. Only God could resolve his confusion and provide clarity on which church was true and which he should join. He was Spirit-led to a grove of trees on a beautiful, bright clear day. He was divinely prompted to kneel on holy ground. This was divine destiny in action. It was a clear convergence between the divine will and Joseph's personal agency. This moment was meant to happen.

Joseph saw a light and two Beings of brilliant glory beyond the power of words to express.

This was a grand theophany—the ultimate mortal revelatory experience. He heard a voice and was called by name. He became a living witness of the perfect Father and His glorified Son. His opinion was not then based on conjecture, speculation, or deceit. He was a living, seeing, hearing, feeling witness with actual firsthand experience of the divine. He was instructed, warned, and given clear and direct guidance. This momentous experience would change his life and the world forever.

Opposition both preceded, accompanied, and attended him after this marvelous moment.

That the account details a visit from the adversary, who came to rant and rave, is a certain testimony that the event really happened and was God-inspired. Both devilish darkness and loving light indicated that Joseph was in the right place, at the right time, with the right desire.

This experience acted as a firm testimonial foundation for the work Joseph would need to do.

It laid the foundation for further sacred communication and provided sure certainty for the many difficult assignments that lay ahead.

Joseph now had the certain confidence associated with knowledge. His was a memorable and overpowering witness.

This was a very personal answer to a private prayer.

God knew Joseph by name and need. What consolation this must have brought to the young man. He knew God knew him! He learned the truth from the ultimate source of wisdom and goodness! Joseph saw that he was truly created in God's image and likeness. This was a very special family reunion between heaven and earth. What relief, love, and happiness Joseph must have felt to have been so treated and blessed!

This was also a response to the deep desires and needs of many others, both living and dead.

I believe Joseph felt relief when he obtained these sure solutions to his problems. This visit answered so many questions. He would also come to feel a great sense of weight upon him by learning a message which would have far-reaching implications for the whole globe. The answer was both a blessing and a burden!

The Prophet Joseph Smith has shown us clearly the inspiring path we must take and the pattern we need to follow to gain the deep personal knowledge of the living God. We benefit from:

Studying sincerely the matters of spiritual import
Determining to ask of God
Going to holy and sacred ground
Kneeling in humble genuine prayer
Persisting through opposition by looking to God for help
Listening, accepting, and following the answers given!

We are not likely to experience precisely what Joseph did as we follow this scriptural pattern of seeking and finding truth. However, we will discover some similarities. We will have sacred opportunities to receive inspiration and revelation that will calm our fears, lessen our doubts, boost our confidence, and foster our determination to stand strong during times of challenge. It is vital that we kneel on holy ground to commune with God and so learn for ourselves the things that are true rather than simply relying on our own intellectual understanding or the seemingly persuasive opinions of those who view Joseph as a fraud. And we will be prepared for the time when we will have divine encounters of tremendous significance to us personally and to our families and communities.

I feel grateful to my Father in Heaven for allowing me to be alive during these great days where the everlasting gospel is restored. These are trying and triumphant times. I am thankful that God has trusted me with His glorious message. I am humbled to serve in His kingdom. I am pleased that I live in this marvelous season of time. Anyone can sail on calm seas, but it takes effort, faith, and patience to sail on stormy ones. I am committed to the building up and strengthening of His kingdom on the earth. I seek to play my part in this divine work wherever that journey takes me, whatever is required and however long the expedition. I am determined to go the distance irrespective of the cost involved in doing so. I feel deep love for this great latter-day work (see Alma 26). My words are as a murky shadow when compared to the light of joy I have received through this restored gift.

I testify of the opening of the heavens to the Prophet Joseph Smith in these last days. This restored gospel is not just good or better, but it is best. It is essential for the highest salvation. We need this restored truth to become the best person we can be. While the people on the earth already have the light of Christ, this is not all that exists. Even this light is under attack in this world. We need to safeguard this light and to promote the higher blessings of the gift of the Holy Ghost, laws, ordinances, covenants, and commandments. The true priesthood and the Holy Temple are necessary to partake of the Atonement of the Lord completely and to become fully Christlike. This is beyond common morality and shared ethics as it involves deep and lasting spiritual transformation. It involves inner comprehension, enhanced perspectives, beautified relationships, and new life.

I believe it is important for us to say and do things in private and public to show our support and sustaining of Joseph as a Prophet. My conviction is that we will never be ultimately derailed spiritually but we will be divinely protected as we openly defend the Prophet Joseph. It does matter if we believe or not, join the Church or not, make covenants or not and live faithfully or not. The spiritual choices we make do matter now and eternally. We are to be different to the world. We use different language, have distinct values, and hold to revealed standards. We think and act differently. Those differences are grounded in restored perspectives. It is this difference that makes us unique and sets us apart, not in arrogant ways but in encouraging and loving ways. This special uniqueness is what we offer to the world. We need to see, live, and proclaim this difference to the entire world. The Restoration has the power to substantially alter the world for the better. Praise to the man who was the instrument for this renewing message destined to change the world forever.

All true prophets follow this same pattern. They ponder and abide by the treasured precepts of the scriptures. So can we. This generation is to have the word of God through Joseph Smith (Doctrine & Covenants 5:10). Hence, we ought to seek earnestly to follow the living prophet in our viewpoint, appearance, words, deeds, and example. By this means we are following the Father and the Son in our day and time. We are thus once again reconciled to God.

5

Laws of the Harvest

THE DOCTRINE OF IRREVOCABLE DIVINE LAW IS REVEALED TRUTH (Doctrine & Covenants 130:20–21). The heavens and the earth are governed by law. Such laws are decreed by the Almighty, whose privilege it is to rule and reign in righteousness as the Supreme Being. We are instructed that He designated an unchangeable standard in the world before this life. That certain and unshakable foundation was the law of cause and effect; action and result; choice and outcome. The law is therefore one of definite assurance. It is that all blessings from God are contingent upon obedience to divine law. All rewards are conditional upon compliance to the laws of the Lord. There neither is, nor can be, any revoking, overriding, or alteration of this elemental truth. This powerful reality makes life knowable, understandable, and reliable.

As we learn God's law, we can live it. Such living becomes an anchor to our souls. A gardener must comply with law in the planting, cultivating, and tending of a seed for it to come to full fruition as a fruitful plant. Likewise, there are laws that must be known and followed for each one of us to gain the blessings that God has ordained for our growth, development, success, and eventual glory.

The Law of Moral Agency

It has become very popular over the last 60 years to see liberty as the freedom to do whatever we want to do. Often agency is viewed as freedom to choose, without regard to the inevitable implications of such freedom. Agency implies choice, it indicates action. However, it also denotes responsibility and accountability. It is vital to discern that agency inexorably includes not simply what we choose to believe and do, but also the consequences, outcomes, results, and ramifications of the choice. If it were not so, then God could not reward righteousness and chasten wickedness. He would simply have to say to us, "Well as long as you make any choice, then you are using your agency correctly." What sense would that make? It would be like equating the offer that Lucifer made in the grand council with the offer that Jehovah made. Jehovah said, "Thy will be done and the glory be thine forever." Lucifer said, "Give me thine honor" (Moses 4:1–2). These are diametrically opposed options. They cannot both be virtuous, righteous, and beautiful. One of them was a proper use of agency whereas the other was a misuse or an abuse of agency. One was compliance with divine truth. The other was rebellion. God could not smile upon both positions simultaneously.

By the same token, our choices are moral ones. They have spiritual implications. They are intrinsically ethical. When we sing "choose the right" (*Hymns,* no. 239), we are acknowledging that agency is intended to be used in righteousness, or rightness. The popular idea that the making of any choice whatsoever, regardless of the spiritual/moral impacts, is somehow automatically approved of by God, is akin to nullifying the distinction between good and evil; right and wrong; good and bad; upright and depraved. Making choices is not enough. Our important choices always have a spiritual component. They need to lean toward what is inspired to be compatible with what God designs for us. Being consciously deliberate is necessary when we are deciding what to believe, how to speak, what to value, how to live, how to relate to others, etc. We need to choose to believe good, to do right, to behave properly, to think purely and to live valiantly. This requires reflective contemplation about why and how we are using our agency.

The Lord said, "If ye *love* me, *keep* my commandments" (John 14:15, emphasis added). Hence, the keeping of the commandments of God evidences our love for God. He did not say, "If ye love me, do whatever you want to do." This is a great insight into the soul of Christ. He loved His Father completely, and thus chose to keep His commandments. He actively decided to show love to His Father by living right, doing good, and being obedient. This gives us an entirely more inspiring view of obedience than it merely being a duty. It is a show of love, a display of affection, a sign of connection. It is about showing respect, admiration, and emulation toward the Supreme Father of our souls. The Son loved the Father with His whole heart, mind, might, and strength. He honored Him, worshipped Him, clung to Him, believed in Him, trusted Him, and served Him. Christ's determination to use His agency well in mortality was an extension of His premortal devotion to His Father. Did the Savior just sail through mortality? Of course not. He faced every possible form of challenge, every conceivable test of character, every imaginable trial of His faith. He voluntarily chose to resist temptation by intentionally choosing to do good instead. He was righteous when He could have chosen sin. He chose to be honest. He decided to be pure. He determined to be courageous. He purposed to be loving. These were real moral decisions because He could have done otherwise.

Why does God command obedience to His voice? Because it is the way His precious children can best live themselves and simultaneously protect and love one another. I do not perceive His invitation for us to show obedience to Him as emotional blackmail or unrighteous dominion. Rather, as the Son of God loves us so perfectly, He levels with us. He wants us to be full of love and joy. He wants us to be in covenant connection with Him and the Father. He wants us to genuinely love Him and have that love as our reason for being true to Him. Our love of Him leads to our keeping His law. It is a relational love of law, life, and liberty! We obtain great joy by spiritually disciplined living. As we control our appetites, desires, and passions in righteous ways, we are filled with love that never fades. As we choose to do good, our agency is empowered, increased, magnified, and expanded. We learn to choose virtue over vice, courage over fear, faith over doubt, work over laziness, sacrifice over selfishness, and love over hate. We become persons of deep and permanent godly character. Our agency is therefore focused to a specific end. This does not imply that we are coerced or forced by God. We are free to choose either good or evil, but not both.

We must make a choice between these two options—we cannot absolve or abdicate our personal responsibility to choose. Every one of us must make a certain choice. Over time the pattern of our choices becomes clear and definite. Hence, to truly be an agent means to be an agent for God. It is to do what He would do. It is to become more as He already is. I do not think we have the divine "right" to do that which is wrong—we have ability to do wrong—but not divine sanction or approval to do so. If we choose to do wrong, we are bound by the consequences of that choice. God is only bound to bless us when we choose to follow the good way.

It might appear strange to compare ourselves to a seed especially in the context of agency. Seeds are acted upon by soil, water, heat, and light. We might therefore perceive seeds as not acting. However, I think the seed is a good analogy precisely because it both acts and is acted upon. Seeds are influenced by their environment. However, they are also living things. They are not like rocks, tables, and cars—which are purely acted upon. Rather, they grow and develop in active ways. They do not stay the same way always. They change in productive and useful ways. So it can be with us. To act through our agency is essential to the development and long-term purposes of our true nature. I love the truth that we are not commanded or *"compelled in all things"* (Doctrine & Covenants 58:26–32). Hence, we are to use our own creativity to bring many righteous things to fruition.

We can therefore only rise above passivity by personally choosing to be moral when we might have chosen immorality instead. We each have the essential freedom to yield to the Holy Spirit, look to our Savior, follow His commandments, and be loyal to His words (2 Nephi 2:27–28;10:23). We are to be wise in gradually becoming spiritually minded (2 Nephi 9:39). Thus, agency is the God-given power to voluntarily act in faith to keep commandments and receive the joy of personal righteousness. While choosing can be difficult, it is also deeply rewarding. There is no real progress without this tremendous privilege. In this process of choosing we learn about consequences and our agency thus expands with proper use or contracts with misuse.

It is also important to reflect on the role of certain kinds of gifts and limitations in life. There will always be those who are smarter, faster, stronger, or better looking than we are. Or those not as gifted as we are in certain areas. These natural gifts vary from one person to the next. A special gift of intelligence, athleticism, musicality, etc. does not necessarily advantage someone ethically. Nor do they automatically spiritually curtail a person. They do not dictate our moral agency. Likewise, a limitation in these areas is not the deciding factor in whether we incline toward light or darkness. Certainly our natural gifts are to be used for good purposes. However, it is our choices, rather than the gifts or limitations themselves, that determine what we become. This explains why people with great gifts or serious limitations can be found either serving good or bad causes.

The core choice we face is between good and evil, or between good and great. All accountable persons have this ability. While we are judged by reference to what we do with our God-given gifts and talents, this is an individual judgment. I am accountable for what I do with my gifts, not for the gifts given to others. Therefore, we all have both gifts and limitations that we need to come to terms with. God is aware of all these natural endowments and what we choose to do with them. Therefore, they do not override our innermost desires and so do not essentially favor us in, or prevent us from, choosing the right. Thus, while genetics and situational factors interact in a complex way with our ability to choose, we are ultimately free to choose the godly life. This is true irrespective of what circumstances exist to make righteousness seem either easy or impossible. We are not judged by reference to gifts and circumstances we have no control over but by choices we do have control over. I see this as evidence of a loving, just, and merciful God. The test of mortality is one we can pass with divine help!

I am grateful to know that following the word of God as revealed through prophetic and personal revelation involves thoughtful and heartfelt compliance with standard, consistent, and useful instructions. Every principle that comes from God has the express purpose of blessing lives now and eternally. He knows what works for us because He has already achieved the perfect state that we are aiming for. He leads us with love, kindness, and when necessary, with direct firmness. The sacred proof the gospel is true comes to those who obey its precepts with regular devoted practice—this spiritual evidence comes with convincing power to the heart, mind, and spirit as it draws us ever closer to God.

The empowering quality of agency is that we are daring designers of divine destiny. Things that are good, positive, uplifting, inspiring, and true naturally inspire more of the same within us and around us. It is wonderful that we are ultimately responsible and accountable for our decisions and lives. The Lord desires that we struggle and grow through our own efforts in what we can do and call on Him to do those things that only He can do. Our proactive power linked with His Almighty power is a mighty combination of influential strength. We can continue to grow in goodness line upon line until we obtain a fulness of agency such as God possesses (2 Nephi 28:30).

Desire is the great determinant of the spiritual life (Helaman 14:30–31). We all desire something. We all have both weak and strong desires. I believe that our desires are not always for happiness. Of course, sometimes we desire happiness and employ the incorrect approaches in aiming at it. However, sometimes we may desire pleasure, ease, comfort, gain, power, or other things rather than happiness per se. Hence, why desires need to be examined and sometimes reformulated. When we recognize that our desires may be displaced, we can change them to align with noble wants instead. The personal gift of agency allows us to have and/or to develop desires for divinity. Gods and angels have different desires than devils. Men live according to the overriding desires of their hearts. Therefore, learning to desire righteousness deeply is core to our development. Christ cultivates righteous desires within us if we let Him!

The stunning reality is that our personal choices over a lifetime either bring us to salvation through Christ or damnation through the devil (Alma 29:4–5). Both spiritual failure and spiritual success are the real consequences of genuine freedom to choose (Mosiah 29:27). I treasure this eternal truth of the highest importance (2 Nephi 10:23). To teach us this principle memorably the Lord reveals the outcomes that follow choices. Consider first the beautiful, edifying, and joyful experiences of those who choose righteousness as their way of life (3

Nephi 17:17–25). Now contrast the tragedy of those who choose wickedness as their way of life (Helaman 13:37–38; Mormon 2:12–15; 6:16–20). It is therefore crucially important to exercise our inalienable ability to traverse the strait and narrow path (2 Nephi 2:27; Alma 30:8). We are to exercise our agency in faith in Christ to do godlike things. We can retain and rediscover continually our individual power to act independently in righteousness.

We learn in mortality that desires are deeply important. What we truly desire becomes the great focus of our lives. As we mature, our desires change. Some things, that we once thought important, become increasingly irrelevant. Other things, previously never considered, start to become incredibly vital. The Lord is very interested in the persistent and consistent desires of our hearts. The deepest longing of the human soul is to enter back into the eternal presence of God. There is so wanting or desire more pure or intense than this and no blessings that surpass these in time or eternity. Our true and lasting happiness is what God labors for. It is what brings Him joy and meaning. It is therefore true wisdom that we learn to live celestial principles in our probationary estate (Alma 1:4).

The Law of Reaping What We Sow

The law of God is that we harvest only what we plant (Doctrine & Covenants 6:33–34). Therefore we ought not to be frightened to do good works. We do not need to worry about the consequences of sowing good seeds. Why? The Lord promises that the sowing of good efforts always leads to the reaping of good outcomes. Always. If it were not for this secure law, salvation would be impossible. As the sons and daughters of God, we can go forward in faith. As the offspring of Christ, we do not need to fearfully concern ourselves with earthly powers and dark forces. Even if both men and unseen enemies unite against us, our cause is secure. The result is assured. We may feel small in significance and timid in outlook. However, we can acquire confidence in the face of opposition because if we are built on the sure rock of our Redeemer's revelation, no amount of pressure can triumph over us. This is the kind of doctrine that fortifies us as we hear, believe, and share it.

THE LAW OF TITHING

The revealed law of tithing is to "pay one-tenth of all [our] interest annually" (Doctrine & Covenants 119:3–7). What a marvelous law this is. This is a perpetual holy law. Therefore, by paying ongoing attention to this law, we will become holy persons. In addition, the land of Zion is made sacred by obedience to this law—that is a mighty promise to the covenant people of God. Our material gifts given to God are a sacred sign to Him of our devotion. Indeed, the land of covenant is truly made "most holy" by loyalty to this law. Further, this is an example for all stakes throughout the kingdom. Thereby each person, family, ward, and stake, is made holier by the continual effort to keep this law of the Lord. Thus, the observance of this commandment is indispensable to establishing Zion throughout all nations of the earth. It also means holiness is lacking in our lives and the kingdom if we do not pay our tithing. If we want more holiness in our lives and homes, we are well advised to make the law of tithing a non-negotiable feature of our discipleship.

"Will a *man rob* ***God***?" (Malachi 3:8–12, emphasis added). To steal from another human is forbidden by both human and divine law. Where then does stealing from God stand from the viewpoint of the Lord? From the Old Testament we learn that the non-payment of tithing and associated freewill offerings by the covenant people meant a cursing for the entire body of people. In the alternative, the Lord commanded the Israelites to pay tithing as a means of stocking the shelves of the Lord's Storehouse, which could then be used to benefit the covenant people and others. The revelation to pay tithing has been given anew in our day and the directives and promises are restored in their pristine purity. We are therefore blessed by this commandment to give to God! In truth, God invites us to put this law to the test. As we do, we find that He will open the heavenly windows to pour out needed blessings upon us.

I have experienced this promised bestowal many times. When my wife and I were newly married we were financially stretched many times. At one point when we had just moved into our first home, I had just started a demanding new job, our son was just a couple of months old, and I was called to serve as first counselor in a busy bishopric.

Our family worked hard to serve and to keep up with all the responsibilities we faced. On one occasion after paying our tithing and other obligations, I remember we had €7 left to live on for the entire week (or about $6.50 USD). We survived based on the simple food storage we had gathered in obedience to prophetic counsel and the availability of the lowest priced bread I have ever seen in the thrift store close to our home! The Lord was at work there.

Another time when we were concluding Church meetings on a Sunday, three people asked me if we needed a lift home (we could not afford our own car yet and so we walked or took the bus everywhere). We literally could not accept three simultaneous offers but were very grateful to receive all of them and avail of one of them! We saw this as a literal fulfilment of the promise the Lord had given that "there shall not be room enough to receive the blessing." The Lord was right. I was not putting Him to the test, for I trusted Him. However, we put His law to the test, and it passed with flying colors! We have witnessed this true promise bear fruit literally thousands of times.

The Lord promises that He will rebuke the devourer for us (Malachi 3:10). This means that our efforts will not be prevented from coming to fruition. Our labors will be rewarded. Our plans will be prospered. Our blessings will be assured. This does not mean we will have no setbacks. However, it does mean that good results will accrue to us. I know these promises manifest in both spiritual and temporal ways. The rich blessings we have seen in terms of education, family, career, and opportunities to serve in the church and community have come in large part because we have diligently tried to observe the Lord's command to pay Him first and sacrifice in offerings for the sake of His children. We are further told that all nations will call Israel blessed and the land of the covenant people will be a delight. This has been fulfilled in our day. A reasonable look at the prosperity of modern Israel shows that the Church is phenomenally enabled with resources to bless the entire world. This directly arises from the obedience of Saints to this magnificent privilege.

The Law of the Sabbath

What a lovely law this is! The Lord commands us to go to the place of prayer on Sunday (Doctrine & Covenants 59:9–10). We are instructed to offer our sacraments to Him. We normally refer to receiving or partaking of the sacramental emblems. To offer is to give something of ourselves, to present ourselves, to supplicate with our souls. We are taught that this holy day is specifically designated by God as a day of rest from worldly work and for us to bring our devotions—our worshipful offerings—to the Almighty. The result of taking this time to consume sacrificial symbols and ponder on holy things is that we become more fully pure, less contaminated with that which is unholy, and more able to resist evil. This day blesses us deeply. The law is that as we set this time apart for focus on our Father, His Son, and the Holy Ghost, we will be less stained with the blot of carnality. I have felt the truth of this beautiful promise.

The Law of Chastity

God's law of moral purity is truly educational. Jacob said that he would rejoice greatly in his people if pride had been their only challenge (Jacob 2:22–28). Imagine that! Pride is quite a serious difficulty. However, the prophet felt that he would have much joy if that were the only thing troubling them. They were facing a much more insidious enemy—promiscuity. Jacob called moral turpitude a grosser crime (a worse sin) than pride! It was the vice that lacked virtue. It was not only immorality in terms of following practices that were not divinely authorized, but also in the rationalizing and justifying of that behavior based on an appeal to the revealed word. The men of that society were saying that because David and Solomon had more than one wife and had concubines, that they were likewise warranted in doing the same. Jacob was clear that this was forbidden. This practice was an abomination because it was not commanded by God *at that time to those people.* Its adoption was therefore not in alignment with a pure and chaste approach to relationships in the eyes of God.

This is strong language. Jacob is teaching that this impure behavior was more serious spiritually than the sin of pride. Surely that is a powerful warning from God that moral virtue is the standard. God always obeys the law of chastity—meaning the law of relational virtue—and we should do likewise. This is a stern reminder that moral rectitude safeguards our purity and keeps us connected with God in a safe and wholesome way. The doctrine of one man and one woman united in the marriage covenant—according to the law of the Lord—is the divine standard given in holy writ and is to be observed unless God specifically instructs otherwise through authorized priesthood channels. When He does instruct otherwise, it will never be to violate holy standards of purity. God's law is essentially virtue laden. It is my view that Christ wants priesthood brethren to strive to be pure in heart and deed.

The Law of Health

The Word of Wisdom is a potent promise (Doctrine & Covenants 89:18–21). The Lord announces that those Latter-day Saints that live in accordance with the principles in the revelation, who simultaneously keep all the commandments, will be blessed in the body with navel health and bone marrow! They will also find the wisdom they seek and the precious knowledge they inquire after. This knowledge will include the mysteries, or secrets of God which can only be known by revelation. These observant Saints will be able to run without becoming exhausted and to walk without losing all their energy. I believe that this ability will be both physical and spiritual. The Saints will therefore be able to perform the physical duties placed upon them. They will also be able to endure spiritually when dealing with the strains of life. This ability to persist without becoming permanently overwhelmed or losing momentum and resolve will therefore be manifest in the lives of Saints that live these wise principles. In the ultimate sense, the oath we receive from God is that we will not suffer untimely deaths from plaques and diseases as we abide in this law of health. This is therefore a spiritual law that benefits covenant disciples both in terms of their bodily health and their spiritual resilience. It is a law of revelation, wisdom, and health.

The Law of Revelation of the Redeemer

There is a revelation that every man, woman, and child ever born on this earth needs to have. There is a law each person needs to have personal encounter with. This is a gift that can come to every seeking and humble person that desires it in righteousness. All gifts of the Spirit are contingent on our asking for them with pure intent. Hence, the gifts come to us from a loving God based on obedience to gospel principles. This special law I am referring to is a law of revelation of a very significant kind. In speaking of this vital revelation, which is not optional for salvation, the Lord tells us about two ways of knowing this truth (Doctrine & Covenants 46:13–14).

Some of God's children receive an actual knowledge by the power of the third member of the Godhead that Jesus Christ is God's Only Begotten Son in mortality and that His suffering/crucifixion paid the price for the sins of humanity. Others receive the gift of believing in the teaching and testimony of those with revealed knowledge, so that they too have the potential to lay claim on eternal exaltation through faithfulness. That means that we must receive the witness of Christ's Divine Sonship either by direct revelation from the Holy Ghost or by hearing the inspired words of those who have had such revelation. In either case, the witness centers on the truth that Jesus is the actual Son of the Highest God. It is of great significance that these are listed as the primary spiritual gifts in this revelation. It is also deeply important that the means has been provided, that all may come to this understanding. God loves each child enough to ensure that this most precious revelation can be theirs. It is only by means of this personal revelation that we can have the foundational strength to survive and flourish through all the storms of life. By so doing we will never fall away from Christ (Helaman 5:12).

The Law of Prospering in Two Lands of Promise

Abraham received promises of covenant lands for himself, his wives, and his children. These were holy lands, consecrated spots of ground, actual physical earth plots on which to dwell. My conviction is that these lands were intended to be places of righteous living. I believe these properties were intended to be sacred, dedicated portions of the earth. Abraham was known as the father of the faithful and the inheritance of his children who were loyal to God was to be a physical and spiritual legacy. He was promised that the everlasting gospel would be preserved through his seed (his children) and that they would share the truth throughout the earth. It is evident that these seeds (children) were to grow to spiritual maturity in these special lands of promise. This symbolism shows that God's plan is that full spiritual maturity can only ultimately happen in the chosen promised land. This explains why the promised land has always been part of the full flowering of God's divine design for the House of Israel. In other words, we do not grow to full spiritual maturity unless and until we have access to a promised land. In my opinion, living in a stake of Zion serves the purpose of effectively living in a promised land community. A country is made holy by the faithfulness to God of those who live upon the land.

The prophet-patriarch Lehi received similar promises to Abraham (2 Nephi 1:5–7). This is the extension of the promises of the Lord from an individual to a family, then to an entire people. Lehi was led through the wilderness (a lone and dreary world) to a place of milk and honey (a land of promised abundance). Many challenges were faced and surmounted in that journey, and the family of Lehi was led to the Americas. Obviously, this land was to be a place chosen above all other lands, in the same way that the celestial kingdom is more choice than any other place in eternity. The Lord promised this land by covenant to Lehi and his seed and others who were divinely led by the Lord there. In other words, these promises—which are covenantal in nature—only pertain to those the Lord designated and guided there. I note that when Laman and Lemuel tied Nephi up, they were no longer being led to the promised land. This was indicative of the truth that Laman and Lemuel had at that point lost the favor of the Lord. Lehi clearly prophesies that the land is only consecrated to those brought by the Lord. This means that those not divinely led do not have the same promise as those who are so led. The Lord is only obligated to bless those who follow His word.

Further, the blessings of liberty are pronounced upon the persons who come to the land by revelation as they live according to the laws of the Lord. They will not be made captive to uninspired entities. However, this is not an absolute, unconditional promise. It is dependent upon righteousness. Those engaging in iniquity—despite the fact of having been led there by the Lord—do not retain the promise of liberty and indeed the land is cursed until they repent. On the other hand, to the righteous the land is blessed forever. Hence, only those who are obedient and/or repentant have the assured promise of the Lord of the reserved blessings of liberty, consecration of the land, and right to inheritance for their children of the blessings of heaven. In like manner, Saints dwelling anywhere on the earth only have the promises of protection and abundance from the Lord to the extent that they put Him and His law first and foremost in their lives.

The scriptures refer to two types of lands of promise—earthly and heavenly. Both can be ours if we know the Gardener.

Mortal Lands of Promise

The key doctrine of a land of promise is that it is given to a people who make and keep sacred covenants with God. A land of promise is of no merit to a people who refuse to keep their promises to God, who neglect their covenants and cast aside their integrity in favor of ambition for mammon.

The people of Lehi were promised both prospering and a new land (1 Nephi 2:20). The Lord prospers His children based on their faithfulness. This prospering is far beyond material advancement. It is fundamentally spiritual. I note that prospering is inextricably bound up with moving toward and inhabiting the American land of promise in this verse. This was and is a land most choice because of the blessings of the Lord that would come upon the righteous covenant people in that land. Without the Book of Mormon peoples and the Restoration from 1820 (which was and is vitally dependent on America for its success) the latter-day kingdom could not exist. The work of redemption for the living and the dead would be impossible!

God told the Nephites that to the extent they kept His directives, they would prosper in a land of promise (2 Nephi 3:4). On the other hand, to the extent that they failed to abide by His instructions, they removed themselves from His protective presence. In His land is abundance. In His presence is joy. His land is one of plenty. His presence is one of peace. To be outside His place of belonging and His place of influence is to be stranded, isolated, and alone. He does not want us to remain in such a condition. He wants us to come closer, draw near, feel of His love, know of His goodness, partake of His blessings, and rejoice in His glories. He wants to endow us with the treasures of eternity!

Enos was taught that the Lamanites would be visited by the Lord dependent on their diligent obedience to the divine command (Enos 1:10–11). That is the law of the harvest! Then Enos said his faith began to be unshaken in God. Thus, he gained confidence in the Lord because He was assured that the divine law was operational in his life and the lives of his brethren. This was the law of moral agency. We can always have confidence in the immutable laws of the Lord. Alma later teaches the same doctrines to those in Ammonihah. He indicates that the long-standing word of the Lord concerning either prospering or being cut off was verified. It was therefore shown, proven, evidenced, validated, or confirmed (Alma 9:13–14).

So it is with modern Israel. We remove ourselves from the divine presence if we intentionally and consistently break the laws of the Lord. Or, if we love His law, then we gain His blessings day by day, week by week, month by month, and year by year. Each person that lives His law benefits by personal prospering. For example, consider a tender revelation to the Prophet Joseph Smith (Doctrine and Covenants 21:7–8). God reveals that He has called and inspired Joseph to progress the kingdom of God on the earth. God knows his diligence and has listened to his prayers. God has seen Joseph cry for the people! God has also brought forgiveness, rejoicing, and gladness to Joseph. God says He will place blessings upon Joseph. It is God that sees and knows Joseph Smith, better than anyone else. He saw both his works and his internal sorrows. He knew Joseph by name and by character. God encouraged Joseph to continue in the work, despite opposition from enemies who had a much more restricted and limited view of the Prophet. God notices our tears, thoughts, troubles, and trials!

A Heavenly Country

Consider the prophet Abraham. He was not content with worldly living (Hebrews 11:8–16). He did not focus simply on that which was seen before him but acted in faith to follow God with long-term vision into the future. He, and others like him, proceeded to new mortal lands of promise where they could worship God. Abraham believed that God could give him a multitude of seed and God did so! However, there is more. These souls were not satisfied with a good life on earth. They desired an eternal land of promise, a lasting place of righteousness, a city of God in celestial realms. The city they sought must be designed by the God of Heaven, it must be based on truth, and it must be better than the temporary promises of a fallen world, or even the opportunity of living in a holy city on earth.

These brethren and their faithful wives and children died without eternal life having been obtained by them, for eternal life can only be obtained in eternity. However, they were persuaded that the promises were true and so they embraced them and knew that this mortal home was not their long-term home. They knew that this fallen earth was not where they ultimately belonged—it was a foreign land to them. They accepted that they were travelers, pilgrims, wanderers—they needed to journey toward the holier place(s) they sought. They therefore stepped across the veil of death with their faith intact.

These are powerful lessons in true faith. Faith means being stretched by God to believe in things that are not yet experienced but will be in the future—sometimes the far future. They may not have fully comprehended the privileges they had access to during the time they were in preparatory places, but in due course they caught the vision of what they had passed through and why. Therefore, because of their genuine, persistent, and undying faith, God was happy to reward them with a family of faith in this life and with an even greater eternal family of everlasting faith in the eternities. Their eternal home was to be a place where all promises would be obtained in their complete fulness, with no limitations. They would obtain a heavenly country of God. This is how God operates. His laws are always ones of faith. The benefits and blessings only fully accrue over time and testing. Waiting, acting, and stretching are always required. This is the heavenly outcome that will come to us as we observe the spiritual laws of the harvest in our lives.

6

A Good Seed in God's Garden

The man Abraham is a great example of a truth seeker (Abraham 1:2; 3:14). Abraham wanted more joy. On that basis he desired the blessings of the patriarchal priesthood—the blessings of eternal family reserved for those who love the Lord with all their souls. He was already a person of knowledge and righteousness. However, he wanted to be a better follower of God and to receive more light and knowledge from heaven. This was highly inspiring to him. He wanted to be a faithful husband and a loyal father. He desired many children who would learn and live the principles of righteousness. He longed to be a preacher of righteousness, a leader with love, a governor who promoted peace. He sought the blessings of Adam, Enoch, Noah, and all the faithful patriarchs that came before him. He desired to receive the necessary teaching and rights to live according to the divine standards of heaven.

Due to his desire, faithfulness, and intelligence be became a high priest after the order of the Son of God, like Melchizedek before him. The God of Heaven thus promised him that his children would be numbered like the stars in the heavens and the sands on the seashore. Not only would his seed be numerous, but they would be bright and brilliant in terms of light, glory, truth, and spiritual intelligence. Abraham is thus known as the father of the faithful (Doctrine & Covenants 138:41). Everyone after him that obtains eternal exaltation in the mansions of the Father therefore must be either of the literal biological lineage of Abraham or be grafted into his family through spiritual adoption. Consequently, all covenant disciples since the time of Abraham are the seed, meaning children, of Abraham. This is important doctrine made known to us through the Prophet Joseph Smith.

Consider these powerful and central truths:

- The Lord confirmed a priesthood upon Aaron and *his seed.* (Doctrine and Covenants 84:18; 107:13)
- Those who honor the priesthood become the *sons* of Moses, Aaron, and Abraham. (Doctrine & Covenants 84:33–44)
- Latter-day Saints are the *children* of Israel and the *seed* of Abraham. (Doctrine & Covenants 103:17)
- Faithful elders and their *seed* will receive a multiplicity of blessings. (Doctrine & Covenants 104:33)
- The priesthood is handed down from father to son—the literal descendants of the chosen *seed.* (Doctrine & Covenants 107:40)
- As with Abraham, so it is with Joseph Smith—in *him and his seed* all the *families* of the earth are to be blessed, contingent on covenant faithfulness. (Doctrine & Covenants 124:58)
- Those who enter and keep the patriarchal order of the priesthood (the new and everlasting covenant of marriage) will enjoy a *fulness and continuation* of the *seeds* forever and ever. (Doctrine & Covenants 132:19)

This vital doctrine of the covenant family is evident in the Book of Mormon also. Lehi was of the lineage of Manasseh, who was a son of Joseph, who was the son of Israel, who was the son of Isaac, who was the son of Abraham. The Book of Mormon is evidence that God keeps His promises to the seed of Abraham. Consider the covenantal promises given to Nephi (Alma 3:17). The great man Nephi was given the certain assurance from God that he, his children, and all who hearkened to his prophetic teachings would be blessed with every blessing that comes to loyal prophets. Also, those who rebelled against the teachings of the prophet Nephi would not be given these precious blessings. These promises were to stand as an everlasting inheritance to the people of Nephi as they followed the prophetic word. The meaning of seed in this verse is clear. It refers to the children of Nephi *and* to any who followed his inspired teachings, even if they were not the biological children of Nephi, on the condition of faithfulness to the covenants of the Lord. *Seed* means offspring, whether temporal or spiritual. This is a key and recurrent theme of the revealed word of God.

These stunning truths point us to a metaphor I mentioned earlier in this book. It illustrates our possibilities in the eyes of our loving God. Alma compared the word of God to a seed. If we allow the word of God to be planted in our hearts (a seed in good soil), continue to nourish that seed (word), and remain faithful, then eventually that seed will grow into a fully grown tree resulting in eternal exaltation (Alma 32). I suggest that each of us is as a seed in God's glorious garden. Each one of us can be a good seed and with proper care and attention can grow into a fully grown mighty tree. The message of latter-day scripture is that we are each invited to play key contributory roles in the rolling forward of the kingdom of God in these last days by this process of spiritual growth.

The goodly garden of the earth is owned by God. His redemptive reaching covers each soul who will let Him reach them. Each of the following symbols from scripture convey these truths. The beautiful doctrines, miraculous stories, and wise precepts of the revealed word show these great truths in symbolic form. This entire earth belongs to the Lord. His purpose is to create life that grows to fulfil its inherent potential. He is the Master Gardener. He has put in place all the conditions needed for us to grow from a tiny seed to a mighty tree. This can only happen in the Gardens of the Lord. In the Lord's Garden, the master is God and the servant is the prophet. We, as sublime seeds can do good deeds in God's garden. We can experience tremendous spiritual growth through struggle. This is an ascent to glory and the scriptures teach how it can happen for us. Each seed must be individually nourished.

A seed planted in fertile soil must struggle through the surrounding darkness (being engulfed and buried in the ground) to grow upwards toward the beckoning light of the sun. For example, consider the transformational experience of King Lamoni (see Alma 19:6). This is beautiful doctrine. God's power brought penetrating light into the mind of King Lamoni. This light was the intelligent truth and astonishing goodness of God Himself. This glorious light removed spiritual darkness from the king. It opened his eyes, mind, and heart to see and sense wondrous things. It broke down the barriers between him and His Father in heaven. He experienced divine reality. His soul was on fire on the inside. The possibility of salvation was now his to behold from the inside of his being. This was pure spiritual light and revelatory illumination. It was so powerful that it caused him to fall to the ground.

This was a personal and deep spiritual experience in which the natural man was subdued—the doubting, cynical, hardened potentialities of his human nature were dismantled, and he was coming to know God experientially and intimately. Ammon himself had experienced something similar previously and he knew that God was at work. The darkness of disbelief, ignorance, confusion, and blindness is to be removed from each one of us individually through personal encounter with the light of God. This light beckons us upward, onward, forward, and heavenward. No wonder that Ammon rejoiced even though others did not understand what was happening. It takes a person who has experienced divinity to sense this experience happening in the lives of others.

Growth must be carefully cultivated—it cannot be forced. Obstacles to growth are everywhere and dangers to the seed abound. However, with proper care, growth will happen. As we turn off the noisy distraction of the world and listen to the Spirit, the music of faith fills our soul and we see things as they really are. The seed will grow into a tree of life—old, large, mature, expansive, and radiant. The fruit will be white, delicious, filling, and eternal. What could possibly be more attractive to the spirit within us than the Spirit of God in both time and eternity drawing us ever closer to the best and most beautiful life of which we are capable?

A Special Seed

Who am I? Who are you? What is our purpose and reason for being? We are children of God. Another way of saying this is to state we are a seed planted in the Lord's Garden. We know this because the Lord has clearly told us so and He does not lie (Enos 1:6). The seed is precious in the sense of having great internal worth and a marvelous divine potential to grow into a mighty tree in God's Garden. It is the intention of the Gardener that each seed become something wondrous and exceptional. This glory is not an unimportant or worldly thing but rather a divine endorsement of our true nature and potential. Although we face the trivial and the mundane our inheritance and destiny is not to be commonplace but rather to be sublime in our achievements. This is not pretentious aggrandizement but rather reflects a divine unfolding of who and whose we truly are. Our nature is great. Our potential is to achieve glorious growth toward majestic divinity.

The Cultivation of the Seed

For this development to occur, the seed needs constant cultivating. To bring about real and lasting growth there must exist the right conditions. Each child of God—regardless of illusory appearances to the contrary—is capable, under certain conditions, of achieving the actualization of their divine nature, potential, and destiny just as each seed in a garden is capable, with correct nurturing help, of becoming something far greater than what it presently is.

Consider how Enos was divinely nourished when his father taught him "in the *nurture* and admonition *of the Lord*" (Enos 1:1, emphasis added). Jacob taught his son Enos that the Lord is involved in the nurturing of our souls—protecting and caring for us while we are growing toward our destiny of great grandeur. We need that divine care if we are to catch the vision of the amazing possibilities that lie within us and around us.

The Nourishing Soil

A seed needs the right kind of soil in which to grow. The soil must have minerals and vitamins that support growth. God has placed us all in a marvelous Garden which has the right conditions for growth. And He has provided a system for each seed to be nourished in its time and season. Although a good seed may be placed in poor soil (as in the parables the master Gardener has referred to in times past), yet the Lord owns the entire Garden and He can infuse soil with ingredients good for growth. The Lord can and does place nutrients in

His soil and He can nourish any seed willing to grow. The Lord can change the soil in which a seed is placed to facilitate its growth. He can change hearts and circumstances (Alma 5). Those willing to grow will find that the Lord leads thirsty men to wells of living water even if the lands they used to live in were sometimes barren with drought.

In His wisdom, God has made provision for each of His children. There is "none to escape" His word and plan according to His timetable (Doctrine and Covenants 1:2). For example, there is a divine wisdom reflected in our becoming aware of the Book of Mormon, as "if it be *wisdom in God* that ye should read them" (Moroni 10:3, emphasis added). Therefore, under His watchful care He knows when we will be most receptive to His will and words. He can tailor the moment of introduction we have to His gospel to align with our readiness. He will send us messengers in defining moments in our lives when we are in a preparation to hear the word (Alma 32:6). When we have this experience, we can sense the mercy of God, ponder His words in our hearts, and ask Him to reveal His truth to us by the pure power of His chosen servant, the Holy Ghost (Moroni 10:3–5). We come to know that the greatest witness we can have comes from God (Doctrine and Covenants 6:23). The supporting soil consists of life experiences which may humble us, followed by receipt of His word, doctrines, covenants, and ordinances revealed to us for our growth heavenwards. As a seed grows upwards by receiving nourishment from the soil, so a child of God climbs the ladder of covenants toward their heavenly destination.

The Water of Life

All seeds need water to grow. Likewise, all individuals need water to survive physically. They also need spiritual water! The Master Gardener knows how and when to water His seeds. This divine nourishment is both essential and life enhancing. The water helps each seed to grow beyond its present size. In the Garden of the Lord, the living water is the life-promoting word of God which sustains the parched soul. It welcomes us to a better place (a promised land) where we can continue to grow and develop. Water gives seeds the oxygen of life.

When travelling through the hot desert of life, we need to drink some cooling water for refreshment and renewal. The physical mirrors the spiritual and emotional. When thirsty, fatigued, dizzy, and feeling weak, we need water to sustain us. At times, this is a desperate and urgent need. We need regular and continual nourishment so that we have energy and strength for the journey of life. We also need those waters to become a part of us so that we can enjoy the abundant life—such as doing the things we love and being able to help others.

The word of God leads to the Fountain of Living Waters and these waters are a representation of the love of God (1 Nephi 11:25). This is beautiful imagery. The living waters is the influential and impactful love of the living God. It is a divine love that refreshes, replenishes, nourishes, and sustains us. This water quenches our thirst, re-enlivens our body, lifts our spirit, and gives us capacity to go forward to face often daunting pressures on our energy, strength, and resilience.

Divine love is essential in the adventure we call life. We need to sense, feel, rely on, and share that love if we are to flourish and thrive. God is the fountain of living waters! He is the perpetual source of true love, of deep encouragement, of caring guidance, and of eternal belonging. He is the original and constant source of all the help, goodness, beauty, and truth of life now and eternally. Without His love, we would always feel undernourished, starving, lost, confused, tired, and alone. To know of His concern and feel of His regard is to feel good about ourselves, others, and life. It gives meaning and purpose to every difficulty we face.

The Living Water is the life affirming power that flows from the living God, the Lord Jesus Christ. His water washes over us to cleanse us from dirt (sin). His water gives us strength when we are weak, comfort when we are discouraged, and knowledge when we are confounded. He stands ready to supply us with bounteous rejuvenation. When we drink of this living water of life, we are filled to overflowing. We are empowered, satisfied, contented, and fulfilled in a way that would otherwise be impossible. Come to the Living Waters. Wash in those waters. Drink from those waters. Live in those waters. Share those waters. And find an entire new life in Christ!

The Beneficial Heat

Each seed needs help in the form of warmth and heat to grow. In the Lord's Garden He provides both. Without heat many seeds will not grow; they will also die. Heat, in the spiritual sense, can be compared to trouble and trials while warmth comes as motivation, comfort, and encouragement that God gives us on our arduous spiritual journey. While a seed may not always appreciate the heat it experiences, it is necessary and beneficial in the long run. Without difficulty we would soon become spiritually complacent and stagnant. Further, challenges are the very thing that so often propel us to increased learning and development. This heat of life comes from the Sun which gives life.

Lifted toward the Sun

Each seed needs the light that emanates from the sun in the sky to grow toward the source of that light. This reaching toward the light is a great symbol. The shining sun is of course a type of the Son of God and His profound ability to illuminate our path, direction, and destination. Christ is the life and the light of the world (Alma 38:9). He is the One that brings life and light to His Garden and to each seed in the Garden. Each child of God needs to live in the light that comes from Christ to grow upwards and thus closer to that heavenly light. Without His light, no seed could grow, develop, and become a great tree. With His light each seed has access to a power far beyond their own. A lowly seed in the ground becomes so much more because of the majestic and radiant Sun in the sky.

There is a magnificent light that shines in darkness. We can transcend spiritual darkness through the loving light of God. There is a noticeable contrast between the light of clear prophetic inspiration (1 Nephi 8:2) and the confusing carnality of this dark and dreary fallen world (1 Nephi 8:4, 7–8). We are to be lifted toward the light. We are to live in the light rather than die in the darkness. We grow toward the light and overcome the darkness of sin and apathy (JS—H 1:15–16; 2 Nephi 19:2; Alma 5:7, 15).

We know:

- Christ is an endless light (Mosiah 16:9) who gives joy to others through a life of light (Alma 28:14).
- The Light of the world (3 Nephi 15:9) has a bright countenance that shines on the faithful (3 Nephi 19:25).
- God is a great, everlasting, and marvelous light (2 Nephi 19:2; Alma 26:15; 36:20).
- Christ is the treasure, life, and light of our world just like we are the treasure, life, and light of His world (3 Nephi 12–18). His great joy comes from seeing us succeed in becoming beings of light ourselves.
- God can bestow much light upon us (Alma 9:19) and make us full of light (3 Nephi 13:22).
- True followers of Christ follow the light (Moroni 7:13–16), voice (2 Nephi 32:3; Moroni 7:25), counsel (Moroni 7:32), and path of God (Moroni 7:33, 45–48).
- We then rejoice in the privilege of discipleship and love God and others with a near perfect love (Moroni 8:16–17).

How illuminating that so much glorious light is readily available!

To become a light to others we must first draw close to the source of that light ourselves. Those who follow Christ's light are good and decent persons. However, His light also draws us beyond goodness into the covenant quest for full and complete discipleship. God respects the principle of agency. Hence, He uses His light to direct and guide us to higher ground if we desire it. Our Lord cares deeply enough about us to speak greater truths to us. Therefore, as we endeavor to share more light with others, we can be a tremendous help and strength to them. Our genuine, wise, and loving care for their temporary and everlasting well-being shines through. Thus, the reaching, stretching, yearning, longing, and improving we each seek is well represented in the upward climb toward the greatest light of all—God's loving light.

The Seedling That Needs to Grow

As wonderful and precious as seeds are, it is not intended that they remain as such. We, as good seeds in God's Garden, are intended to germinate and grow beyond ourselves gradually but surely. As a seedling we have started to receive nourishment and to grow. I like the idea of us being a soaring seedling in the sense of making real and substantial progress. There is nothing to stop a seed from growing in God's garden except for the seed itself. All the conditions are in place and God will not forget us or neglect us. We can begin to fly high as we reach higher and higher heavenward.

Compare the Word to a Seed

Alma Chapter 32 is an excellent exposition on how the word of God within us can become something mighty. I am grateful that it helps us to better understand Lehi's dream.

Poverty-produced humility made the people ready to listen to the word of God (verse 6). I think of my growing up environment in a place called Darndale. We lived in Primrose Grove—how ironic and yet appropriate that this would be so named. It was a poor area of social housing. However, it had some ripeness for hearing the word of God. My mother accepted the word with gladness and our great spiritual journey began.

The poor needed to learn spiritual wisdom (verse 12). That is precisely what Joseph Smith, himself in difficult material circumstances, needed to learn—the restored wisdom given only by God (Joseph Smith—History 1:12). It is also what we needed to learn in our Primrose Grove setting! The symbolism is rich. God brings us to a Garden Place and He gives us new information with which to deal with and transcend our mortal circumstances.

It is more blessed to truly humble yourself because of the word of God (verse 14).

To *choose* humility is better than to be *compelled* to be humble (verse 15). Resistance and stubbornness put us at risk of rejecting and neglecting the word. Alternatively, acceptance and conscientiousness make it highly likely that we will embrace and cultivate the word. The attitude we take at every step of this journey makes a phenomenal difference to the outcome.

To believe in God's name is equated with believing in God's word (verse 22). This is the case because the name of God is the perfect representation of His word!

The desire to believe works in us (verse 27). In other words, desire is not passive acquiescence. Rather, it produces action, effort, and persistence. It is active.

A true and good seed is planted in the soil of our hearts and will grow within us and enlarge our souls if we let it (verse 28). We are to give place for the word—make room for it, welcome it, value it. The word of God never leaves us the same!

The word magnifies, develops, enlarges, enlightens, expands, and increases the person it becomes lodged in (verse 29). It tastes good and sweet. It increases our faith. This is a joyous thought. The word makes us better, stronger, wiser!

A good seed swells, sprouts, and grows (verse 30)—this is the test of goodness, this is the measure we judge the seed (word) by. Does it grow? The good word always strengthens faith. We know the seed is good by the fact that it grows!

We are sure the seed is good in this process (verse 31). That is a great antidote for worry and anxiety. Sureness, clarity, certainty—these evidence that the seed is good!

The word swells our souls, enlightens our understanding, and expands our minds (verse 34). It allows us to see things we had never perceived before and it helps us to become developed in new ways. It is soul enhancing. In fact, this is how we obtain a perfect knowledge that the seed is good.

This is real, good, and discernible (verse 35). This is a light sponsored process. It tastes good to us. It is enjoyable. It is real. It can be felt, experienced, and observed by ourselves and others. It is an actual process of growth and magnification.

As we have exercised faith in planting the seed, we now know the seed is good (verse 36). Growth starts at the very beginning and manifests itself over time. We are rewarded for our initial efforts.

Alma teaches us that a tree is growing inside us (verse 37). This is not just a seed, as wonderful as that is. It is intended to become a fully grown tree. This is potent symbolic language. It is great imagery and sublime metaphor! We become stronger, larger, more developed, more mature spiritually. We grow into something more than what we were previously. As we perceive the growing seed within us, we will comprehend that we are becoming a tree. We realize we need to nourish the seed/tree with great care/much care so that it gets root, grows bigger, and becomes fruit yielding. We clearly still need faith as the process of development takes time and patience. It is not an immediate transition from a seed to a tree.

If we neglect to nourish the seed/tree then it gets no depth, gets scorched by the heat, withers, and we remove it ourselves! (verse 38) As we are responsible for planting the seed, we are likewise responsible for facilitating its growth. We have control over whether the seed grows or not. Christ wants us to learn responsibility for our lives!

Our failure to nourish the seed/tree is not because it is bad, false, or undesirable (verse 39). Rather, it is because the ground we have lodged the seed in—the soil of our heart—is barren. There is no receptivity to the word, nothing to welcome, sustain, and develop it.

Without nourishment and hopeful faith, the seed/tree cannot and does not become productive (verse 40). In other words, an eye of faith is critical to nourish the fledgling word within us.

Great diligence, patience, and faith allow the tree to become eternal (verse 41). We nourish the tree over time so that it will flourish always.

Finally, we are reminded that the word of God takes deep root in us and over time we enjoy the benefits that come (verses 42–43). Long-suffering care allows us to partake of the most precious, sweet, white, pure fruit to the point of full fruition, satisfaction, and filling. This is a nutritious and tasty feast of the most wonderful kind. The fruit is the great reward and it is worth the price paid.

There is superb doctrinal richness in this symbolism. Why is it so important that we grow into a tree? What is the significance of the Tree of Life? Well, we have several scriptural passages that greatly clarify our understanding of the meaning of this truth. Let us consider when Jehovah appeared to the prophet Moses (Exodus 3:1–8). In this account Moses was looking after the animals of his father-in-law—which is itself a great symbol of being a spiritual shepherd to the Father's flock. He journeyed to the divine Mountain of Meeting. The heavenly messenger appeared to him in the middle of a "burning bush." While a bush is smaller than a tree, the idea is similar. The flame of fire is also interesting. It is evident that Jehovah appeared to Moses in this encounter (see Moses 1:17). I note that when Christ appeared to Joseph Smith, His eyes were as a flame of fire (Doctrine and Covenants 110). Thus, we have here a divine encounter between Moses and the premortal Jehovah. God is symbolically associated in these verses with a light-bearing bush or tree of fire. He is a living fire, a burning light, a messenger of love filled with luminosity!

That is remarkably comparable to the Tree of Life idea as recounted in Lehi's dream. Christ is a refining fire, a being of great purifying light, a holy personage, and a person of deliverance. He plans to bring the covenant children of Israel to a goodly land flowing with milk and honey. This promised land is a place where the family of the patriarchs can practice their faith in a garden setting—a land of abundance. The Tree of Life is therefore the ideal representation of the Messiah—He who saves Israel from death and slavery and brings them through shedding His own blood to a place of peace, prosperity, and posterity now and eternally. I love that Moses was told to remove his sandals because the ground was holy. To me this signifies that God wanted Moses to be respectfully reverent and to directly touch the holy ground—not to be separated from that which was holy but to be in immediate contact with it.

Jesus Christ is the *Word made Flesh*. Indeed, "*the word is in Christ unto salvation*" (Alma 34:6). He is therefore the great Seed planted in God's Garden. He grows into the Tree of Life, from which the fruit of eternal life is plucked. In other words, Christ is the living manifestation of the love of the Father spread forth and shedding itself throughout the world to give humankind the most delicious, pure, and beautiful fruit that exists in time and eternity—eternal lives (See 1 Nephi 8, 11, and 15). Christ is like a great tree of love. When I put up my Christmas tree each year in December, I see it as a visible symbol of Christ in my very house, among my family. The lights on the tree are like the fruit on the tree. The presents under the tree are like the great gifts He gives to my family because of His atoning love.

We are to plant the word of God in our hearts. What word? Well, the true message that Jesus is the Christ, the Only Begotten Son of God. He is the Seed (son) of the Tree (Father). As we plant this doctrine in our hearts and minds with permanent love, it lodges within us and takes root in us. To what effect? Well, the seed within us grows until it becomes a tree. From this tree, the fruit of everlasting salvation is plucked. This salvation is essentially bound up with the idea of eternal families. In other words, the offspring of deity are to become procreators in the eternal plan of salvation. There is to be an eternal line of gods, springing forth from the great Tree of Life, the Father of our Souls. The family of Christ lives forever. Hence, the Father's family is everlasting!

In essence, we are also trees of life—speaking allegorically. In other words, we are symbols of the love of God as manifest in our coming into the mortal world to perform our sacred ministry. What is that ministry? It is to gather Israel (The Tree of God's covenant people) home to the promised land. It is to invite the family members home after the long dispersion and scattering. It is to beckon the prodigal to return. It is to rescue the weary traveler. It is to bind up the battered soul stranded on the wilderness way between being lost and being found. It is to go after that which is lost and bring them back on our shoulders rejoicing. It is to restore the connection of the wanderer to the Shepherd of the Flock. It is to preserve the fruit of the Tree—the children of God—for an everlasting and exalted inheritance in the never-ending family of God.

7

Brought into the Light

A SEED KEPT CONTINUALLY IN DARKNESS CANNOT BECOME WHAT IT is intended to become. While seeds begin covered with dirt, at a certain point, they need to break free from the dirt that enshrouds them so that they can grow beyond their present status. They need to be brought into the light and experience the growth capacity that comes to them only through interaction with the world of possibility that is presented to their view.

In like manner, there is such a thing as having a veil over our eyes so that we do not see all things as they really are. The man Enoch was called by God to preach to people whose eyes could not see the spiritual truths God wanted them to see (Moses 6:35–36). Even Enoch, who was called to serve God, needed to have his eyes opened. He was instructed to anoint his eyes with clay and then wash them so he could see. Was Enoch physically blind? I do not believe so. What would he be able to see through this process that he could not already see? Why cover his eyes with clay first—surely that would make it more difficult to see, not easier? As in many things, God works in ways that initially appear contradictory to perceived wisdom.

Enoch was to anoint his eyes first. This was an ordinance. It was a physical act with symbolic and spiritual significance. Usually, religious anointings utilize oil. This symbolizes the conferral of a divine or holy office upon a person such as a priest, high priest, or king. It is in indication of a special appointment, a commission of authority, a delegation of divine power. In this account Enoch was to place clay on his eyes as a sign of the natural, non-transparent material of this fallen earth. Then he would wash away these particles which limited his view. Upon doing this, he would be able to see. Obviously, he would be able to see physically. However, there is clearly a different type of sight being referred to here. He could see with new eyes. He could see spiritual things. In fact, we are told that he could then see the spirit children of God—notice this, he would be able to see "spirits," not just mortal bodies. The natural man sees the natural body, but the spiritual man can see the spirit body!

There are those who do not think we have a spirit at all. That is because their spiritual eyes remain closed! Those seeing with unveiled eyes see themselves and others in their true and complete nature—they see their spiritual identity. In other words, things not visible to those whose view remains clouded by the dirt, dust, and muck of this natural world. Things not apparent to those whose perspective is limited by earthly senses. In this process, Enoch became a seer. This means he could then see things God unveiled to his sight—things uncovered, revealed, made plain, made understandable to him.

Interestingly, the use of the word "also" suggests that perhaps Enoch could see the things of God with his natural eyes (meaning mortal eyes) after having his eyes washed clean. However, he could "also" now see things that mortal eyes—even after spiritual washing—could not see unless God permitted it. I believe this brings important additional perspective to the story. Every mortal person needs to have their spiritual eyes opened by God. However, even this divine opening happens in steps and stages. Even good men and women need further endowments of spiritual sight before they can see greater spiritual things. Even covenant disciples of the Lord only receive greater spiritual sight by degrees. The greatest gift of spiritually "seeing afar off" comes to seers only on specific approval from God. No spiritual gift is greater than that of seership in this life.

It makes sense that each of us need to have our spiritual eyes opened to see and comprehend the things of God. One of the most important doctrines in this connection is the spiritual gift of discernment. We need to have a finely tuned ability to distinguish not only obvious good from definite evil, but also to discern between those things that are good and those that are great. We need to know what is trivial and what is vital. This is particularly so as the world becomes more awash with options and information ranging from the crucially important to the benign to the deeply insidious. The revelations provide clear insights on this key theme. We must have our spiritual senses and mortal eyes enlightened to see more clearly.

One of the most important spiritual gifts we can possess in this life is the ability to discern between those competing ideas which come from God (good) and those which originate with the devil (evil). The revealed word enlightens us that some ideas are true, virtuous, valuable, fruitful, beautiful, healing, and useful to us while others are not (2 Nephi 15:20). The everlasting gospel encompasses every pleasing beauty, jubilant pleasure, and bounteous joy. The wise truth is that happiness always follows righteousness, and this message is needed in our day when many confuse good and evil with each other (Mosiah 2:41; Alma 41:10). The Prophet Joseph Smith had a keenly developed ability to discern spiritual truths. I believe this was due, in part, to the doctrinal flood that filled his mind through the revelations he received.

Seeing with New Eyes

It is noteworthy that the Book of Mormon specifically shows us that God views us very differently to how some in the world see us:

How God Sees You	How the Worldly See You
As precious (Jacob 2:21; Alma 31:35)	As worthless or an enemy (1 Nephi 11:35–36)
With joyous, genuine, everlasting love (1 Nephi 11:17, 22–23, 25)	With an attitude of mocking, finger pointing, and scoffing (1 Nephi 8:27–28)
As worth correcting to help you (Helaman 15:3)	With scorn (1 Nephi 8:33)
Gives you many opportunities to repent and to grow (1 Nephi 8:37)	Is willing and quick to cast you off (Alma 30:60)

Truly, without God there would be no light, law, or life at all whether spiritual, temporal, immortal, or eternal. We need His light to see all things, including ourselves, in a proper perspective. God knows all things and has all power (2 Nephi 9:20; Mosiah 4:9). God is, unlike us, not surrounded by any mortal mists of darkness (1 Nephi 8, 11). He is no longer being tested as to His desires and choices. He has advanced beyond the temporary and the unknown into the realm of eternal clarity and certainty. God discerns all truth perfectly.

God temporarily and wisely permits many things He does not endorse. He is an all-powerful intervening actor and circumscribes the bounds of all other partially powerful beings in time and eternity and of matter itself. God places His children in a very real situation where temporary and eternal losses are not only possible but actual. God works in so many ways both small and large to bring meaning and happiness into our lives. Of course, while we can know much about God, we do not presently fully comprehend Him or His ways (Mosiah 4:9). No mortal can do that fully even with the help of divine revelation, although by inspiration we can understand God in a personal and powerful way (Jacob 4:8–10). Thus, of necessity, there must be a leaning on Him which is based on faith, revelation, and trust rather than rational explanation or personal knowledge alone. It is reassuring to know that whatever we face in our lives can ultimately be turned to the glory of God and our blessing. This is a message of structured order, planned opportunity, creative vision, and majestic destiny.

Our eyes can be opened spiritually as we learn incrementally how to see the thoughts, desires, and motives of people. There are so many concepts used in the revelations which describe the gift of discernment. Let us consider how we can differentiate between kinds of beings and distinguish their types of influence upon us.

Perceiving the Nature of God:

God is a being of glory (Jacob 4:4) and light (2 Nephi 19:2; Mormon 8:16).

The light of His goodness is discernible (Alma 32:35). In fact, His influence is as daylight when contrasted with the dark night of the adversary's impact (Moroni 7:15).

He has rich comprehension (understanding), and His word is quick (sharp, insightful, intelligent, vibrant) and powerful (Helaman 3:29).

His practice is to openly share His ensign of light with the world (2 Nephi 15:26) and His direction is readily available to us (Ether 2:5–6).

Recognizing the Characteristics of the Born-Again Person:

The spiritually born-again person is illuminated (Alma 5:7), enlightened (Alma 24:30), spiritually able to see (Mosiah 3:5), lives according to their conscience (Alma 29:5), has a brightness of hope (2 Nephi 31:20), is alive in Christ (Moroni 8:12) and lives in the day of preparation with a repentant attitude (Alma 34:31–33).

They have received knowledge from heaven (Helaman 14:30), divine instructions (Ether 2:16), directions from God (Alma 37:36–37), and inspiration from heaven (3 Nephi 6:20). They are caught away in the Spirit (1 Nephi 11:1), receive revelatory communion from the Spirit (Jarom 1:4), and are guided by the Spirit (Mosiah 2:36).

They have authority to speak the word of God with power (Helaman 5:18), and they declare divine doctrine (3 Nephi 11:40).

They resemble the Savior in their exemplary behavior (3 Nephi 18:16). They are holy persons doing holy deeds and speaking holy words with authority, power, and clarity (Words of Mormon 1:17).

They can often perceive the hearts of others (Mosiah 13:11), and discern the thoughts and desires of others (Alma 18:18; 3 Nephi 24:18). They have the capacity at times to reveal that they know the hidden thoughts of the minds and hearts of other people (Jacob 2:5).

They know they are accountable to God (1 Nephi 10:1; Moroni 8:10) and accept His judgment (2 Nephi 9:46). They know that their works follow them (3 Nephi 27:10–12) and that they are known to God (Alma 60:10).

Their motive is to glorify God (Ether 12:4) and so they judge righteously (Alma 41:14).

Seeing the Tendencies of the Natural Person:

The natural man or woman does not know the dealings of God (1 Nephi 2:12). Indeed, they are often spiritually in the darkest abyss (Mosiah 27:29). Hence, their minds are darkened rather than enlightened. They do not comprehend the ways of the Almighty, as it seems to be irrational foolishness to them (2 Nephi 28–29).

Their mode of life tends to focus on competing with others, trying to obtain worldly prizes in any way they can, and harming themselves and others in the process.

They dismiss spiritual truth due to it being inconvenient, onerous, demanding, unpopular, and difficult.

Their motive is focused on self-promotion rather than the glory of God or the blessing of others.

Detecting the Traits of the Adversary:

The adversary is a being of darkness who cannot abide the light of God's glory (3 Nephi 8:21–22).

He does not understand the sacrificial love of God.

He wants us to deny God (2 Nephi 28:5), be angry with God and His truth (2 Nephi 28:28), to pervert the right way of the Lord (2 Nephi 28:15), and to revile against goodness (2 Nephi 28:16).

He encourages people to rob the poor and persecute the meek (2 Nephi 28:13), to contend with their learning (2 Nephi 28:4), and to have rage inside of them (2 Nephi 28:20).

He wants us to be pacified and lulled away into a sense of carnal security (2 Nephi 28:21). He does this by whispering flattering words to us (2 Nephi 28:22) such as saying there is no God, no morality, and no afterlife, so there is no accountability to God or anyone else for our choices. He wants us to indulge in hedonism, irresponsibility, procrastination, and selfishness.

If we listen to his enticements consistently, we become grasped with his awful chains (2 Nephi 28:19) and thus he cheats our souls (2 Nephi 28:21).

His initial motive to ascend and exalt himself above all others is seen in a deranged obsession to bring everyone below him through misery and oppression (2 Nephi 24:13).

Consequently, it is evident why the Lord contrasts the great differential between His way and the way of the world. The tree of life gives us eternal life while the spacious building offers certain eternal death (1 Nephi 8, 11). To know God for ourselves is to personally travel the path to eternal life for ourselves—no one else can make that most important journey for us. To have eternal life we must be willing to give up all worldly things. We must jettison wickedness from our inner selves so that we can become spiritual vessels of joy (Alma 22:15). All good and beautiful things in this world come from God. However, relying on the wisdom of men exclusively for salvation leads to spiritual darkness (2 Nephi 9:28–29) and excessive materialism can lead us to unbelief and to forgetting God (Jacob 2:18–19). Consequently, everything we learn in this world should be judged by how it squares with the revealed word of God (2 Nephi 28).

We are to overcome spiritual death through possessing a great desire to see things as they really are. For those privileged to receive the everlasting gospel in mortality, their eternal destiny depends on their response to the truth in this mortal life. Those who love spiritual light in this life will continue to do so in the next—they are the righteous (the good) (Alma 34:34). Each of us has a perfectly fair opportunity to prove ourselves during literally thousands of premortal, mortal, and post-mortal tests both large and small over a long period (Alma 13). Each new day is an opportunity to repent, and anyone can choose to change the direction of both their mortal, and spiritual lives. The Redeemer is the keeper of the gate to the celestial world, and He will allow us to pass by Him if we merit it (2 Nephi 9:41). God offers all individuals every blessing according to His divine timetable and in conjunction with their personal desires (Moroni 10:3–5). One day, we will see clearly how God has prepared every needful thing of eternal worth. In this life we are to live by the light of faith (Alma 5:15).

Discerning the Distinction

We can find protection from our enemies both seen and unseen by fortifying our discerning defenses. The ongoing conflict between good and evil is one of words and ideas as well as attitudes, desires, and behaviors. It is a contest of testimony and faith as we are placed in a situation to decide in whom and in what we place our trust for eternal salvation. The strait and narrow path of bounded discipline and godly grace gives us not only pleasure in appropriate measure but also spiritual safety, real happiness, and everlasting joy.

Through experience, we come to "see" the goodness of the Father and the love of Jehovah. God governs by loving law and ordained order. We can also "detect" the motives of the evil one. The adversary enslaves by chaos, anarchy, subterfuge, deceit, confusion, and arrogance. God leads but the adversary misleads. God fishes for our souls through His capacity to touch the very deepest parts of our nature with His tremendous loving outreach, unfailing devotion, and loyalty to wholesome principles. God teaches, embraces, blesses, lifts, connects with, and changes us for the better. The enemy seeks to flatter us, use us, and destroy us.

We are seeing in this fallen world an effort at apostate mutiny, an attempted spiritual coup, a movement to dethrone God. The devil is the main source of temptation, deception, and distraction in this world. There are potent enticements of all types, kinds and degrees which are in essence spiritual counterfeits to Christ, seeking to take us away from the path of righteousness. Some of these are evidently evil while others are much more carefully disguised and subtle. The adversary offers us temporary pleasure followed by enduring entrapment and sorrow. Anti-Christ and anti-restoration doctrines in all their forms are exposed clearly in the examples of Korihor, Nehor, and Sherem. Such teachings award people with no good thing (Moroni 7).

The enemy of our souls wants us to act in ways that are bad. He:

- Entices people to do secret works of darkness (2 Nephi 9:9). He loves combinations covered in the cloak of conspiracy.
- Has power to work sorceries, magics, and other evil works (Mormon 1:19).
- Invites all others to do evil works but never to do good works (Moroni 7:17). His angels and mortal followers do likewise.
- Promotes the work of spiritual destruction (Alma 27:4; Helaman 6:28) and advocates war as a work of death (Alma 43:38).
- Advocates the secret combination evil works of murder, robbery, and destruction which serve his purposes (Helaman 2:4; 3:14; 11:28).

In contrast to these devilish designs, heaven plays no part in promoting and advancing such deadly derangements. The covenant people of the Lord are warned not to engage in works of darkness or abominable doings (2 Nephi 25:2). We can undermine the adversary's power of deception through intentionally drawing close to Christ. He is the enduring light that shines in darkness and suffered to save us (2 Nephi 19:2, 6; Mosiah 14:3–6). There is a vital distinction between the living God who has firmly founded atoning love for the people of God (1 Nephi 15:36; Helaman 5:12) and the strange and vain baseless wisdom of the world which fights against God and His people (1 Nephi 8:26, 33).

Latter-day revelation shows that divine commandments are not revisable opinions or temporary social norms. Rather, these are operative spiritual laws that influence us constantly and eternally. God governs by laws which are the parameters He has set for circumscribing the actions of intelligent beings under His guidance to help them to become as He is (Alma 42:15–26). These laws have an impact on both our spirits and our physical bodies. The nature of God is that He enjoys being righteous because His commandments naturally bring happiness (Helaman 13:38). His very nature is joyful!

Spiritual laws can be ignored for a time, but not suspended or destroyed through rational argument, lifestyle choice, or clever legality. Korihor falsely claimed that "whatsoever a man does is no crime"

(Alma 30:17). However, many behaviors are sins under divine law. Living life in a worldly way carries with it no promise of eternal life. I am grateful that keeping commandments is an inherently enjoyable thing to do. All sin harms both the sinner and inevitably ends up hurting others indirectly or directly. God endorses principles that promote peace and eternal joy. Hence, He despises sin because it detracts from these beneficial blessings. Worldly attempts to rewrite divine law—like the great and spacious building—will eventually fall because humans cannot change laws that we did not create in the first place. We can reduce the threat of danger to our souls by knowing true and pure doctrine. We can also avoid doctrinal dilution by sharing courageous truth—including to ourselves when we need to be reminded of divine teachings in our own times of challenge.

There is a great difference between the reliable iron word of God (1 Nephi 11:25) and the confusing darkness of devilish temptations (1 Nephi 12:17). It is good to hold fast to the promise of sure and certain results based on the immutable word of God (Helaman 5:12). If we are willingly humble and submissively teachable, we will be receptive to the safeguarding truths, transformational powers, consoling solace, desirable goodness, great delights, beautiful majesties, and miraculous benefits of the restored gospel. We will rejoice in these. Universally available truth is right whether in the light or in the dark, in public or in private, for one person or for everyone. The true doctrines of God are to be kept pure by us (2 Nephi 28:7–9). Of course, it is always time to stand up for truth as there is always hope that some will hear and repent (Alma 26:26).

Illuminating Inspiration

Revelatory instruction helps us to see more clearly and empowers us to act better. It illuminates the covenant way and inspires us to choose wisely:

- When faced with the darkness of ugly immorality we can turn on the light of beautiful purity (Mosiah 12:21). We can gravitate toward the abundant spiritual life of light that Christ offers. Enlightenment dispels doubt about which path we should take.
- When faced with the darkness of weakness and defeat we can turn on the light of strength and endurance (Mosiah 9:17).
- When faced with the darkness of temptation and guilt we can turn on the light of righteousness and repentance (Enos 1:6).
- When faced with the darkness of ignorance, confusion, doubt, and despair we can turn on the light of knowledge, testimony, faith, and hope (Mosiah 12:27). The true gospel is the ultimate message of light. It is at its best when life is at its darkest.
- When faced with the darkness of worry, loneliness, and sadness we can turn on the light of comfort, companionship, and happiness (Mosiah 12:23).
- When faced with the darkness of fear and laziness we can turn on the light of courage and work (Mosiah 13:3).
- When faced with the darkness of pride, anger, hate, conflict, lies, and ridicule we can cultivate instead the light-filled qualities of humility, kindness, love, peace, truth, and forgiveness (Alma 61:9).

Alma gives us a beautiful expression of testimony about how the Son of God can truly change our spiritual night to blessed day (Alma 36:18–21). Christ lights our view so we can distinguish the narrow path of light from the broad way of darkness.

QUICK TO OBSERVE

I love how Ammaron was able to discern that Mormon was "a sober child" and was "quick to observe" (Mormon 1:1–4). The man entrusted with the plates "saw" that the young Mormon was a spiritually responsible and astute child. He therefore gave him a commission for an event some 14 years into the future. Imagine that! You get a priesthood leader asking you to do something in 14 years-time! That requires a high degree of faith and trust on behalf of the person making the assignment, a pronounced degree of conscientious in the person receiving it, and a real devotion to duty on both sides. It also requires the person called to remember the things they were asked to do. Mormon would need to observe what was happening among his people, remember these events and lessons, go to the place indicated in the future, take charge of the sacred records of the people of Nephi, and then add his observations to the sacred plates. What a heavy and important responsibility to give to a ten-year old!

There are great lessons here. One is that it takes discernment to recognize the capacity for discernment in others. We can also reflect on the great importance of being quick to observe—quick to notice, fast to see, alert to that which is central. We can follow the example of Mormon and become attentive to things that matter most. Therefore, we can acquire the capacity to be:

- Quick to see, discern, perceive, notice spiritual things.
- Quick to follow inspired direction and counsel.
- Quick to choose to act in obedience now to prepare for future opportunities and obligations.
- Quick to repent of things that hold us back from the opportunities that lie ahead of us.
- Quick to observe the lessons learned from the behavior of those around us.
- Quick to remember God's involvement in our lives through other people.

The divine word teaches that as the heavens are higher than the earth, so the Lord's ways are higher than man's ways (Isaiah 55:8–9). While the thoughts of men align with this telestial natural world, the thoughts of God correspond with the celestial spiritual world. As rain cleanses, the sun warms and shines, clouds inspire, and stars glow, so God's manifest goodness and genius lifts us above the grasping, conniving, insular, greedy, and plotting ways of the carnal man to the higher, loftier, holier, cleaner, and grander ways of God. Everything about God elevates our understanding and reach to a greater vision of beauty, intelligence, culture, excellence, dignity, and achievement. God inspires us to dig deeper, reach higher, endure longer, exemplify better, and pursue nobler.

The scale and scope of God's work in His Garden encourages us to believe in great and amazing things beyond the confines of our human imagination. This new understanding helps us to see the earth as a reflection of God's great intellect, beauty, power, purity, and love. The earth is full of wonders in sight, sound, taste, touch, and smell. It is aesthetically majestic. It is scientifically amazing. It is a place of great meaning and significance. This reflects the grand architecture of its great designer. It is a place of growth, life, and abundance. It is stunningly breathtaking.

Triumphing over the Temporal

We need to personally discover and remind ourselves of the distinction between the transitory world we live in and the eternal world that awaits us. The paradoxical irony is that we are dual beings subject to temporary trials, challenges, and temptations but we also long for, and sense, an inward connection with the infinite. We feel inside that we are eternal beings, at least in terms of our spirit selves. I love the wisdom of the statement by then Elder Dallin H. Oaks: "We are all tempted to desire that worldly quartet of property, prominence, pride, and power. We might desire these, but we should not fix them as our highest priorities" ("Desire," Apr. 2011 General Conference).

We are confronted by two seemingly contrasting realities:

Perspectives	Desires	Relationships
Time or Eternity	Commit Sin or Do Good	Temporary Relationships or Eternal Families
Mortal Body or Eternal Spirit	Brief Pleasure or Everlasting Joy	Disease/Illness/Decay/ Death or Beauty/Health/ Immortality/Resurrection
Shifting Opinions or Unchanging Truths	Lying or Integrity	Tribulation or Peace
Confusion or Clarity	Fads & Fashions or Doctrines & Principles	Pressures & Demands or Patience & Calm
Transient & Trivial or Crucial/ Significant/ Meaningful	Worldly Power or Unending Dominion	Time-bound Roles or Eternal Ministries of Service
Fleeting or Permanent/Lasting/ Forever	Urgent or Vital/Crucial/ Important/ Essential	Earthly Careers or Eternal Destinies
Contingent or Absolute	Material Gain or Treasure in Heaven	Earthly Bread & Water or the Bread of Life & Well of Living Water

I believe that our stifling orientation on the world can be overturned. It is essential to have clarity about our true nature, identity, ability, capacity, and purpose. Replacing paralyzing confusion with clear thinking is paramount. Thereby we can be centered, and know who and whose we are, rather than being blown about by every wind of false doctrine. We have a deep need to awake to the amazing goodness of God (2 Nephi 1:13). We all must emerge from the darkness of the world incrementally. To live in the pure light we first need to know where to look, as we always gravitate toward what we continually focus on. The source of our guidance is important, as is the direction we travel.

Imagine for a moment that we are active participants in Lehi's dream:

- Where are we located in this vision?
- Where are we headed?
- Who is the subject of our gaze?
- What is the object of our desire?
- Are we looking at the tree?
- Are we situated in the swamps or feeling our away about in a dark place?

If necessary, we can change our desires, alter our course, and go toward the fruit that is within our grasp if we want it. We can soften our hearts and strengthen our resolve to cast aside the enticements of a moment for the truths of eternal worth. To orient our life by turning to face the Lord instead of someone else, is to perceive life and ourselves differently.

We can arise to God and be godly men and women (2 Nephi 1:21). Temperance, moderation, clean air, heavenly music, wholesome food, good books, reflective journals, positive thoughts, kind words, and uplifting activities can create a new life within us and shape our environment in marked ways. This can alleviate so many of the troubles that drag us down. We can obtain an astonishing awareness of truth. All the spiritual senses will allow us to be immersed in the joy of enlightenment rather than swallowed up in the cesspool of sin. We can develop our capacity for discernment. Confusion and conflict will then be calmed. Certainty will wash over us and create peace within.

Other Faculties to Be Enlarged

As it is with our eyes, so it is with all other faculties:

- Our ears—that we may hear deeper truth, more beautiful music, and more powerful sermons.
- Our feelings—that we may sense deeper emotions.
- Our intelligence—that we may learn more quickly and remember more lastingly.
- Our Insights—that we may discern better, detect more wisely.

- Our creative abilities—that we may create better.
- Our imagination—that we may perceive more possibilities to do good.
- Our hearts—that we may have more purified desires.
- Our hands—that we may labor more consistently and do greater works.
- Our tongues—that we may utter more sublimely, speak more profoundly, and preach more perfectly.
- Our words—that we will reflect better the excellence of God. We will be better prepared to speak languages of edification.

The Edification of Sacred Music

As we sing the special words of our holy hymns, they are lodged in our hearts and minds. We learn true doctrine. Both the music and the words combine to lift us to sublime heights. We are inspired by faith in our loving Father. We are in awe at the love of our Messiah. We are touched deeply by the Holy Ghost. I cherish the doctrine of coming out of darkness into God's marvelous light, such as in Hymn No. 1, *The Morning Breaks.* Our Father in Heaven wants to flood our lives with light. His Son also wants us to bathe in glory. They desire to fill this world with light. Their ambition is to overcome error with truth, to replace hatred with love, to banish falsehood by promoting truth, to replace darkness with light, to turn ignorance to knowledge, and vanquish badness with goodness. They have revealed their glorious plans in these latter days in a new commission, a distinct charge, a restored revelation. These are days of the culmination of all things. These are days of majesty and glory, of power and prophecy, of might and sacred brilliance.

Truths Discerned

As I have sought the gift of discernment that Christ possesses, the Lord has opened certain truths to my understanding:

We need to be touched by the hand of God to feel things we have never felt before. We can come forth in a newness of life. We can experience all the material senses of sight, hearing, feeling, touch, and taste AND all the spiritual senses of insight (the sight within). Our immersive experience in the truth will give us general understanding, detailed knowledge, and holistic comprehension. We can then recognize falsehoods by learning to think as God thinks. We will have our minds opened, see with new eyes, perceive beyond material reality (2 Nephi 21:3), and sense new dimensions of understanding. We surely will have our tongues loosed by God to speak in praise of Him.

Discernment is needed for us to make wise and righteous judgments. Without it our judgments are often rash, incomplete, biased, etc.

Revelation is not synonymous with revisionism. Revelation often goes against our personal preferences (especially where these represent natural man tendencies not yet transcended in our lives) and yet is in alignment with God's long view purposes. Hence, we can detect further revelations better if we accept and understand the ones we have already and if our desire is to be submissive to a will more noble than our own.

Scriptural stories are not just literary devices. Although they contain many allegorical teachings, they also contain literal elements. It takes discernment to see this. Sometimes the literal and symbolic are not mutually exclusive.

The choice to sin brings trouble into our lives. This is especially the case where sin is intentional, repetitious, serious, and non-remorseful. There is such a thing as evil. Otherwise, true goodness would be impossible. Hence, there is a burning fire associated with breached conscience/destruction of corruption and a holy fire associated with purification. God cannot save us "in our sins," meaning where we stubbornly refuse to repent (Helaman 5:10). If He did, agency would be null and void. Related to this is the truth that there are different degrees of heaven in eternity (Doctrine & Covenants 76). This makes perfect sense to me, because we each gravitate toward the level of goodness we consistently desire. God accommodates us according to our choices, even though He initially offered something higher for us than what we ended up choosing for ourselves.

While generous grace is available to us, it is also true that we don't want to become complacent by thinking, "All is well in Zion" (2 Nephi 28:20–24). We need to keep grace and works in balance in our lives simultaneously or we will become spiritually lopsided. Just as two sides of a mathematical equation with an equals sign in the middle must be equivalent, justice and mercy must meet in perfect alignment in the Lord's system of salvation. Only when we work in unanimity with the Lord can the spiritual scales of balance be perfected. The Lord sees patterns, forms, connections, relations, and links in all things. We are not intended to be isolated, alone, and separate. Our sealing to Him makes us total, complete, holistic, and perfect.

Hence, the Lord tells us to "awake and arise" (Mosiah 3:2; 4:5), "arise from the dust" and "break off the chains with which ye are bound" (2 Nephi 1:21–23). Truly, the sleeping giants need to be disturbed, alarmed, and awakened. The Lord wants the entire world to wake up! This awakening must start within us individually. We cannot wake others up until we are first awake ourselves.

Just as our spirits are eternal, so are love, power, truth, wisdom, and beauty. They are everlasting principles!

The Light of the Lord

I am grateful beyond words that I have been brought into the light of the Lord. I rejoice to live in a world where angels minister, where stones shine, where bread is multiplied miraculously, where visions of the past happen, where prophecies of the future occur, where metal plates are used to record sacred encounters, where the blind are made to see, the deaf made to hear, the lame walk, and the broken are made whole. I would not want to live in a world with no knowledge of premortality, no promise of eternity, no possibility for forgiveness of sin, no literal bodily resurrection and no hope of eternal wonders promised to those who believe that God is a worker of miracles. I want there to be a God. I am grateful that He is real and He wants there to be a "me" in this world. He made me and I love Him for that. He made you too and He wants you to be in His world!

8

Forest of Nourishment

I LOVE THE MODERN REVELATION THAT STATES THE PROMISES OF family salvation made to our fathers are to be planted in the hearts of their children (Doctrine and Covenants 138:47–48). Where better to instill such memorable past promises than among future posterity? As the word of God is like a seed (Alma 32), so the seed of God's word is to be planted in the hearts of God's children. That word includes that their Father in Heaven and mortal fathers have not forgotten them. They love them, know them, remember them, think about them, are concerned for them, and want to be with them eternally. It is a deep feeling, a profound desire, a marvelous doctrine. That is why it must be deeply lodged in the hearts of the children so it can find deep roots there. It finds a permanent home there.

The word thus planted is one of abiding love. However, it is also that families can live together in love eternally in a strong covenant bond. Such a message is not easily forgotten nor is this bond easily broken. These doctrines of family love, family connection, and family longevity are core to the temple work that now suffuses the mortal and spirit worlds in majestic ways. This work of salvation redeems the dead, it seals the children to their parents, it unites that which is separated and restores that which is lost. Were it not for this restored priesthood work, made possible through the Lord Jesus Christ, the whole planet earth would be cursed, barren, useless, and wasted at the second advent of the Lord! How important the family is to God in time and eternity!

If a seed/tree represents one person, then what is the symbol for a family? It is a forest. A forest of trees is a part of God's good garden. The trees in a forest are intended to support and sustain one another. Families are essential to God's eternal garden—His everlasting Kingdom. We are endeavoring to do far more than simply help individuals to develop personally strong spiritual reflexes. We are seeking to bring families to eternal spiritual heights. It is naturally desirable to want to be part of a strong loving eternal family. Family salvation is the most physically important, spiritually poignant, emotionally significant, and deeply beautiful doctrine of the restored gospel.

The Book of Mormon contains two family stories. This sacred record was a major unifying device that the Lord used to bring the family of Joseph Smith together as the firm foundation for the restored church. It can likewise help each of us to build a lasting family of faith. I believe that one of the ways Joseph learned how to strengthen his family was from scriptural examples of strong faith-filled families. The good and remarkable news of the latter days provides for families to be sealed together in lasting harmony. The unity in righteousness the Lord seeks to cultivate in families will come about fully as each person becomes devoted to righteous living in their own lives.

The Pattern of the Lord

The Lord starts with the end in mind. His vision of saving souls comes from His understanding of what it means to be saved Himself. The Savior wants to shape us to become the kind of person that He is (3 Nephi 18:25). He uses a developmental process to help each willing individual and each humble family advance from a state of fallen nature to a state of holy saintliness (Mosiah 3:19). He does this by sending missionaries of The Church of Jesus Christ of Latter-day Saints into the homes of people to teach them the restored gospel, principally from the Book of Mormon, in plainness and power.

My mother was a single mother raising three boisterous boys in an extremely poor area of what was then a very poor Ireland. When the missionaries came to our door in 1975 my mother welcomed them and their message with great acceptance. She joined the Church and endeavored to raise her boys in the gospel. We faced troubles and afflictions of every kind including great persecution from some because we were religiously different. I can say frankly that we had many bittersweet experiences—like all families do—but some of these were especially pronounced due to our circumstances at the time. There were highs and lows; good and not so good times; advances and setbacks. Despite facing difficulty, I was a happy child. I am certain that to my mother the challenges seemed insurmountable at times. It certainly felt that way to me. But my mother persisted with courage and determination and in the process taught me the value of being true to what you know to be true.

On two occasions all the windows in our house were smashed by some who did not like that we were members of the Church. We could not afford to replace the glass after the second event so we had our house boarded up with wooden panels for months while we continued to live there. I remember this experience vividly. On another occasion someone tried to burn our house down while we were out at a church activity. We came home to find the inside of the front door had been heavily charred, although we did not know that initially. It took us many minutes to open the badly burned door but thankfully the fire did not go any further. This was a miracle. Another time I will never forget was when my mother's life was threatened by a gang of angry teenagers—gratefully we were protected by heaven. Further, we regularly listened to mocking from those who called us "Mormons" in a disparaging way. Nevertheless, we had the very real protection of the Lord and we were greatly blessed because of the gospel. We had many happy moments and came to sense over time that the Lord was intervening in our lives for His purposes.

I will not be ashamed to meet the pioneers and the Prophet Joseph Smith in the life that follows this one, because I know what it is to experience deep, persistent persecution and yet not use it as a reason to abandon God. I know that God does intervene at times to protect and preserve the lives of His children, as I have had that experience on more than one occasion. It is in times like these that our faith in God and support from loved ones sustains our tired bodies, weary souls, and watered eyes. In due course, we were blessed to move to a better area. God has prospered us in many ways since then and although opposition has always been a feature of our lives, our faith in the restored truth has been a shining beacon in a sometimes-dark world.

Crucially, our mother made sure that we practiced (under direction from the prophets) the daily reading of the Book of Mormon. It laid a foundation of love in my heart for this inspirational book. It is a better book than it may appear at first. It has lifted my weary soul, altered my perceptions through moving insights, brought hope and peace and beauty into my life and been a constant guide and help to me. It has been a treasure trove of doctrine, knowledge, and comfort to me. It has given me a new and improved life because its words have become part of me. When I think of the devotion my mother showed I know that she is one of those that the prophet Alma referred to as being foreordained before the foundations of this world (see Alma 13:3) to receive the everlasting gospel in Ireland in these latter days. I am grateful that she continues today through tender tears to triumph over trials. I now see the family purposes of the Lord with clearer understanding than I did as I child.

During mortality, many people have family and relationship experiences that are troubled and difficult. Many long for a love that is reciprocated. Many hope to love and be loved in genuine and lasting ways. The temporary troubles we face in relationships in this life will one day yield to sublime joys, if we learn the lessons we encounter from both poor relationships and good ones. I am grateful that family extensions work in both directions. In those very painful situations where couples are unable to have children of their own in mortality, they remain part of the family extension which reaches backwards to those before them and forward into eternity. Connectivity always goes beyond our own situational circumstance. We can learn to jettison unhealthy attitudes and behaviors. We can continue in patterns that we observe to be good. In my view, the faithful will one day know relationships that are truly loving. Think of the most blissful relationship you have ever had and think on the fact that this is but prologue to the ones that God will provide you with in the eternities—if you truly desire such.

Called beyond Comfort Zones

When I was a little child, I did not know my biological father. He lived in the United Kingdom, away from my family. In a certain sense, he might as well have lived on a different planet for all I knew about him. He was a stranger to me and my two brothers. Nor do I recollect discussing him in our home much. He simply was not a fundamental part of our lives. I do remember getting birthday cards from him, and although I did see photographs of him, he really was an enigma to me. I suspect my brothers felt likewise.

However, around my 10th birthday, my mother mentioned that our father would like to visit us. She asked us what we thought of the idea. To me that was both a scary and exciting suggestion. I thought he was impertinent, given his clear absence from our everyday lives up to that point. I felt partially resentful of him. On the other hand, I felt interested in knowing about him and using my own perspective to see what he was like. We consented to his visit. It was a most unusual experience to meet him. It was like having a guest in the home or meeting an uncle for the first time. I found him to be good natured, jovial, humorous, and witty. He was flirting with my mother and that was strange to my boyhood eyes as I was protective of her. I also saw in him a man who could be kind, thoughtful, and charismatic—these were things I liked, and I was surprised by that. I saw in him some worldly attributes and boyish traits. I thought to myself "who is this strange man that gave me life, that I resemble in some ways and yet is almost completely unknown to me?"

Overall, it was a worthwhile experience, and it gave me a new perspective. I understood him and his life a little better than before and I liked him. There was a gentleness about him that I did not expect. There was also some sadness I saw in him. I have not forgotten that empathy gives us a new vantage point of what others are going through in their lives. From then until his death, we met on several occasions. He even came to my wedding. He seemed very touched by the fact that I would invite him given how distant we had been throughout our lives. He remarked that he was proud of his boys. I sensed in him a measure of regret about how things had turned out.

I am aware that there were times in my teenage years when I felt hurt and embarrassed by his absence—it made me feel somehow unwanted, and unloved. I admit to feeling many times the hurt that other boys had their father, but I did not. It certainly made me feel that I was losing out on something special. I even felt this way at church—at young men meetings and camps. No one wants to feel abandoned by their own father. I was grateful to dear, concerned priesthood brethren who stepped in to accompany my brothers and I on father and son outings in a measure of compensation—that lesson of love stayed with me.

However, I did outgrow those painful feelings and came to see differently as I matured. Through time and experience I came to terms with the reality of my experience. I held no grudge against my earthly father. I learned that ability to forgive from my mother. Never once did she say anything approaching a disparaging remark about him—even though their relationship had obviously not been what either of them had initially hoped. We can learn so much about how to love others even when relationships are imperfect. I wish to explain why and how the restored gospel has helped me.

Due to being distant from my earthly father, I initially found it difficult to relate to my Father in Heaven. Not in conceptual terms but certainly in terms of personal understanding and comprehension. This makes it easy to see how I found it challenging to grasp the reality of a loving, speaking, concerned, and interested divine Father. I can also see how other people, especially those with similar personal backgrounds to me, might feel that God is distant, uncaring, and unknowable.

I am grateful to report that some key spiritual experiences allowed me, through revelation, to come to sense the actual reality of our loving and devoted Father in Heaven. I can relate these firsthand experiences because while they are precious, there is nothing about them that is inappropriate to share as part of my sincere testimony. They are quiet and reverent events—as opposed to being flashy or especially unique. They are genuine spiritual experiences without fanfare or worldly acclaim, but which nonetheless have come to mean so very much to me personally. These events have impacted me in deeply profound ways and have opened my spiritual mind, eyes, and heart to the truth of our Father in Heaven.

I have learned that our Father in Heaven is our best friend. He seeks our best interest—genuinely and eagerly. He wants our growth and development for our sake. He is committed to the plan of immortality and eternal life. His friendship is one that encourages real and lasting improvement within us. He is trying to get our attention. Do we hear Him? (Doctrine & Covenants 1:2). His faithful and loving voice is speaking to us. He wants to shower great treasures of knowledge and wisdom upon us. His guidance, direction, and help are available in abundance (see 3 Nephi 27:27–29). He is the supremely great and generous gardener of our eternal souls. To have a real, personal, deep, and abiding knowledge of our Father is a need of vital importance. It is crucial that we come to know who He is, what He is really like, and what His purposes and plans for us are. This knowledge is fundamental to our salvation.

Gospel Nurturing at Home

All those who learn about the restored gospel are taught:

1. Through the First Vision and all the other revelations to the Prophet Joseph Smith we are established with a firm personal testimony that God is the *literal Father* of our spirits, that Jesus Christ is the *living Redeemer* of our souls and that the Holy Ghost is the *Testator* who witnesses deeply to us of divine truth, and comforts and guides us (Alma 18: 24–35). Indeed, the Godhead are part of a family as they consist of one Father and two sons who love, sustain, support, and testify of one another (3 Nephi 11:32; Mormon 7:7). We are to become as perfectly one as they are (3 Nephi 12:48; Moroni 4:3). What family harmony! The very notion of family stems from the core doctrinal truth of the Godhead. Each person is shown how to gain their own testimony of the Book of Mormon and that the gospel has been restored in its fulness to the earth in a new and complete endowment of truth and righteousness. We are to transcend any hesitance we might have about spiritual things through the knowledge endowed upon us from on high. A testimony is a witness through the power of the Holy

Ghost that the restored gospel is true. This personal divine revelation forms the basis of our spiritual journey throughout life (Alma 18:40).

2. The *knowledge* of God's plan for our happiness and salvation which includes the vital elements of the *creation*, *Fall* and *Atonement* (Alma 18:36–39).
3. To *act* in accordance with divine principles, meaning to keep commitments, obey commandments, be converted, make covenants, and develop consecration. As Nephi stood on an exceedingly high mountain holy place (1 Nephi 11:1), we are invited to establish lives of holiness through the three unique sacred places which are the *home*, the *church*, and the *temple.*

All converts to the church and all members need to know the doctrine that plays a crucial role in the conversion process. In the home we make personal commitments in the sacred privacy of our own hearts to study scripture, pray, and attend church. In the home the parents who join the Church learn to govern the family in righteousness. At home, children are taught the gospel and continue throughout life to learn and teach the gospel. The home is the foundation of the spiritual life and the main place for ongoing discipleship. At home I have read, studied, and pondered the scriptures and learned they are both true and powerful. Those words have brought goodness, truth, peace, comfort, hope, and happiness into my life (Mosiah 2:41). Whether we learn the restored gospel at home from our parents or from missionaries as converts, we learn the same principles.

When people keep commitments, they are better prepared to live commandments. In the home we are taught to keep the commandments of God. When our missionaries enter the homes of people to teach them, they follow the example of Abinadi, who taught the commandments one by one to King Noah and his priests. Why? Because we cannot live commandments we do not know. Even if we know them, we still need to be reminded about their importance (Mosiah 12–13). Indeed, Abinadi taught the Mosaic Ten Commandments as a prefiguring for the essential atoning ministry of Christ. In doing this he changed the life of Alma the Elder who later became a prophet himself and the father of a prophet and great missionary Alma the

Younger (Alma 5:11; Mosiah 13). Our keeping of His commandments as a lifelong pursuit reflects our deep love for God, others, and ourselves. We are to teach the commandments, for doing so leads others and ourselves to the fruit of the tree of life (1 Nephi 8, 11; Alma 32). Hence, teaching people to obey and repent through Christ is what inspires and allows them to want to live a godly life. The family is the key setting for teaching such foundational faith in the ways and laws of God. Our children are more likely to want to obey God as we teach the word of God in clarity and confidence (Alma 31:5).

We are taught in the home how to forge faith in the revealed concept of the family. We have scriptural endorsement and prophetic approval for the divine family pattern. The children of God can be clear about their divine identity, can seek fulfilment in divinely approved relationships and can move closer to the family ideal that the gospel holds up as the perfect standard for all. We can learn the lifting power of love. We seek to protect our children both born and yet unborn against tragedy. We learn that love and law are essentially connected and so we seek to bring the message of hope and salvation to all because we love them. We are to help all to see the divine in themselves and come to a personal knowledge that they can have a fulness of gospel blessings within the bounds the Lord has set. It is precisely because moral purity is a divine commandment of love that we teach the more excellent way of the family ideal that only the true gospel makes possible to every person in the world. We preach the universal need for obedience and repentance (Mosiah 4:10).

Patriarchal Priesthood

Patriarchal authority and power is from the Almighty. It is authentic, genuine, and almost tangible at times. Its influence is compelling. It has power to heal, lift, warn, guide, protect, and bless us. Indeed, "the doctrine of the priesthood shall *distil* upon thy soul as the *dews from heaven*" (Doctrine & Covenants 121:45, emphasis added). It may appear imperceptible but it is real, heaven sent, and nourishing. It is no accident that the patriarchal priesthood runs in families. It requires priesthood to bind families eternally in exalted links that can never be destroyed by time or death.

Cherishing Covenants

Home life is vital to the development of family faith in God. However, in general there are no saving ordinances administered in the home or under the direction of the parents in a family. This is because ordinances go beyond commandments into the realm of covenants. When we accept the commandments to be baptized and confirmed we are essentially accepting the word of God personally and institutionally (Mosiah 18:8–10). Priesthood keys held by governing officers of the Church direct the administration of the saving ordinances. We can lessen spiritual danger by choosing to make and keep covenants with the Lord. We promise to do His will but we have the opportunity for repentance if we fall. God promises us special blessings for our faithfulness. Christ always establishes a covenant-based Church among His people (Mosiah 5:5).

While civil marriage between a man and a woman may be honorable, it is preparatory in nature. Of course, such temporal marriages can display great love. However, God has a loftier plan in store. Making legal contracts alone does not require love of the Father, faith in the Son, moral worthiness, or priesthood ordinances. For example, people can be married legally without being moral or without being baptized. However, the standard of God is higher. Our missionaries teach all people to live the law of chastity and to enter sacred covenants (Mormon 9:29). Though a couple who are legally married and are chaste can be baptized, they will still be invited to be sealed one year after baptism. Civil marriage is not yet a celestial marriage under priesthood law. To partake of gospel ordinances, we need to be qualified in our personal lives. We are to strive to develop the celestial love of Christ within our relationships.

The purity provided by repentance and obedience is to come before we experience the spiritual blessings of baptism and temple sealing. Thus, the spiritual qualifications for an eternal family are both personal worthiness and priesthood covenants. This is in addition to the love between the parties. Love, worthiness and priesthood ordinances and covenants are all necessary for our families to become truly and deeply rooted in the saving embrace of Christ. Every person learning about the gospel needs to know this.

In considering the idea of covenants, allow me to use an illustration. A "contract" refers to a legal agreement between parties which requires the parties to do something for each other. A covenant is a contract with a significant spiritual dimension. We might compare eating food to a kind of covenant. When we eat a piece of fruit, the vitamins and minerals are absorbed into our bloodstream. In a sense, this eating of the fruit is a form of spiritual contract. It is an agreement that benefits both the person and the food. The fruit has its purpose fulfilled of being consumed. We are benefited by the nutrients that come into our bodies. They are used to keep us alive, giving us necessary energy to fuel our cells and muscles. To contract with food in this way is to allow it to have access to you. For the food to benefit us, it must be internalized and digested. If we do not eat it, or only eat a portion of it, it will not be helpful in the way it might have been. Eating good food is both a tasty and nutritious activity. The food keeps us alive physically. This permits us to keep working and serving in this spiritual probation. Hence, eating physical food is a form of spiritually beneficial activity!

We can compare gospel covenants to a form of contract to eat food that is good for us. In this analogy, we covenant with God and our loved ones to act in certain beneficial ways toward them and they likewise promise to act in helpful ways toward us. If we allow ourselves to have regular interaction with God and our loved ones, and allow ourselves to "contract" the good things they are sharing with us, then those good things enter our lives positively. Our immune systems—our defense mechanisms—will allow these beneficial gifts to come inside us and be part of us. They go to our inner selves. Just as food is needed to sustain life, so, in like manner, will attention to our covenants influence our entire life. In this sense, covenants or spiritual "contracts" permit us to influence and be influenced by the people we value most deeply and who can bring the most "life" to our lives, including God.

The covenants are the same for both men and women (although obviously each party brings distinct abilities and expectations to the arrangement) and both come under the protective, saving and blessing embrace of the priesthood (Mosiah 5:1–8). The priesthood is shared openly between all members of the family in terms of its blessings and promises. We can be willing to let other family members unload their burdens in conversation to us—this is a personal ministry of extending hope and healing (Mosiah 18:9). Although the baptismal covenant is made once in the waters of immersion, the ordinance of the sacrament allows us to renew the cleansing impact of our baptism through a weekly renewal of covenant (Moroni 4:3; 5:2). Thus, we can retain a remission of our sins which gives us both relief from spiritual pain and a new healthy life (see Alma 5). For covenants to be eternal we need to become qualified in our capacity to keep them. Obviously, we always require repentance in mortality, and such is available thanks to our merciful Savior. While we are not perfectly obedient in mortality, we can strive to be genuinely faithful to our covenants for our mortal lives (Mosiah 4:30). We can feel the healing balm of beautiful bonds that come through Christ-like covenants.

The Soul Stretching of Marriage

Marriage is a precious covenant involving obedience to God and loving kindness toward our spouses (1 Nephi 7:1). God is interested in deep substantial love, eternal happiness, and lasting responsibility. The true love of the heart linked with a determined resolve to do our solemn duty and the bolstering of spiritual priorities makes us strong through all the difficult challenges of family life. It involves the divine power of God—He who is our help and strength all the days of our lives (4 Nephi 1:11). As we grow to achieve our individual divine potential our marriage becomes more united, selfless, and happy. It is an everlasting love protected inside a continuous covenant with endless rewards. Can anyone doubt the great spiritually based covenant love that Lehi had for his wife Sariah and vice-versa? (1 Nephi 2:4). Spouses can experience unifying togetherness. Male and female spirits are similar in so many ways. However, our differences can be celebrated as a means of making us stronger together. The partnership is mutually reinforcing based on synergistic understanding, cooperation, reliance, and harmony (1 Nephi 5:1–9). We seek to be the best version of ourselves and endeavor to help our spouses to become their best self also.

Even with all the education of growing up in a family, we still have lessons to learn in marriage and parenthood. My wife and I got married four months after we started dating. We had to give three months' notice of our intention to marry legally, so I had to get the legal papers submitted soon after we started dating and before I asked Veronica to marry me. Faith is a principle of action and power! We got married three times within the space of two days—in the legal registry office, by our bishop in the ward building, and finally in the temple. These were three distinct ceremonies. While each was sweet in its own way, I sensed that the greatest opposition, and hence the greatest spiritual power, accompanied the third of these marriages. A ferry delay of 14 hours meant getting to the temple much later than planned. The stress of that situation was immense. However, there was a powerful spirit in the temple. The priesthood power of the sealing ordinance was prevalent. The difference between temporal weddings and celestial ones was profoundly clear to me at that time.

I have learned valuable lessons from being married:

Effective communication and planned budgeting and "unselfish love" are underestimated skills. Marriage was certainly a baptism of fire from my perspective as it presented an educational course for me which I never fully anticipated.

For introverts like me, the closeness of marriage provides challenges in terms of trust, intimacy, and feeling confined. However, there is also the richness of feeling cared for uniquely. It is not that introverts do not like relationships. It is that they put so much into them that it causes them exhaustion.

Excessive and persistent stresses test marriage partners deeply. We are taught by such experience in a way we never could be without it.

All aspects of married life are important—relationships, finances, church, work.

We grow upwards through both struggle and joy.

My wife and I have learned that each of us is far stronger as a couple than we are alone. We know God is always there to help us when needed (2 Nephi 9:10). Of course, the beauties of life such as happy moments, good memories, true friends, small miracles, sweet spiritual feelings, and the nearness of God have been comforting consolations. The gospel adds a dimension of concern and stability to relationships that is beyond unaided human ability to replicate. I am grateful to have a wife who has set her sights on the kingdom of God in preference to the values and standards of the world. She has done this amidst many trying circumstances both before I knew her and since we met. Her independent devotion to the truth attracted me to her because those who love righteousness are naturally drawn to others who do likewise.

This is seen in the example of Sariah who was like Lehi and followed him and similarly with Nephi and his wife (see 1 Nephi). The light of truth unifies those who love truth in the bonds of mutual spiritual love. The gospel certainly acts as an anchor to keep us safely grounded and as a sail to lift us heavenward. We ensure that the Book of Mormon and the other works of divine standards are daily guests in our home, following the divine guidance given to Prophets in these turbulent last days regarding the strengthening of families through infusing our family life with God's revealed word. Our hope is to rise to greater heights of achievement through that key prophetic principle. Following the prophet brings power to individuals and families.

In scope and scale, the grandeur of celestial marriage is clearly breathtakingly beyond what we can presently fathom. It is the mosaic of infinity. The quality of celestial marriage is superb and unsurpassed. For marriage to reach its full splendor both wife and husband must want to be together and be worthy of it. A temple sealing then involves shared sacred power, love, truth, and righteousness. In the resurrection, which is the everlasting union of body and spirit, eternal literal marriage relationships become possible (Alma chapters 40 and 41).

In God's Likeness

Our Heavenly Parents are perfect. They care deeply about their children and their salvation. We are especially honored to bring to Christ those special souls entrusted to our care as our children. Parents are wise when they remember that their covenants include not only each other but their children also—we have a solemn responsibility to bring our children up in the nurture and admonition of the Lord (1 Nephi 1:1). As we follow the injunctions of prophets, we learn to love our children more deeply and teach them by word and deed more powerfully and consistently.

Women are masters at helping their children grow to a happy maturity through righteous nurturing. This supremely important work of a lifetime yields marvelous dividends. If all women in the world raised their children to follow the Lord, we could have a world full of men like the two thousand stripling warriors—imagine that! (Alma 56:47–48). Obviously, God intends fathers to be conscientious, loving, and devoted spiritual leaders of their children. Alma corrected his sin-attached son Corianton honestly but also humbly and lovingly. He also showed great confidence in him by not giving up on him and teaching him (Alma 38). No other work has ever given me a fraction of the joy that being a father does, with all its triumphs and frustrations.

God derives His joy from helping us to find and possess true happiness. The Savior Himself is the example we are to follow in all things, including in family relationships. Our Savior is called the Everlasting Father, meaning He is the father by spiritual rebirth of all who come to His gospel by covenant (2 Nephi 19:6; 31:13). He is the Only Begotten of the Father (2 Nephi 25:12). He is the Messianic Son of God. He is in the Father and the Father is in Him (3 Nephi 9:15). During His transformative visit to the Nephites, the Savior taught and healed the families, blessed and prayed for the children, and wept and witnessed as angels came down to minister to the children (3 Nephi 17:21–25). What an example to us of how the Savior ministers to families! The Savior commanded husbands and fathers to pray to the Father in the name of the Son regarding blessing their families always (3 Nephi 18:20). We know that the Lord atoned for individuals but also that a prime purpose in doing so was to exalt entire family units.

When I had the privilege of baptizing and confirming our son Thomas it was a remarkable experience. We both stood on holy ground. I felt the great authority and power of the priesthood as I stood in the baptismal font with him and performed that sacred saving ordinance. As I laid hands on his head to bestow the gift of the Holy Ghost upon him, I was touched deeply with emotion and touched beautifully by the Spirit. There was great spiritual power present, and I was particularly touched because of the great love I felt for my son. We felt genuine joy and a special sense of the sacred that day in seeing him progress in such an eternally significant way. This is like what those at the waters of Mormon knew and testified of—that the priesthood binds us together in spiritual love and unity (Mosiah 18:13–14, 21).

A Priority of Prophets

We desire to save souls, especially those of our own families. True and strong faith is both an individual concern and a family priority. The greatest blessings come through righteous humility and unity in families. Parents, and especially fathers, can and must teach their children faith in the redeeming Christ by word and deed. This is the great burden and desire of Book of Mormon prophets through more than two thousand years. The Lord reaches one person through a profoundly life-changing spiritual experience and then that one person reaches out to many others. Parents pass a torch of truth, legacy of love, and fortress of faith to the hearts, minds, and spirits of their children. Let us reflect on how family members can have a great influence for righteousness on other family members.

Abraham was the father of Isaac, Jacob, and Joseph and was even called the father of the faithful—meaning all those who embraced the everlasting covenant and were true to it. He blessed all his children and indeed all nations of the world according to the everlasting covenant. This covenant would be meaningless without the Atonement of the Son of God (1 Nephi 15:18; 17:40). Abraham wanted his son Isaac to know the meaning of the Atonement. Abraham offering up Isaac was a representation of God the Father offering up His Only Begotten Son as a ransom for all (Jacob 4:5). Indeed, Lehi's entire family are the seed (children) of Abraham, Isaac, and Jacob through his son Joseph. The redemption of that family which was to be wrought by the Son of God was known in this family line long before the Savior ever came to earth. The righteous seed of Abraham would bless all nations of the earth with the true gospel (3 Nephi 10:17; 20:25; Mormon 9:11–12). The Prophet Joseph Smith received the new and everlasting covenant—which was the restoration of the saving Abrahamic Covenant—the covenant to save the faithful family of the House of Israel eternally (2 Nephi 3:7).

Likewise, the great concern of the Book of Mormon prophets was to create Christ-centered families forever through protective and enhancing covenants. Jacob teaches that every person, including married couples such as Adam and Eve, would have become sons and daughters of perdition forever without any hope of resurrection or joy were it not for the Christ who atoned (2 Nephi 9:4–13). Consequently, their bodies were saved from death and their spirits were saved from hell. Further, their very real physical and spiritual marriage was saved from all forms of death by the Savior. Thus, the Savior overcomes sin and death to allow for eternal lives through eternal family. Salvation in the full sense is for spiritually united families. Eternal families, eternal righteousness, and eternal joy are only possible because of the atoning sacrifice, which we benefit from through restored priesthood covenants and ordinances.

Consider the following heart-touching examples:

We see that Lehi comforted his wife and taught his children. He wanted nothing more than his wife and sons and their families to partake of great joy through the Atonement of Christ (1 Nephi 8:12).

Nephi believed in the Messianic prophecies given by his father Lehi and desired to gain an understanding of these saving truths for himself by the deep power of the Holy Ghost (1 Nephi 10:17; 11:1).

Jacob wanted his son Enos to have eternal joy through faith in Christ (Enos 1:3).

Jared asked his brother to ask God to not confound their language so that they might remain a united family of faith (Ether 1:34).

King Benjamin taught his sons and people the masterful Messianic prophecies of their fathers given by the Lord (Mosiah 1:2).

Benjamin's son, King Mosiah, did likewise (Mosiah 6:3, 6–7).

Alma the Elder prayed in such great faith for the redemption of his son Alma the Younger that an angel came to call the rebellious son to repentance. As a result, Alma the Younger had a marvelous experience in coming to know the Son of God and thereafter was devoted to God (Mosiah 27:14–30).

Alma the Younger wanted his son Helaman to remember that Jehovah delivered their fathers from bondage (Alma 36:1–3). Alma also explained to Helaman how in his own time of desperate spiritual need, he remembered his prophetic father Alma teaching the people about the Atonement of the Son of God, Jesus Christ (Alma 36:17).

Alma wanted his son Shiblon to know that salvation came through Christ (Alma 38:9).

Alma taught his son Corianton that Christ would come to take away the sins of the world and he commanded him to turn to the Lord with complete devotion (Alma 39:13, 15).

Ammon taught King Lamoni the teachings of the Fathers from Adam down to Lehi and his children regarding the revealed word of God (Alma 18:36–37). In connection with these events, Abish, a Lamanite woman, was given an opportunity to defend the true faith (Alma 19:16).

The life of Ammon was literally preserved because of the faith of his father, Mosiah, who trusted Ammon to the Lord in his mission among the Lamanites (Alma 19:23).

As a result of this inspired mission of Ammon, King Lamoni bore testimony to his own father, under threat of death, about the divine calling of Ammon as a prophet of the Lord (Alma 20:14–16).

We are taught that Captain Helaman called the two thousand stripling warriors his sons and they called him their father (Alma 56:27, 46). Those young men were actual descendants of Laman, the eldest son of Lehi. Now, that is interesting! Those young men had been taught with conviction by their mothers that God could indeed be trusted in every particular of life and death, and they believed! (Alma 56:47–48)

Helaman walked after the righteous ways of his father Captain Helaman (Helaman 3:20) and wanted his sons to build their lives on the rock of the Son of God (Helaman 5:12).

Nephi, son of Helaman, walked in the righteous ways of his father (Helaman 3:37) and testified that almost all the fathers of the people of Lehi were prophets that had testified of the coming of Christ (Helaman 8:22).

We are tenderly instructed that Mormon, as a distant yet pure descendant of Lehi, praised Jesus Christ for bringing the fathers out of Jerusalem and allowing them to know and preach about the redemption of God for His people (3 Nephi 5:20).

Samuel the Lamanite prophet, in fulfilment of prayers and prophecies, testified to his brethren the Nephites of the resurrection of the Son of God and many saints of the meridian day (3 Nephi 23:9).

Mormon desired that the prayers of faith of the saints of the house of Israel (family of the faithful) for their children to be gathered to the redeeming knowledge of Christ, through the covenant made possible by the everlasting priesthood, would be fulfilled as God remembers this everlasting covenant (Mormon 9:37; Ether 13:11). Mormon prayed for his son Moroni to be kept always in the grace of Christ and that his son would endure faithfully to the end. He also wanted his son to be lifted upwards by the Savior (Moroni 8:2–3; 9:25).

We can do likewise.

The Crucible of Affliction

Of course, families face challenging troubles of every kind and degree. These are stark realities in a world of real choice, certain trouble, and opposing alternatives. God faithfully provides the way through (not out of) all difficulties, even if sometimes that takes much time and patience. As we come to understand the plans of God, we come to see God, others, and ourselves in a very hopeful light. The restored gospel is a joyful way of life. It is a way of thinking, seeing, acting and being that can transform people from being the grossest of sinners to being the most humble of saints (Alma 26).

A Mighty Change of Heart

After we make covenants, we are on our way to conversion, which is to become new in Christ. Conversion is not spiritual boredom. The receipt of the ordinances brings about conversion (Alma 23:6). We are to experience a mighty change within ourselves, meaning acquiring a divine nature through the Atonement (Mosiah 5:2). The profound change of heart is a transformation of status, identity, character, and substance. Thus, we become saints. We then increasingly align with the divine in our perspectives, attitudes, values, behaviors, motives, intentions, desires, beliefs, actions, and characteristics. We are nourished in Christ. We will never have to leave Heaven once we get there because it will be within us (Alma 7:23–26).

We become able to be filled with heavenly attributes just as our Heavenly Father and Savior already are. This life is an abundance of joyful optimism through Christ in that we continually receive more light and truth. Divine attributes become part of the fabric of our souls everlastingly. The truths and promises are then solid tangible actualities, discernible verities, and soul pervasive realities that encompass our entire being (Mosiah 5:15). As we live by these wonderful precepts, we thereby become much more able to foster these same attributes in others (Alma 26:22).

After we are converted, we are ready to venture forth to learn about ultimate devotion to God in the form of consecration (Omni 1:26). Through priesthood ordinances and covenants we gain access to the authority, power, and blessings of God. In the temple we promise to be consecrated to God. We take upon ourselves the name of Christ in the full and complete sense for time and all eternity unless we blot out that name through our transgression (see Mosiah 5:11). The temple ordinances are crucial for living to our ultimate spiritual potential in this life. There we commune with God, feel His love, learn reverence, show respect, sense spiritual peace, serve unselfishly, and know joy. It is a holy and sacred place, the pinnacle of the kingdom of God on the earth and the great symbol of the celestial kingdom. The temple leads us to Christ and to the Father. God there infuses our lives with divine power to lift us to a higher level of divinity. The Lord appeared at the temple in Bountiful, as that was where His saints were! (3 Nephi 11)

Our inheritance in the Kingdom of God comes as we belong to the family of God through the new and everlasting covenant. Such covenants, of course, would have no saving power were it not for the Atonement of Christ. Every person that enters the new and everlasting covenant with sincerity has a personal conditional promise of eternal life now, which will become guaranteed if they continue in lifelong obedience to God. To give the ordinances and covenants lasting validity we must prove our devotion to God through enduring obedience. No one falls automatically into salvation or finds the process easy. As the reward is great so the price to obtain the reward must be great also. For example, God made a binding covenant with His servant Alma that he would have eternal life. The mortal precursor to this type of life was that Alma was commanded to serve God, minister in His name, and to offer salvation to those who would follow God (Mosiah 26:20). Those who are obedient to God have the inspired promise and testimony of prophets that they will obtain eternal life (Alma 7:16).

We must be tested in our attempts to achieve consecration. The adversary will try to overpower us through various means as we approach God more fully. Our enemy seeks to replace our true spiritual Father. He seeks to rule and reign over us all by getting us to worship or follow him. He is the father of contention (3 Nephi 11:27) and the father of all lies (Ether 8:25). His followers are like he is and are also called sons (and daughters) of perdition. When inspired by the adversary, families are united in profound sin and error. Just as some parents teach righteousness to their children, other parents teach wickedness to their children by their willful rebellion against God, Christ, and their true servants. Unfortunately, some families thereby promote unity in sin and carry on the work of hatred, wickedness, and carnality (4 Nephi 1:38–39; Mormon 6:6). This brings damnation upon families unless they repent (Mormon 7:5). Thus, the adversary, who can never have an eternal family of his own, seeks to enlist us as his alternative family and to deprive us of exalted family blessings. He is downcast forever because he has no wife, no children, and no eternal glory. What possibly could be worse than this!

I see this experiential and lifelong process as a triangle of consecration shown below. May we all stay on this path of peace, or having come off it, may we find our way back to the loving embrace of our eternal family.

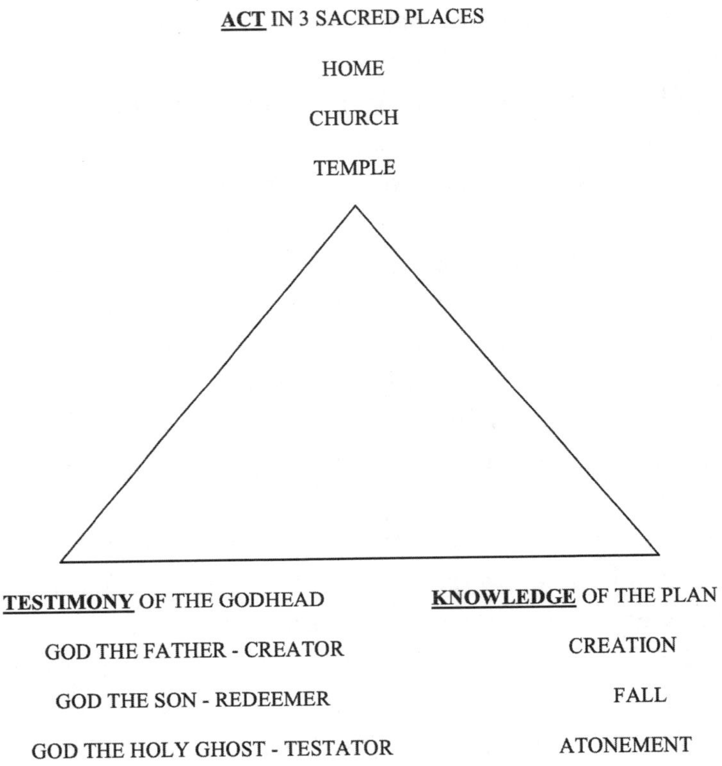

9

Drawn toward the Sun

I WILL NOW REFLECT ON THE PRONOUNCED MORTAL EDUCATIONAL development which helps us to become more like our Heavenly parents. When viewed from the vantage point of eternity, these schooling experiences are essential to our growth toward divinity, just like a seed must struggle through the darkness to reach toward the light.

I remember the very first day I attended school as a four-year-old child. I was crying incessantly because I did not want to leave my mother. I recollect running out the door after her and she brought me back to the school. This happened several days in a row. Gradually I was okay, but I still remember the trauma even after forty-five years. This represented my fear of abandonment and loss. It also showed my comfort with the familiar and how change scared me. I also remember this as the period of my life when I became sensitive to other people being alone although I was only between 8 and 10 years of age. I felt sympathy for them and resolved to comfort the individuals I would come across in my life that would feel alone.

This was a key formative time for me. I remember feeling nervous around people, especially girls. Initially, I felt that I did not deserve anything good in my life. I did not feel particularly important. That was devastating. I wrestled with those issues for all my growing up years and well into my twenties. Due to my fears, I distanced myself from others in protective fashion. Some may have thought of my aloofness as contempt. In truth it was grounded in fear. My shyness was not dislike or animosity, it was based on low self-esteem. My introversion was not evidence of pride or being uninterested in others—it reflected the fact that I got my energy from inside myself rather than from other people. My love for others is in fact deeply felt. I feel things profoundly deeply. This was true, even as a child.

However, this is not the end of the story. I am glad to report that I have overcome my fear of abandonment and I am deeply comfortable in my own skin. I believe the primary reason for this is because I know that my Father in Heaven loves me. I love to hear His voice and sense His love in my life. It moves me to a great and profound sense of peace and certainty. I also know my Lord Jesus Christ. I have felt of His love and known of His goodness. Even if no other person on the planet approved of my faith, this would not change the reality that I know the Lord loves me. This has provided huge impetus to me. I cannot explain how much my connection with them has reassured me. While I am still quite introverted, I have a confidence grounded in knowing who I am, based on divine identity. This has been the most important identity of my life. I can stand on my own ground because I know that God stands with me.

I have another story about my time in my first school. While there I was reasonably good at mathematics. However, in the very last year of being in this school, I became friends with a boy that was new to the school. He had little or no interest in education and influenced me negatively. I started having less interest in studying. This meant that when I did the entrance exams for secondary school, I was placed in a class of students whose interest in schooling was mixed. In addition, when I moved to secondary school, I unfortunately made "friends" with another boy whose sole purpose in life was to have fun. His influence rubbed off on me. I then continued even more to not take my schoolwork seriously and caused trouble for my teachers by not paying attention and causing distraction to others. This impacted my grades in everything—especially in mathematics—which continued to plummet downwards.

Ironically but mercifully, someone in leadership decided that I was capable of better than this and determined to move me in with the better performing students for my second year. I presume this was based on the notion that someone able to distract an entire class through humor must have a reasonably high level of intellectual capacity, even if for the moment they were acting immaturely. Of course, I still had not woken up to my need to change. Thankfully, in my second year, I had a teacher who directly confronted my clowning around. She said, in essence, "smarten up." I was shocked. I thought I was smart. I did not comprehend that others might view me as being foolish. I remember that day as a defining day in my life.

I immediately began to get my act together and become a serious student. Overnight, I went from class clown to attentive learner. I told my "friend" that I needed to concentrate on my studies and while we maintained something of a relationship from then on, it was essentially reduced to a distant association. While this friend continued to play around, I was on a mission to prove to myself and others that I was capable. I had substantial amounts of lost ground to make up and had to work very hard to do so. I found that the classmates I admired were way ahead of me and so I worked exceedingly hard. In due course my grades rose dramatically. Although I was now associating with a new group, I was in a mathematics class at ordinary level rather than higher level. I worked hard and ended up getting an A grade in my main mathematics exams at age 15. I was thrilled.

However, I believed I was capable of more. I approached the teacher of the higher-level mathematics class and asked if I could move to his class. My teacher and the new teacher agreed. When I went in, at first I was lost. I thought I would never learn the material. The level was so much higher than I was used to. However, I was motivated to succeed. The Lord had given me a chance to improve, and I did not want to waste it. My new teacher was exceptionally good at teaching and that really helped me. Also, I was introduced to a new friend. This young man was phenomenal at mathematics. He was simply astounding in what he could do. I made friends with him and started to sit beside him in mathematics and science classes.

My life was never to be the same. I was inspired by his example and it encouraged me to dig deep and to work even harder and to give answers in class. He was never condescending to me. He never said, "Thomas, you are not as good as I am and will never be able to do this." He always showed support to my efforts. Even though he was significantly better at mathematics that I was, he recognized my ability on its own terms. After spending many hours learning from him and studying for hours each day in homework, I am pleased to report that I scored well in these subjects in my exams at age 17. That achievement—assisted by wise teachers and a true friend—has had a significantly important impact on me. It is unlikely you would be reading this book if these kinds of cultivating experiences—which were heaven sent—had never happened and changed my life in such a beneficial way. I am convinced that it was divine intervention that allowed me to experience the tender mercies of having these opportunities to become something more than I thought I ever could.

There are few people in this world that I have admired, respected, and loved more than that gifted and generous true friend. He gave true meaning to the idea of friendship. He was hungry to learn. He was thirsty for knowledge. He loved to show interest. He played basketball the same way he studied—with enthusiasm and excitement. I never heard him use bad language. He never disrespected women. He was what many would consider the ultimate nerd or geek. He spoke with a refined accent and hailed from a well-off family. He received much by way of insults from others because of the way he lived his life. I never once saw him bend to the crowd or lessen his devotion to learning. I am a better man for knowing him. I will always love him because he showed me that there is a better way to live than gravitating toward a life of mediocrity. His influence made me a better student, a better friend, and a better person. I met him some years later when both of us attended the same university! He was still the very supportive man I had known years before. I appreciate that man deeply.

There is a message in this story. We each radiate an influence on others. We can be a poor and bad influence or a great and good one. I had both types at school and I know from experience which one I prefer. I prefer the friend who helps me to incline toward greatness. There is, of course, one person in eternity who is the greatest example we could have in time and eternity of what we can achieve. That is the Lord Jesus Christ. His invitation to you and I is sublime, powerful, and life changing. Like my good friend, who saw potential in me and worked to bring it forth, our Lord, on a much deeper, higher, and important level, sees in us that which is only latent potential now. He discerns that we can do great things and become truly good with His remarkable help. It is the perspective that the Son of God has of us that we need to come to see, believe, and live according to. His radiating influence upon us can transform the vantage point of how we see ourselves and every aspect of our lives.

In this second school I attended—aptly named *Mount Temple* Comprehensive School—I had numerous formative experiences. When I started going to school dances initially, I was afraid to dance as it was embarrassing. However, when I started to dance, I realized I loved it. I love the sense of expression that comes with dancing, especially freestyle. I retain that love to this day. I loved finding solutions to complex problems in my studies. I had feelings ranging from great excitement to great frustration. There were happy and sad times. So much of my life has been like my schooling—a smorgasbord of feelings, events, people, and experiences. I remember the girls that touched my heart. I have never forgotten that this was a preparation for me to sense how God feels about His children. He sees each one in dynamic, living color. He sees what is hidden from view within us, what others do not see, and even what we often do not perceive. God was watching over me, even when I did not see that.

Lessons Learned

The lessons I have learned throughout my life which have opened my eyes to God's nourishing nature include the following:

We often only learn what we like by trying things out. God will guide us, but He expects us to take an interest in seeing what we are good at through effort and experimentation.

The longing for adventure, for newness, for travel has been a part of me for as long as I can remember. Of course, there is a time for daydreaming and a time for applying ourselves. Dreaming of beautiful exotic places and exciting adventures is not enough. It needs to be joined by practical efforts to make a useful contribution to this world. Then we can have both!

I have enjoyed watching people as they come and go at airports. It is intensely interesting to me to see the deep emotions involved when people say goodbye and hello to family and friends. We can learn remarkable things by observing others in the enormously important times of their lives when their true feelings are manifest. Our happiness and sadness at airports offer us a small indication of what we will feel when we come again into the presence of God and loved ones in the life after this one.

Life is a great education for us in thoughts, words, ideas, and actions. We can learn to like education and love learning. The desire to improve our lives is a good wish. To enjoy flourishing and doing hard things well is something truly precious.

We are all tempted to abdicate responsibility for our lives to someone or something else. It is not always easy to do the right thing and be hard working, conscientious, and focused on goals and action. However, the greatest progress occurs as we dig deep and accept personal accountability to move our lives forward. God will sustain us as we try.

God is interested in our relationships, education, careers, opportunities, and privileges. I have seen Him guiding me to improve my outlook and circumstances in all these areas.

We all face doubts, isolation, disconnection, and loneliness. There is no immunity from this in life. However, God has prepared a way for us to find faith, togetherness, tenderness, and belonging. I sometimes surrendered to fear, shyness, and low self-esteem. I sometimes stayed in comfort zones as that was safer. However, we learn through trying and certainly I have grown due to contact I have had with others. I have learned to grow beyond fear with courage and faith. My incorrect script of life gave me false views about relationships and about life that unfortunately meant I lost some opportunities. I am so grateful for change and now I hope I do not waste my opportunities. I engage in relationships differently now. I know God understands why I was less than a brave and loving person at times in the past.

We each face the challenges of pride, of learning how to lead, discovering the nature of true friendship and having to confront others in constructive ways.

Mortality will present each one of us with experiences that open our eyes and broaden our knowledge. We are wise to take advantage of learning from and tutoring the people we associate with. I have benefited from reading the thoughts of great thinkers and discussing with people the great questions of the soul. These contributed to my understanding of significant and meaningful subjects.

We need to learn to believe in ourselves more. Every one of us is more capable than we think we are. We can conquer fear and doubt about our real worth and capacity. This is something God can teach us.

It can be difficult to break through our self-constructed shells of protection if we are more concerned with safety than we are with development. Growth comes with new opportunities, different experiences, and novel tasks. God seeks our growth rather than our comfort. Comfort has its place, but so does challenge. We need to push ourselves to achieve our limits. This is true in all things. Complacency can hold us back from glory.

As a career manager for over twenty years, I experienced the difficulty presented by constant demands for my help. It was simultaneously thrilling and exhausting, involving both immense joy and deep heartache. I could listen to others share their challenges professionally and personally and I enjoyed being able to help them in that way. We all need to be listened to sometimes. I also had the opportunity of being thrown into the deep end, metaphorically speaking, when I worked in an office with a chaotic structure, limited training, some temperamental colleagues, and a general negative atmosphere for several years. This was an exceedingly difficult experience. However, with effort and prayer I eventually rose above it and became competent and confident in the very same place. I know that our good attitudes can improve harsh environments. This has been a truly life-changing experience as it has caused me to grow in so many inconvenient but vital ways.

To discover joy in serving others is the gateway to a whole new inner and outer world.

We need to discover a harmonious balance between seriousness and fun.

The peace we can control is that of knowing we are living according to our spiritual and moral conscience.

We all long to be special, different, and unique. I believe each of us is distinctive in time and eternity. We therefore need to use our gifts in whatever form they come to share our light with the world and by so doing to bless lives. God can magnify our talents in ways that will astound us.

On Wings of Wonder

For the first anniversary of our marriage, my wife bought me a gift I treasure deeply. It was a flying lesson! I had been fascinated by flight my entire life and this was a very thoughtful gift. Given my lifelong fear of heights, it is ironic that I wanted to fly an airplane. It was a wonderful experience. It was quite scary as I felt like I would fall out of this fragile device. The trees started to look like broccoli as we ascended high in this machine that felt like it was the weight of a feather. It appeared the wind was flying us. I felt like I really belonged in the clouds. I have seen the world differently since that encounter. In so many ways this is a great symbol for our spiritual growth. We are nervous but we experience exhilaration that we never knew was possible previously. We sense the glory of the skies. We perceive an enlarged view as we grow toward the beckoning lights in the heavens.

Revelation and Reason

I have learned in my growth toward heavenly things that God rejoices in both that which is known by divine uncovering and that which we become acquainted with through intellect. His nature is revealed in both our perspiration and inspiration. I am deeply grateful for revelation. To sense that inspiration which I know came through me—as opposed to coming from me—is a marvelous blessing. I love to detect spiritual intelligence touching my mind and heart. I have experienced this many times and I rejoice in the beauty and transcendence of it. I also love reason. I appreciate rationality. I am grateful to be able to think, examine, explore, analyze, and question. I see no fundamental conflict between true revelation and true reason. These both testify of the glory of God and the majestic possibilities for humanity as the offspring of deity.

I am grateful for the hundreds of discussions I have had with my wife, son, mother, brothers, missionaries, and friends on topics such as feelings, forgiveness, finances, church history and doctrine, philosophy, mathematics, movies, gardening, poetry, and numerous other subjects. Each of these conversations has refined my understanding and improved my ability to articulate core concepts. I am grateful for the rich resources of knowledge at our disposal in this world of wonder. We literally have access to a flood of information that has come to us from the research, study, and pondering of great minds in so many fields of enquiry. We are blessed with treasures of knowledge! All these sources of comprehension and wisdom ultimately trace themselves to our Father in Heaven and His Beloved Son.

However, if we allow ourselves to be confined purely by reference to viewpoints that can only be conceived in intellectual terms, we close the door to anything that is beyond our present capacity to articulate and explain in purely rational terms. This is spiritually precarious for us as it eliminates anything miraculous from serious consideration. In this sense, human standards—in morality, tradition, or reason—obviously cannot be the ultimate foundational basis for anyone to build a life of devoted faith on, no matter how plausible they sound or appear. This is because true faith will always require something additional to intellect. It will always be a test of character, of morality, of spiritual discernment. It will always demand some faith—the assurance, evidence, or spiritually based proof of those things which we believe in but which are, for a time, beyond our certain sight.

Without consistent and ongoing personal revelation, we run the risk that our viewpoints will be based on shifting opinions rather than on eternal truths. This is certainly the time in the history of the world where the elect according to the covenant need to remember the importance of holding consistently to the iron rod. When the winds inevitably blow and the storms inexorably rage, any weakness in our knowledge and understanding makes us spiritually vulnerable. God has given us a resilient way to avoid such spiritual downfall. True religion is thus God-made not man-made. Revelation teaches us that the correct way, truth, and life must be God's way. It cannot be a way devised or comprehended by man alone.

In my own life, I have approached God with numerous personal questions I needed guidance on and found the answers to be direct, powerful, persuasive, and very helpful. That to me is clear evidence of revelatory outpouring. It is so logical to me that I would never have received a divine witness of Joseph Smith and the Book of Mormon by the Spirit when I was a young boy if he had been a false or fallen prophet and if the Book were the work of men. Revelation is the beginning, middle, and end of our faith—there are a multitude of counterfeits but no satisfactory substitutes for it! I know that the Church has my best interests at heart. However, I have been lied to by the adversary and misled by humans numerous times. I have been hindered by my own shortsightedness. I now clearly see the difference between relying on revelation and trusting something else regarding matters of eternal import. We are so blessed to have been instructed from heaven! The Lord has taught us how to discern truth from error (Doctrine & Covenants 50).

Of course, relying on revelation does not imply that we do not ever use reason. We use it daily! Reason is a gift from God. It is evidence that we are created in His likeness—He is a thinking God. We are intelligent because He is. We are logical because He knows perfect logic. We use rationality to read, learn, study, ponder, consider, and review. In fact, we use both mind and heart, spirit and body, study and faith, to learn the lessons of the Lord. If we deny reason and simply focus on what we perceive to be spiritual promptings, we run the risk of being led astray. Balance is needed. The two witnesses of reason and revelation bring us to truth.

Let us use reason, wisdom, and experience to carefully consider all viewpoints that are presented to us. As we reflect on all things, we can use the Lord's protective mechanisms to our advantage. Then, we will be kept safe from either an excessive focus on reason to the exclusion of inspiration or a view of revelation that excludes reasonable thinking. If something sounds wrong and feels wrong, then our mind and heart are both unified on the issue. Conversely, if both thought and feeling align in saying something is correct, then we are on safe ground. I know my faith is based on revelation and is also rationally defensible (at least to a degree). As we put the answers from God first, then the gospel makes marvelous reasonable sense!

10

Pruned to Flourish

This mortal life is one of remarkable perfecting. This is especially so when we come to know the sacred purposes of our lives. To strive for spiritual excellence, social development, emotional growth, intellectual progress, and physical mastery is to grow in all the ways we are capable of. Our complete personal growth involves faith, testimony, and talents. It requires commandments, covenants, and character. Our education is multifaceted and lifelong. It demands stretching. I am convinced that doctrinal reflections, experiential musings, contemplations on our relationships, and regular pondering are needed if our holistic development is to be maximized.

We came to this earth for many special purposes. We can triumph over the exhaustion that comes inevitably with deep challenges by immersing ourselves in the nourishing news that God knows what He is doing. To choose to follow God also means we choose to reject the adversary (Alma 41:13). We can only show our true desires for goodness if the opportunity for badness is simultaneously available (Alma 41:7). Hence, mortal life is essentially a very compacted series of difficulties to be overcome through purposeful effort. That is the great growth advantage of this short life. It is one thing to learn by theory in the boundaries of a safe classroom. It is a different matter to learn by personal experience in the arena of daily living. We learn how to make choices, often hard ones, and then to deal with the consequences, which can be significant. (Alma 41:14–15). The final judgment will be one that we will not personally dispute—we will be where we are because of what we have consistently chosen to become (Alma 40:25–26).

A Poor Spot of Ground

I think of my own life as an example of the doctrine of "a poor spot of ground" (Jacob 5:21–23). I have experienced an outpouring of instruction and edification in three Gardens—Home, Church, and Temple. I grew up in a place of much poverty, crime, and social deprivation. It was an especially poor subsection of what was then a very poor country. Stolen cars, gang conflict and other types of trouble were regular occurrences. The obstacles against my development appeared pronounced. My family faced constant opposition due to being church members. Of course, there was also friendship and community spirit. It was a bittersweet learning experience. Miraculously, we survived, flourished, and became stronger through defending our faith.

We lived in *Primrose Grove*. That was no accident. The Lord intervened to turn a very challenging situation into a growth experience. The Lord is interested in helping us to overcome obstacles and to bloom where we are planted. This is not just a catchy slogan. It is a powerful verity.

I attended *Springdale* Primary School and later *Mount Temple* Secondary School.

We subsequently lived in *12 Mount Olive* Park and *Huntstown Wood*.

My wife and I now live in a place that means river meadow of glory.

In each of these areas I experienced profound challenges within and externally. I also experienced many miracles which bolstered my faith in vital ways.

Greatness Is Born from Struggle

To grow in stature requires growing pains. To become something more than what we presently are, we must shed our lesser self. To rise in achievement demands that we overcome obstacles we have never faced before. In the realm of spiritual things, there is great advantage in facing and surmounting difficulty. The muscle that is exercised grows stronger. The faith that is challenged can become deeper. The heart that is hurt can know a new kind of love. The mind that is tested can become sharper and wiser. It is in trouble that we find who and what we are. We learn patience when we must wait for things we desire deeply. We cultivate longsuffering when the darkness persists longer than we expect. We nurture understanding when we encounter limitations. We come to know character when our resolve is tried.

Great afflictions can turn us to God in humble sincerity (Mosiah 24:10). In like manner, difficulty can soften our hearts, mellow our spirits, bend our stubbornness, quash our pride, and decrease our vanity. It can also help us to develop greater compassion, sympathy, empathy, and love. Greatness is born out of struggle. The struggle for the light within to conquer the dark. The struggle for courage to overcome fear, for kindness to dismantle harshness, for selfishness to give way to caring for others. The struggle to replace ambition with service, to surmount doubt with faith, to replace vengeance with forgiveness. Let us rise above natural weakness, ascend above the tendency to give up, move beyond the inclination to demand instant relief from sorrow, and grow closer to becoming the majestic person that lies latent within us just waiting to be nourished. God can help us to learn and grow from every challenge we face.

Some of the challenges we may experience throughout our lives are as follows:

Internal Issues

Fear of animals, confined spaces, heights, nightmares, responsibility, and water.

Feeling angry, ambushed by evil, beyond love, disturbed, disgruntled, depressed, frustrated, incapable, imperfect, like a failure, low self-esteem, powerless, slow, stuck, self-contempt, trapped, unimportant, useless, unworthy, and wishing for death.

Having career disappointments, financial setbacks, and learning difficulties.

Experiencing bodily weakness such as chronic conditions, headaches, infections, nose bleeds, paralysis, skin problems, serious illness, and travel sickness.

Relational Issues

Fear of people who are angry, beautiful, dangerous, emotionally manipulative, intelligent, in authority, negative, pessimistic, violent, vindictive, and wealthy.

Feeling abandoned, accused, bullied, betrayed, criticized, controlled, derided, disparaged, disrespected, dismissed, embarrassed, forgotten, humiliated, hopeless, hated, ignored, invisible, left behind, laughed at, misunderstood, not listened to, opposed, overwhelmed, overlooked, ostracized, penalized, punished, persecuted, rejected, snubbed, silenced, singled out, taken for granted, taken advantage of, undermined, used, undervalued, unfairly treated, usurped, and weak.

Having poor people skills, relationship breakdowns, and trust issues.

Experiencing abuse, condescending treatment, being mocked and maligned, being misled, insults, persecution, and violence.

I frankly admit that I have experienced all these things at one time or another—and others—in my nearly half a century of living in this fallen world. These things have been difficult to bear. I suppose that most of us have experienced these kinds of things at times in our lives. These experiences are not pleasant at the time—they are jarring to us. They are confusing and often debilitating. They test us because they often (if not always) breach our expectations, wishes, dreams, and hopes. I also know at times I have treated others in some of these ways. That is something I have felt deep sorrow for and tried deeply to change. I have been grateful for the goodness of God in helping me to transcend such behavior.

However, I have also been educated by these experiences, mostly in terms of recognizing that these are not ideal ways of living. I have been instructed in patience, perspective, forgiveness, mercy, understanding, courage, etc. because of deep and persistent challenge. It may appear ironic but I am thankful for thorns, troubles, and tears. Each difficulty has polished and refined me to be something more than I was. I thank God for the confidence He placed in me by stretching my soul. The internal difficulties are common to man. By confronting these we may learn how to become a wiser and stronger version of ourselves. In terms of the relationship challenges, it is not that God endorses poor treatment of others. It is that we so often learn what not to do by seeing the negative impacts upon ourselves or others of poor ways of relating. We learn from the bitter how to prefer the sweet.

Of course, I have also had many thousands of wonderful, beautiful, instructive moments that have taught me great things. I have endured through the rains, the floods, and the tempests and learned great lessons and felt great joys. I have learned important lessons as an individual, son, brother, friend, priesthood holder, missionary, student, husband, father, employee, priesthood leader, hospital patient, dreamer, exerciser, and writer. I have discerned good and evil, right and wrong, and desirable and undesirable from observing how different types of choices yield to different kinds of outcomes. I have learned that the experience we call mortality will, if we have ears to hear and eyes to see, prune our souls so that we clearly detect the kind of people we really want to be and the kind of relationships that make for more of a heaven rather than a hell on earth.

I now see clearly that the symbols of my spiritual journey were everywhere—although I did not perceive that at the time. Living in allegorical groves, springs, woods, temple mounts, olive mounts, and places of glory—although accompanied by difficulties of every kind, type, and degree—has also been rich with opportunities for growth and development that have stretched me, refined me, polished me, educated me, and pushed me to become more than what I was before. I know by direct personal experience that environmental factors—although they most certainly impinged on me and were something of a stumbling block—are not so strong that they can permanently and decisively prevent us from becoming a good seed in God's Garden. As flawed as I have been, I know that God's cultivating hand can reach into the poorest spots of ground, for I have known that firsthand.

I think of the times in my life when someone gave me a genuine compliment, or a handwritten note of appreciation for something I had done, or had spent some time listening to me or asking me about my interests. These were very important and poignant (if sometimes rare!) moments for me. I know this was personal cultivation by the Lord, working through mortal people. Without these lifelines, life would have been almost impossibly difficult for me many times. I have come to know deeply that each of us is really like a seed—we need affection, warmth, concern, protection, and nourishing, especially in our formative stages, if we are to survive and thrive.

We are well served by understanding ourselves and by being able to teach others about the crucial role that opposition plays in the divine plan. We have been taught why opposition exists and how it can be faced, learned from, and transcended in spiritually productive ways. Every great personal quality that we can acquire will require effort to obtain. Resistance to greatness comes both from within, and from the world around us. Consider the following vital questions in your own life:

- What are some of the difficulties I have encountered in this life and how can these teach me great lessons?
- How have setbacks helped me?
- What is my deep purpose on earth?
- How can I become the person God wants me to be?

It is helpful to locate such questions—and therefore the answers—within this overall structure of each of us being like a good seed in God's Garden. We can sense that our growth is developmental. God only teaches us "line upon line, precept upon precept, here a little and there a little" (2 Nephi 28:30). God gives us knowledge and understanding by ordered degrees, by proper sequencing. He gives small lessons for us to learn incrementally. These truths build upon one another gradually and steadily. Each pruning experience can teach us something valuable that we need for our growth and progress. As we listen to God—in all the ways He can teach us in word and deed—we obtain divine wisdom and are ready and prepared to receive further instruction from Him. That is both a true and hopeful message.

Counsel with the Lord

The Lord sees us as His apprentices. He is training us in gospel governance. The restored gospel gives us wise cautionary counsel in terms of how we as servants deal with being governed by other servants and how we are to cope with challenges we face when opposed in our efforts. We are wise to override our limited wisdom with the Lord's divine system of priesthood government. His wise and loving instruction is relationally perfect—He could not be a better God than He is. He could not be more loving, wise, or instructive than He already is, for He is perfect. In our efforts to influence the Lord and the Church there is a crucial distinction between counselling with the Lord (which promotes agency) and counselling the Lord (which hampers agency). This depends upon the spirit and motive in the person who either seeks to counsel the Lord or who seeks to take counsel from His hand (Jacob 4:10).

Counselling with the Lord is a righteous form of action that takes place when we follow the injunction to involve the Lord in our daily lives. We do not tell Him what to do but rather use our own judgment and seek His guidance, direction, and correction. For example:

- Nephi had *genuine desires* to learn but did not make impatient or inappropriate demands of the Spirit of God (1 Nephi 11:1–11).
- Nephi asked where he should go to find ore rather than telling the Lord to provide tools (1 Nephi 17:8–10).
- Enos *pleaded* for merciful forgiveness of his sins rather than demanded such (Enos 1:1–8).
- The brother of Jared *humbly petitioned* the Lord to touch the stones rather than telling Him to sort out the lack of light problem (Ether 3:1–4).

- The sons of Mosiah *requested permission* to serve as missionaries to the Lamanites (Mosiah 28:7–8)

All these sincerely sought divine help and were grateful for it when it came in whatever form it came. This process is one of refinement and growing up into an experiential understanding of the ways of God.

As we seek to gain knowledge from the Lord, we are given sacred information to test our personal spiritual integrity. We are taught that sharing such with others in the wrong context can be very harmful to them (Alma 12:9–11). The Lord decides with whom to share His treasures, when to do so, and how to do so (Moroni 10:3–5). As we prepare ourselves, we are qualified to learn from His master teachings. We are even invited to share our own proposals with the Lord. God discusses matters with His humble servants to teach and train them (Jacob 5). This is how we become spiritually mature. We learn to think and feel like the Lord in our own minds and hearts.

However, it is wise to avoid directing the Lord or His chosen servants. Otherwise, we are counselling the Lord (like Lucifer did in Moses 4). The Lord invites us to give suggestions to Him on His work at times. However, He does not appreciate being instructed or commanded by men, even well-meaning ones, on doing His work (Jacob 5). While we should make righteous petitions to the Lord and genuine suggestions to improve things in the kingdom are to be encouraged, we should avoid allowing our own agendas to get in the way of the Lord's will. What is best for the kingdom is more important than getting our own way.

It takes real spirituality to defend the faith against attack, to love those who do not love us in return, to believe in the best version of ourselves and others, to have patience amidst potential chaos, and to show kindness amidst situations of tension and anger. We can stem the tide of spiritual confusion by desiring to be loyal to the Lord's church and to principles of integrity and goodness. Hence, there is a vivid contrast between the strait and narrow path of discipleship on the one hand (1 Nephi 8:20) and the strange winding roads and forbidden paths of worldliness on the other (1 Nephi 8:28, 32).

11

Nurtured through Connection

Let us consider places of Holy connection, especially the Church and temple of God, in time and eternity. These are intended to be gardens of developmental holiness where we progress from innocence, ignorance, sickness, and weakness to knowledge, understanding, health, and strength.

Holy Places

My holy places are where I have had sacred experiences that have moved me deeply:

- The baptismal font, where I was washed in the waters of new life.
- The patriarch's home, where I was blessed to see myself in a new and improved way.
- The dedicated church buildings, where I felt holiness and received life-changing instruction.
- The homes, where I have spent many happy hours drawing closer to God and my family.
- The London/Frankfurt/Preston/Salt Lake City temples, where I have seen the things of God with new eyes.

- St. Anne's Park and Phoenix Park, Dublin, where I have walked, pondered, and connected with God literally hundreds of times.
- In the mission field, where I walked on hallowed ground and changed for the better in monumental ways.
- Lough Ennell/Lough Owel and Lough Derraveragh in Ireland, where I have found peace in numerous times of challenge.

I am humbly grateful for these gardens of contemplation, where God has touched my life.

Lough Ennell Forest in the Midlands of Ireland—A place of quiet tranquility for me.

I am aware that some people think that spirituality is useful while religion is not. It is increasingly common for people to view organized religion as unnecessary at best and dangerous at worst. It is helpful to look at the doctrine of why the Lord has a church and has commanded us to be a part of it. I see no essential incompatibility between devout spirituality and true religion. Religion gives structure and order to the work of God. Spirituality gives life, vitality, meaning, and purpose. To say that spirituality and religion can coexist is comparable to saying a spirit can live within a body. While a person can be spiritual without being religious, just as a spirit can live without being embodied, it is true that religion without spirituality is lifeless, just as a body is dead without the spirit that animates it. Ultimately, of course, being spiritual without being religious will not bring the fulness of blessings—just as spirit and body separated cannot receive a fulness of joy (Doctrine and Covenants 93).

Why does God have an organization? The Church is like a hospital. Let's suppose that you have a serious injury to your head, and you travel to the emergency department to seek treatment. This hospital, however, is very different. It is not well organized. There are no signs over the doors, so you do not know where the entrance is. There are no signs inside giving directions to various areas of expertise. There are no head injury specialists/doctors there at the time you arrive. There are no timetables or set surgery hours so no one has any idea if a doctor who might be able to help you would arrive. The cleaners do not always turn up so there are lots of dirty areas in the hospital. Some of the workers tell you that they are concerned for health but that they do not believe in organization.

How confident would you feel that you would be able to get the treatment you needed to save your life? I think the answer is obvious. Of course, this scenario I have outlined seems ridiculous on the face on it. Whatever inefficiencies there are in real hospitals, it is highly unlikely that there are many hospitals in the world that would be comfortable operating in these kinds of conditions. Patients would not stand for it! It is evident from the above exaggerated example that organization is very important to our lives. We simply could not live for very long without a high degree of order and structure. We often take this for granted, especially in our multifaceted and highly complex world. However, life would truly be uncertain and deeply frustrating without clear expectations around rules and regulations. They give us security, calm, and assurance in circumstances that would otherwise involve constant worry.

In like manner, the Church organization and structure gives clear direction, guidance, and clarity to the spiritual life that would otherwise be chaotic. We have a sense of knowing who our leaders are, where to look for help, what is required of us, and how to conduct ourselves. We are reminded of commandments, covenants, and ordinances. We learn about duty, service, responsibility, followership, leadership, administration, public speaking, teaching, and so many other things. We receive blessings, make friends, learn how to counsel with others, and are given numerous opportunities to contribute of our time, talents, and testimonies.

The Church of Jesus Christ of Latter-day Saints

The Lord has organized His Church with us in mind. It is His Church and He is the ultimate Saint! He wants us to belong to Him. He wants us to know with certainty where He can be found, where His word will be spoken, where His laws will be sustained, where His love will be felt, where His scriptures will be safeguarded, and where His power will be manifest in full measure. The Church of Jesus Christ of Latter-day Saints has been a garden of great belonging and growth for me. I will now share some of the experiences I have had that have blessed my life greatly. I credit a phenomenal part of my growth and development to the Church and the opportunities it has blessed me with. I know and feel so many wonderful things because of the true Church of the Savior.

Called to Hear

I attended the dedication of my chapel in 1980 by President Ezra Taft Benson, president of the Quorum of the Twelve Apostles at that time. After the benediction, the noise level in the chapel was noticeable and excessive. President Benson stood again at the pulpit and said that the building had been dedicated to the Lord and that we should show respect and move out to the foyer to visit. I was struck to the core even though I was not talking. My mum and I went immediately out to the foyer. I have never forgotten that experience. Even now, I prefer to be silent or whisper in the chapel.

Presented with a Newness of Life

I was baptized when I turned eight years of age, in the font of the Finglas Chapel in Dublin, Ireland. The building was directly across from the Glasnevin Cemetery—the baptismal font really was on a level with the grave! I was afraid of water at this time (truthfully that fear has never entirely left me) and I felt extremely nervous about the water. Nonetheless, I was excited as I felt strongly that it was the right thing to do. My branch president baptized me. He was calm and confident—the comfort we can give others is very real! I was very thankful for his gentle reassurance. I felt wet when I came up out of the water, but I did not feel particularly different from before. However, when I was confirmed as a member of the Church and received the gift of the Holy Ghost, I felt a wonderful feeling inside of me. I felt like I was having a bath on the inside. It was refreshing, renewing, and cleansing. I sensed a beautiful warmth inside me.

As a child I often felt very ordinary and not very special. However, this rare experience was a gift from God. I knew that I must be of great value to Him if He would allow me to feel this way. The special feeling did wear off soon, but when I reflect in remembrance on the event it always reminds me of what the baptism of the spirit feels like and how wonderful and precious it is. I have often contemplated this and it gives me a self-worth boost, especially in challenging times. I am grateful that I was washed in those clean waters on that day and came forth in a newness of life. I am so glad that I experienced the baptism of fire that gave me a feeling of being clean on the inside. That was forty-one years ago. I still feel the excitement of this spiritual adventure. There have been many highs and lows in that time. I have struggled many times to keep the eternal laws of love at the forefront of my life. Nevertheless, I am deeply grateful that I have endeavored to abide in that divine covenant and have felt the surety of the promise of having the Holy Ghost poured out upon me. My covenants mean far more to me today than they did then. I rejoice in being a covenant follower of Jesus Christ.

Invited to Higher Ground

I have been richly blessed and uplifted by being instructed by true prophets and apostles. I now share some of these experiences which have given me a much greater vision of how the Lord nurtures us, for His representatives have nourished me in inspired ways.

When I was 13 years of age, I attended a meeting with President Thomas S. Monson of the First Presidency in Belfast. This was a remarkable experience. I was impressed with his joyful happiness and obvious love. It was a shock to me that such a man lived in this world where I saw much that was the opposite of what this man so clearly radiated. He was very naturally spiritual.

When I was 17 years old, I attended a meeting with Elder Boyd K. Packer. He said, "Do not come to America. We do not need you there. Stay in Ireland." That caught me off guard. He was so forthright and bold. The sense of spiritual presence, priesthood power, and personal purity emanating from that man was very distinctive and very apparent to me. I could feel it, just as I can feel the heat from a warm fire. Also, that year I attended a meeting with Elder Jeffrey R. Holland and Elder Kenneth Johnson of the Seventy. I was due to work that night but when I heard of the meeting, I strongly desired to go so I swapped shifts with someone else and went. I was so glad that I did go because I found myself being hugely impressed with these brethren. Elder Johnson was confident, charismatic, and happy. He called me up to the front and asked me questions on my priesthood progress. I was nervous and needed some prompting to answer his questions. He thanked me for all my efforts. I was blessed by that experience. Elder Holland impressed me with his knowledge, power to motivate, and great teaching style. These were men I wanted to emulate.

I attended a devotional presided over by President Gordon B. Hinckley in Ireland when I was 23 years old. I was extremely impressed by him. He had a clean countenance that radiated light. He had authority, conviction, and love. He was funny, confident, and certain. For his age—85 at the time—he was full of spiritual strength. It was one of the most powerful testimonies of the Savior I have ever heard and felt. There was no doubt in my mind he was a prophet. He taught us how to stand with pure confidence in the divine presence.

When I was 28, I attended a fireside with Elder Richard G. Scott. He preached with great spiritual power about the Atonement of Christ. He was captivating. I was riveted on his message for the entire time he spoke. The force of his testimony was undeniable. He had what I would call intense spiritual charisma. I remember being sad for three days after he left because of the feeling of returning to the normal world. I missed his influence of light.

Each of these pivotal experiences has been important and memorable for me. The momentous aspects of these visits involved the following elements:

- Beauty, goodness, love, light
- Courage, conviction, devotion
- Example, enthusiasm, energy, power, purity, persuasion, motivation
- Righteousness, sanctification, strength, spirituality
- Testimony and warning

I could use more descriptors but suffice it to say that these brethren—and others over the years—were living witnesses to me of true discipleship. Their impact on me was to encourage me to get my life in spiritual and temporal order, to become my best self, to serve others consistently and to endure to the end in righteousness. It would be exceedingly difficult to portray the definite and lasting influence of all these brethren on me, my choices, and my life. I am deeply grateful that we are prophet led. Again, this has evidenced abundantly to me clearly the love of the Father in allowing me to feel of His divine influence through these special witnesses. Indeed, "by their fruits ye shall know them" (Matthew 7:20). These men have inspired me to draw closer to the living Father of us all—what greater witness could any of us have than this to indicate that these men are truly heaven sent? I have remembered their words and more especially the spiritual feelings associated with being in their presence. That has rescued me during tough times and protected me from making potentially shortsighted decisions. Seeing how these brethren treated me helped me to see better how Christ views me.

Commissioned to Bless

I had a head cold the day I was to receive the Aaronic Priesthood on my 12th birthday. I thought that by getting the priesthood I would be immediately healed. I made the effort to go even though I did not feel that good. I was not healed physically on receiving the priesthood. I nevertheless felt that I had done the right thing. I had precious opportunities to pass, prepare, and bless the sacrament during those early years and was blessed to be able to serve others. This formed a foundation for priesthood service in my life. Christ sees young men as having a significant role to play in their youth!

I received the Holy Melchizedek Priesthood in 1991. I was ordained by my older brother Michael. I know that he desired to be in tune for the event and he made some special preparations to be ready for the ordination that surprised me. He walked from our home to the church building—11.5 kilometers (over 7 miles). That was a significant sacrifice at the time. He was joined in the circle by the district presidency and branch presidency (this was prior to the formation of our stake). I do not recall the words spoken but I do remember distinctly the feeling. The ordination was prophetic in nature. It was authoritative, assured, and comforting. I appreciated the spiritual power of the experience and the strength of my brethren. This gave me confidence to go forward with my commission and a clear sense of heavenly endowment. I have often thought that the Lord graciously blessed us with an experience beyond what we deserved. His greatness compensated for our immaturity. Our sincerity was rewarded by His manifest goodness. How generous are our Father in Heaven and His Son!

Privileged to Leave My Comfort Zone

Three weeks after turning 18 years of age, I entered the Missionary Training Center (MTC) on the grounds of the London England Temple. I was assigned as a district leader to assist six other missionaries. I was nervous but grateful to have the opportunity of conducting meetings. I learned that people look up to those in leadership and expect them to lead. It was nice to be able to feel like I was making a difference. What a Church this is to place such confidence and trust in young and inexperienced people. It greatly facilitates their growth! During this time, Elder M. Russell Ballard came to the MTC. This was a brief, but memorable meeting. We got to shake his hand. He talked about how the boundaries were coming down in Europe and how the work of the Lord would go forward and that we would be a part of that. I was impressed by his certitude and the sense of destiny that awaited us in this holy work. This was a tender mercy of the Lord to me.

After the MTC, I travelled to Birmingham to serve. It was life changing. It was an emotional roller coaster. I was up and down. I was nervous and childish. I was also confident and mature in some ways. I liked getting to know the sisters and the children in the wards and branches. I was genuinely impressed with the confidence of my mission president, President Chappy Winstanley. He was bold, forthright, and knowledgeable. He was a natural leader. He played basketball with us and told jokes but also taught with great spiritual power from the scriptures. He was consecrated, diligent, and balanced. I was in awe of him. He hugged us and prayed on one knee in interviews. He was vastly different from most leaders I had known up to then and subsequently. I wished I could have loved people more and given them more of a chance to change. I was still wrestling with many limitations at that stage in my life. Some of my companions were very loving individuals and expressed their love to me. They prayed for me. That touched me significantly!

During my mission I was impressed by many of the local leaders and members I met and especially by the General Authorities such as Elder Holland and Elder Johnson when they visited the mission. Elder Johnson (who was an Englishman) had a magnetic charisma about him and radiated light, peace, joy, warmth, and love. I wanted to develop those attributes myself. Elder Holland very much inspired me to raise my vision of what was possible for me. He motivated me to be a better man. His gift for teaching was phenomenal and he had vast knowledge, understanding, and compassion. His wife radiated love and happiness. I wanted a wife like her someday! I wanted what they had, as they were well on their way to celestial life. They seemed to be living as heavenly persons on earth. That was a motivation to me!

The day I turned 19 years of age I began to train a new missionary. He was older than me. I had more confidence than competence. I was not sure what to do. Nevertheless, the experience did help me to grow and mature. One lesson I learned is that of spiritual focus. My companion and I had been distracted by seeking spiritual experiences for ourselves when we should have been focused on helping others to come to Christ. During my personal study one morning, the Lord revealed to me as I read the scriptures that we were out of line. We were both directly and gently reproved for seeking our own will. I also learned that the Lord honors His authority system—as the presiding elder I got the revelation. I shared it with my companion, and we changed the focus of our attention away from ourselves to others. This is a lesson I have never forgotten. Christ wants us to focus primarily on helping others!

The gospel is truly the perfect message of inclusion as God seeks to bless all His children with all they are willing to receive. The entire world needs repentance desperately. I love a person when I offer friendship but I love them most deeply when I offer them the restored truth as that will bless them far more than even a precious friendship could. The latter-day ark of the covenant—the true church—is the best and safest place to be for anyone and everyone. How grateful I am that I was permitted to be a missionary for the Lord!

Set Apart to Teach

I am grateful for the many times I have been able to teach the gospel to others. I love teaching gospel doctrines. As I have prepared to teach, I have learned much. I believe I have learned more than those attending my classes. As I have stood to teach, I have shared principles I did not know before I stood to speak. This is because the Holy Ghost has given me insights at the very moment it was needed. I have consistently found that in my desire to inspire and encourage others, I have been edified myself. I have very much enjoyed teaching key and powerful doctrines such as the importance of divine revelation and the Divine Sonship of our Savior. I felt the Spirit many times. I like to be able to create an atmosphere of loving learning.

An Opportunity to Record and Protect

I have served twice as a clerk and twice as a stake auditor in the kingdom. When I was called to these duties, I really had no idea what I was supposed to be doing. However, with effort and time I learned key things:

Leaders are genuinely interested in the people. Leaders do magnificent work behind the scenes that most people never see. They do it out of love. As I have watched leaders closely, I have observed that they mirror examples that are worthy of emulation. We do not appreciate these fully at the time. One of my bishops taught me of the importance of having a plan in life, making good choices, being healthy, laughing, working hard, keeping positive, and being loyal to God and the Church no matter what. It was only later through my own experience that I sensed the truth of this wisdom.

So much of the Church is important administration. It is great when it is performed well. Otherwise, it causes challenges. However, administration should never ever take preference over ministration.

The Lord loves law and order. He is a God who places order upon chaos. Our keeping of correct and timely records is a sign to the Lord that we are paying close attention to His intervention in the lives of His children. These "written memories" serve many core purposes of reminding us of the hand of God in our lives and will inspire others who come after us to remember the great goodness of God. This explains why keeping records is so difficult for so many people—because it requires great effort and yields great dividends.

The adversary sees the potential of leaders and he hates them, which is why he works extra hard to derail them from the covenant path. He knows that if they fall, then many people may be weakened by their example. We need to cultivate the close companionship of the Spirit to keep us safe and happy.

I was grateful for the opportunity to gain experience in these callings. I tried to be diligent and devoted. I have not forgotten either the overt lessons or the implied ones.

Challenged to Administer

I served as a ward mission leader twice. It helped me to develop my leadership skills. I learned about the bounds of authority, how different people perceive the role of the Church differently, and how crucial it is to maintain resolve even when things are moving very slowly. Being a leader is not easy, but it helped me to become new. The process of refinement is almost imperceptible, but it is real.

Chosen to Minister

When I was called as an Elders Quorum president the first time, I was nervous but grateful. I was sometimes unsure of what to do and made mistakes, but I tried hard. I endeavored to help my brethren grow and bore testimony to inspire them. The Lord can only use what He has. We are weak vessels in the hands of the expert potter. He has tremendous confidence in us. He knows that while we can become polished giants, we nevertheless often fumble toward greatness.

When I served as first counselor to a bishop, I received more visible responsibility. I was quite nervous about sitting up on the stand and being in front of all those people. It was exceedingly difficult at first. I have shied away from people so often in the past that it became second nature to me to do so. I had confidence in the gospel but not in myself so many times. I have learned that this was a call to a higher place and to become a better priesthood man. I was stretched by the difficulties I encountered in this call. A valuable experience containing joy and pain. Inviting others to come to Christ sometimes involves serious personal heartache. It helped me to become more tolerant of the weaknesses of others. I became more loving and compassionate. I sensed the dislike of some for calls to loyalty, obedience, and duty. This was tiring and I had much responsibility—sometimes I felt like the actual bishop due to being so busy! However, I was able to do some good and grow in my experience. I matured in this role. It was good for me and a very necessary preparation for what I would yet experience.

My next leadership role was serving as first counselor on a branch young men's presidency. I am frank to say that this was extremely difficult as we were dealing with seven emotional teenagers, especially because the unique circumstances meant I was heavily relied on. Those youth tested my character hugely. I failed at times and succeeded at others. I was glad that I endured that trial. I was desperate to help those young men, irrespective of resistance. That calling caused me deep worry and stress. Sometimes when our love is deep, so is our frustration. The Savior knows how we feel!

I then served for a second time as Elders Quorum president. I felt the desire and authority to teach, testify, and promise. I felt strong in my conviction. Inspiring people to act and change their behaviors seemed to me at that time to be an exceedingly difficult challenge. It was so easy to feel that I was making no difference, but I kept going. Home teaching did improve during that time, and I was grateful for that.

I soon discovered that this was only a prelude to what I would yet encounter in more demanding callings. For example, my decade of service as president of a branch would help me to see others through the eyes of Christ more clearly. It was an education in understanding that has become significantly embedded within my soul. I loved that opportunity to work with people personally. It was demanding and beneficial. I came to know with greater comprehension that Christ ministers personally to the one!

It has been my deep privilege to struggle upwards in the quest to be true to the sacred leadership charges that God has given me. These experiences of ministering to others for days, weeks, months, and years softened my heart, bolstered my love, challenged my limitations, tested my patience, and helped me to face frustration with determination. I do not believe that I would be the man I am today (incomplete as I am) without these growing experiences which have come to me directly through membership in the true Church of God.

This church is the greatest organization on the face of this planet in what it can do for every man, woman, and child that takes the opportunities afforded to them through it.

Admonished to Account

I had a personal priesthood interview with Elder David Bednar many years ago when our stake presidency was being re-organized. I was one of the brethren invited to attend and give my recommendations for a potential new stake president. I was impressed by how quick and direct Elder Bednar was at getting revelation in terms of the questions he asked me. I felt like I was accounting for my behavior and stewardship to an ordained servant of the Lord—it really was a mini judgment. I was incredibly grateful for this as it gave me a sense of the importance of being prepared for my final judgment when that time comes. I also noticed his sense of clarity, focus, determination, and energy. The gospel makes us good on the outside and inside. Our resolve to serve is strengthened by truly knowing we are responsible and accountable to God for our actions. Christ delegates so much to us and we are empowered by acting in the roles given to us!

Asked to Rejoice and to Comfort

In my Church experience I have spoken at both weddings and funerals. For the weddings, I really enjoyed speaking about the full romantic promise of love that blossoms through the restored gospel. God knows about true love. I celebrate the rich magic of spiritually grounded love. For the funerals, I felt the deep spiritual guidance in knowing what to say and how to say it, in a way that honors both the person who has passed and the great God who has a perfect plan for that person. The feelings of comfort from such opportunities have assured me that God engages in the days of our lives on which we rejoice and/or mourn. He is near to us as He wishes to share in our rejoicings and console us in our afflictions.

Obedient Works and Merciful Grace

The revealed word teaches of the need for both obedient works and merciful grace. We can become conscientious through our covenants. Our baptismal covenant and the sacrament are both clearly associated with water and its symbolical value in drawing us heavenward. There is a clear distinction between the living waters of spiritual life (1 Nephi 11:25) and the filthy waters of spiritual death (1 Nephi 8:32; 12:16). I cherish the covenants made available through the Church. These covenants warmly invite us to rise in righteousness.

The deep experiential knowledge of Jesus Christ comes only through making and keeping sacred covenants (Mosiah 4). Through covenants we promise to show generous comfort to the sad, compassionate love to the lonely, and healing devotion to the distressed. We certify our desire to be willing witnesses of God in all situations and so will have the Holy Spirit with us in this life and eternal life through Christ in the eternities (Mosiah 18:9, 13). We follow on earth the divine pattern of physical ordinances laden with spiritual significance. Through literal baptism in water, we are symbolically partaking of an abundance of spiritual life in Christ. As we are immersed in the literal companionship of the Holy Ghost, we can feel the wonderful reward of calming peace, hopeful certainty, and joyful love that the gospel offers us daily. Eternal life is a continuation and elevated expansion of the righteous life we strive to develop on this earth. We are cleansed, healed, and made holy through sacred spiritual ordinances suffused with divine power.

Only through the Atonement of Christ is salvation of any type, kind, or degree possible. With our willing acceptance of the Atonement through our works (especially gospel ordinances), we can become qualified for the celestial kingdom of God. While we deserve justice when we are obedient, we only deserve mercy when we repent because of our great Messiah. We use our desires and divine endowments together in harmony to do the will of God. We are saved through a covenant agreement with God, through which we receive His purifying and enabling help. We can prevent the threat of secular relativism from ensnaring our soul by drawing on Christ's priesthood power. There is a contrast between inspired people who are prayerful, desirous, beckoning, concerned, exhorting, preaching, and prophesying (1 Nephi 8:8, 12, 15, 36–38) and worldly minded detractors who adopt the role of mockers, pointers, scoffers, and scorners toward those pursuing the covenant way (1 Nephi 8:27–28, 33).

Gathered into the Garners

Ammon and his fellow missionaries brought the Lamanites into the fold and garners of God (Alma 26:4–7). What does it mean that thousands were brought into God's fold? Well, the shepherd welcomed them into the divine fold—the place that sheep find pasture and rest. What about being gathered into the garners? The garners are the place of security from the elements and predators. To be not wasted is to be used for the purpose for which the sheaves were intended. They add to the storehouse of the Lord. They are not lost, stolen, destroyed, or spoiled. They are preserved for the day of need. These garners are in essence, holy temples. Temples are sacred places where we can experience treasures of revelation, the warmth of grand insights, and special sanctity. They are houses of the Lord. They are schools of Holiness. They are holy homes where we are taught new things, instructed in divine patterns, edified by sublime ideas, loved without dilution, protected from falsity, included in lofty designs, and valued highly. We literally walk, stand, and kneel on holy ground.

I love that the temple is described as "a house of prayer, a house of fasting, a house of faith, a house of learning, a house of glory, a house of order, a house of God" (Doctrine & Covenants 109:8). I believe that we should perform each of these functions in the temple! We pray, fast, evidence faith, learn, partake of glory, follow divine order, and come to know God more deeply:

We pray in righteous unity in that Holy House so that others might be blessed. Likewise, they pray for us.
We sometimes fast from food and water in that sanctuary. This can make us more spiritually receptive and pliable.
We show faith because we receive knowledge and understanding we did not possess before we walked into that precinct of light.
We learn doctrines, principles, and patterns that are both new and precious.
We partake of glory by being surrounded by light and receiving revelatory truths that educate and inspire us.
We follow divine order as the temple is the ultimate place of law and order where we patiently follow in reverent ways that which is clear and structured.
We come to sense God in a higher, more meaningfully rich way.

Consider the words of Hymn No. 5, "High on the Mountain Top." The temple intentionally invites those in the world to come to the Holy Mountain. The temples of our God are purposefully situated upon a high place so that all may see the beckoning light of that holy place. The restored ordinances and covenants can propel us to a higher vision of what God is trying to do within us:

He remembers His promises to the ancient people of the Lord.
He gathers all who will have Him as their God into His fold of safety and protection.
He teaches us of His ways in His house of light.

Those living in mortality and in the world of spirits are to be instructed in the very same truths and powers as presented in the Holy Temple (Doctrine & Covenants 138). All are to be instructed in the same doctrines, partake of the same ordinances, make the same covenants, and receive the same blessings.

As I came forth in a newness of life in baptism when I was a young boy, so those in the spirit world are "born again" when they receive these same ordinances by proxy in the House of the Lord. In truth, we are instructed that the earth will be smitten with a curse in the last days unless the welding link of baptism for the dead binds the fathers and the children—"that a whole and complete and perfect union, and welding together of dispensations, and keys, and powers, and glories should take place" (Doctrine & Covenants 128:18). Hence, perfection within the gospel covenant requires the entire binding of all saints throughout all time together. Revelations previously withheld from the worldly have been, and will be, freely given to humble saints of this day. The comprehension of this glorious doctrine of one Zion for all the righteous people of the earth will send our hearts soaring and give our minds encouragement to ensure this great work to be done by latter-day Israel is done. May we gather to that sacred space to obtain and to share all the principles of eternal life offered there so lovingly and freely.

Those who worship faithfully in latter-day temples have the following promises:

> They will grow up spiritually in the Lord, receive a fulness of the Spirit, be organized according to the laws of God, and be ready to obtain all needed blessings (Doctrine & Covenants 109:15).
>
> They will be gathered with other saints of Zion, which will protect them from the spiritual storm and global wrath associated with the last days (Doctrine & Covenants 115:6).
>
> They will experience refuge, safety, and defense by divine decree due to the ordinances of the House of God (Doctrine & Covenants 124:36).
>
> They will be crowned with eternal exaltation in the celestial kingdom of God (Doctrine & Covenants 132).

I have known many people over the years that worry about family arrangements in the eternities. I believe that family members in the eternities will be able to see each other even though they may be in different kingdoms. I believe the ministering that happens between the celestial and terrestrial is a family ministering (Doctrine & Covenants

76 and 88). Service on ethical and moral issues gives common ground for such ongoing family relations. This is different from the priesthood seal that pertains to exaltation. It is the connection of loving concern. I see a distinction here. The sealing of families is for the purpose of eternal salvation in the highest heaven. Those who, for whatever reason, seek a non-exalted glory for themselves will, in my opinion, be visited by those who live in celestial glory, who will be permitted to visit their loved ones to share their love. This is comparable to those on the earth who are temple goers being able to visit those who are not. The family members cannot go inside the temple, but the temple goers can visit their family members outside the temple. The bonds of love are not always exactly synonymous with the bonds of priesthood power, because we can have love without priesthood but we cannot have priesthood without love. That may give us great consolation to not worry about those things outside of our control.

The Church of the Firstborn

There are core doctrines associated with those who belong to the Church of the Firstborn:

They are individuals from every nation of the world that have chosen to be gathered to God's restored Church and Kingdom by the "good news" ministration of holy high priests who were ordained by angels with power (Doctrine & Covenants 77:11).

They become part of a covenant body which has the privilege of communicating with heavenly beings, such as angels, the Savior, and the Father (Doctrine & Covenants 107:18–19).

They are those who overcome the world by faith, live true to the faith, become "just" persons through Christ, and are sealed by promise to eternal life (Doctrine & Covenants 76:53–54).

They are taken up in a cloud at the last day with the saints of God, to be with God and to receive celestial glory (Doctrine & Covenants 78:21; 76:102).

Their glory is the highest and holiest glory that can be obtained (Doctrine & Covenants 88:5).

They are spiritually begotten through Christ and hence become partakers of the glory rightly belonging to the Firstborn (Doctrine & Covenants 93:21–22).

Indeed "they who dwell in his presence are the church of the Firstborn" (Doctrine & Covenants 76:94–95).

The Church of the Firstborn is therefore distinguished from The Church of Jesus Christ of Latter-day Saints. It is the Church of the Lamb of God, who was the Firstborn spirit child of God in the eternal realms. This is the heavenly Church of the Lamb. It consists of those who are covenant disciples of the Lamb, who have taken upon themselves His name and retained His name in their hearts (see Mosiah 5). These are faithful, valiant, covenant makers and keepers. They truly belong to His Church, not just technically as members on the records. They have moved beyond apathy, indifference, and casualness. They have overcome laziness, fear, and indifference. They have put on courage, purity, and consecration. They have a well-developed quality of love. They are transformed to the point that they belong to their Lord in eternity. Hence, to be part of the Church of the Firstborn we must be born again to the full extent. They are part of His celestial covenant kingdom in the worlds that are everlasting. It is the eternal fold of God, from which we will never be removed, as we have drawn close to the Shepherd. This is thus the fold of the Firstborn, the ultimate home of belonging. It is the place of great and full joy. It is the home in which we will always find peace, rest, happiness, and worlds without end.

12

An Enemy Hath Done This

DURING HIS TEACHING MINISTRY, THE MESSIAH SPOKE TO A GREAT multitude in a parable about a sower of seeds. The seeds fell among different types of ground (Matthew 13:1–9). It is evident that the sower is God, or His servant. The seed is the good word of God. The soil is where the seed is placed to grow. It is the ground (meaning the heart) of the person receiving the message. A soft heart is receptive to God's word. I understand the Lord's interpretation of this parable as follows:

Wayside hearers—They hear but do not understand the word of God, then the enemy catches the seed that was essentially cast out by the hearers (Matthew 13:18–19). It is apparent that falling by the wayside is comparable to situations where the word of God does not reach the core of the person. The word is not central to the person's life.

Stony-place hearers—They hear it and accept it happily, but the word does not go deeply within them, so they endure for a time, but when opposed for the word's sake, they are in due course upset (Matthew 13:20–21). Falling upon stony places is comparable to situations where the word of God is resisted by the receiver. There is little or no soil of receptivity and hence no depth of delivery. When opposition in the form of heat (pressure, challenge) comes, the growing seed simply withers. In other words, it dries up and dies.

Thorny-way hearers—They hear the word but their concern with worldly things, including the false promise of material treasures, hampers and overcomes the word so that no fruit can be produced (Matthew 13:22). Falling upon thorns is comparable to situations where the word of God is met with hostility. The hostility overpowers the seed. Anger against the word of God literally overcomes any chance of the word growing within a person.

Good-ground hearers—They hear the word and comprehend it, they then bear fruit, some to the extent of a hundred times as much, some sixty times as great, and some thirty times as productive. Thus, all of these are productive with the word of God, some even yielding the most beneficial bounty that is possible (Matthew 13:23). The JST clarifies that because of their receptivity these persons both understand the word and endure tribulation they encounter (JST Matthew 13:23). Falling upon good ground is comparable to situations where the word of God is met with a listening ear, an open mind, and a soft heart. This ground always brings forth fruit. The amount of fruit brought forth depends on the willingness of the person.

The enemy of God works consistently to entice people to ignore the word, rebel against it, resist it, attack it, or, having accepted it, to then make it an incidental part of life or to stay with it for a period and then abandon it. Our enemy does not want the seed to bear fruit and will use whatever means he can to prevent its growth. A fruitful seed is a threat to his kingdom. Hence, the need for each of us to hear and hearken with our spiritual ears so that we are aware of the ploys to destroy the power of the word of God within us. A seed that does not bear fruit is a tragedy. Its whole purpose is to grow and multiply. The absence of good fruit represents the lack of fulfilment of our true purpose.

After the Lord gave the parable, His disciples were confused as to why He used parables if His message was to be understood. It is apparent from the explanation of the Lord that He used parables to conceal mysteries from those who were spiritually blind and deaf (Matthew 13:10–17). Alternatively, He explained the meaning of the parables to His disciples in clear language because He wanted them to know and understand the mysteries of the kingdom. The reasoning is quite simple. Although the ones hearing the parable, but not the interpretation, could physically see, hear, and understand, their spiritual faculties were closed off to obtaining truth. They did not comprehend the meaning because of their hard hearts, slowness to hearken, and unwillingness to see what the Lord was trying to teach. This was a problem of desire which impacted their ability. The apostles were different. They wanted to follow the Lord and sought to comply with His teachings. Their motive was good and so the Lord detected that their hearts, minds, eyes, and ears were open to truth, receptive to wisdom, willing to learn.

Interestingly, those that refused to receive the new instruction from the Lord lost the old instruction also (JST Matthew 13:10–11). In other words, they thought they had salvation already but their unwillingness to be taught of the Lord meant that the truths they thought they knew could not benefit and bless them. To reject further spiritual light from heaven is to have existing light removed. It is to lose light and have our minds clouded over by unbelief and darkness. On the other hand, those who seek more light and knowledge retain what they already have and gain further light and truth, which richly magnifies and blesses them. The truths of heaven are not static in our lives. They are either growing within us or diminishing—just like a seed is either growing or shriveling. Light leads to life; darkness to death. The Lord indicated that many holy persons would have loved to hear the Lord speak in person in mortality but did not have that opportunity because of when they lived. Sometimes we do not perceive the greatness of the teachers and the teaching that is available to us. We need to open our eyes and hearts to God and whatever He seeks to teach us—especially when it flies in the face of our previous conceptions. I would have loved to have heard the Lord preach in Jerusalem and Bountiful. I always hope I will have an open mind and a soft heart to hear His truths—including any stretching doctrines He seeks to share with me.

The Lord proceeds to tell the people other parables pertaining to the kingdom of God. The parable of the good seed portrays that in the kingdom of heaven, good seed is always grown in the garden of the Lord. However, during times of darkness, sleepiness, or distraction, an enemy sows tares among the good seed. As the wheat grows upwards, so do the tares. The wheat is productive, but it is not alone. The servants of the master wonder where the tares came from, as they did not plant them there. The master reveals that "an enemy hath done this." The servants want to gather the tares straightaway. However, the master of the house prevents this because to uproot the tares immediately would be to uproot the wheat also. He commands that both wheat and tares be allowed to grow to full fruition until harvest time. Then, the reapers will gather the tares into groups for burning and the wheat will be preserved in the storehouse (Matthew 13:24–30).

The Lord gives the meaning of this parable to His disciples after He sends the people away. He explains that Christ is the sower of the good seed. The field is the entire world. The good seed are those in the kingdom of God. The tares are offspring of the devil—meaning those who believe his lies and promote his insidious purposes. The enemy is the prince of darkness. The harvest is the end of this world when a great separation of wheat and tares will happen. The reapers are angelic ministers who will in due course remove from the world all who promote the works of the adversary. They will be placed in a fire where their sorrow and hatred can no longer contaminate the field. At that day, the righteous of the kingdom will obtain a grand and radiant glory with the Father of the harvest—our Father in Heaven. The Lord then warned that if we have the capacity to hear anything, we should hear this parable, learn this word, know this reality (Matthew 13:36–43).

The clear meaning is that the adversary of our souls encourages the planting and mixing of bad seed among the good. Both types of seed will grow to full maturity and then both will be divided into one of two bundles—one of good wheat and the other of bad tares. The difference will be obvious to the reapers. We thus learn that the Lord only ever grows good seed in His garden—all bad influences are therefore of enemy kind. It is critical that we discern the goodness of God's garden, His servants, His plans, and His eventual triumph. If we listen to any message in this time, we surely need to listen to this sobering prophetic promise.

The parable of the mustard seed teaches that in the kingdom of God a small seed, even the smallest of all seeds, if planted in a place and taken care of, will grow into a great tree, even the greatest tree, to the point that the birds will find rest there (Matthew 13:31–32). The core idea is that the kingdom will rise in great ways, to surprise all who witness it and will be a place of nurturing and protection. Let us give place to be amazed at what the kingdom of God has, and will yet, achieve.

The parable of the leaven teaches that in the kingdom of heaven the leaven, though small, can influence a much larger body that it is placed in. This is intended to indicate again that the kingdom will grow in unexpected ways. However, it seems to also point at the idea that Christ is the hidden bread of life, concealed from view, but He will impact the entire body—meaning the totality of humanity. Indeed, His resurrection must inevitably directly influence every man, woman, and child that has ever lived. It is evident that Jesus is declaring Himself as the revealing Messiah, the Prophet of Prophets, the great teller of secrets (Matthew 13:33–35).

The parable of the treasure teaches that in the kingdom of God, the real treasure is hidden from view. Those who find it keep the news secret, then they sell all their possessions to buy the field. There are those who understand that the treasure is available to us, but we must value it highly and give all else away for it. This reminds me that the Lord often told people not to share the fact that He had healed them. Perhaps this was a way of keeping the sacred secret of His Messiahship hidden from those who had no intention of selling all that they had to obtain that field of treasure (Matthew 13:44).

The parable of the pearl shows us that in the kingdom of heaven a trader who desires many pearls comes upon one single pearl and, realizing its great worth, sells all his goods to acquire it. The principle is that we might desire many things, even many valuable things in life, but there is one thing far more important than any other single treasure or even than all other riches combined—that is God's true treasure—the pearl of great price. A wise trader knows that this is worth more than all other pearls combined—even good ones (Matthew 13:45–46).

The parable of the net reveals that in the kingdom of heaven every kind of fish is invited to come. When the kingdom becomes full, the fishers of men gather the good fish together and return the bad fish to their proper place. At the end of days, angels of God will divide good people from bad ones. The bad are cast into the fire where sadness and anger dominate (Matthew 13:47–50). The world refers to the children of the wicked (JST Matthew 13:49–51). Thus it is that wickedness begets wickedness. The world and the kingdom of God are not synonymous. The world fosters the bad while the kingdom of God promotes the good.

After sharing all these parables the Lord asked if He was understood. He then explained that in the kingdom of God, wise scribes recognize treasures both new and old. The Lord was approving of those who accepted the historical word of God *and* new revelations. However, uninspired students of the scriptures who merely copy that which is already revealed do not accept that which is new and revelatory. Hence, these uninspired scribes cannot comprehend the parables about the kingdom (Matthew 13:51–52), whereas the apostles are to be instructed in the new law and covenant.

Then the Lord went to His own synagogue. The people were shocked at His wisdom and impressive works. They viewed Him as an ordinary man, belonging to common people, having a human mother, mere men for brothers and sisters that lived in the village. They therefore could not comprehend how He could know and be something more than ordinary. They were upset and offended by Him. He responded by saying that prophets receive honor in faraway homes and lands. He did not do miraculous works there because the people did not believe He was anything other than a mere man (Matthew 13:53–58).

It is evident from all these examples that the Lord does not conform to our expectations, match our wills, act according to our demands, or confine Himself to our understanding. He wants to teach a higher law, show a better way, preach a greater doctrine, and to advance a more noble cause. The kingdom of God will always be marked by power, growth, influence, and joy. It will always be opposed by some and embraced by others. The adversary will always be found sowing doubt, discord, disbelief, and dissension. However, the true servants of God will always preach that the kingdom can and will rise to its glorious destiny and that we can be a part of it if we desire consistently to be so. The receipt of miracles is so often limited by our unbelief, not by His. He would do wonders among us. As we open our hearts and minds to His great doctrines, we will know miracles that will happily shock us to the core.

Great Pollutions upon the Land

It is interesting to me that chemicals, pesticides, and herbicides, etc. can pollute natural soil, water, plants, and animals. This is analogous to the idea that drugs, impurities, alcohol, tobacco, sugar, etc. when placed in human beings can be poisons that lead to suffering, illness, abnormality, and death. The Garden of the Lord is often polluted both physically and spiritually. The Lord has warned us that in the last days there will be great pollutions upon the earth. These pollutions are immoral breaches of the divine laws of honesty, integrity, chastity, and valuing of life. These abominations are diversions from the laws of the Lord. Many people will preach that we can do whatever we desire to do as the Lord will still save us. We are warned that such teachings come from those who are in "the gall of bitterness and in the bonds of iniquity" (Mormon 8:31). They are trapped in the chains of sinful behavior.

I find it interesting that the Lord refers to significant sins as great pollutions. Hence, the breaching of the commandments of God around honesty, virtue, upholding the sanctity of life, etc. is considered by Him to constitute pollution and abomination. This evokes thoughts of contamination and despicable behavior. This makes the earth dirty. We are warned that many mortals will preach that it is permissible to lie, cheat, steal, commit adultery, etc. as the Lord will not hold the doers of these deeds accountable for such at the final judgment. The prophet warns us that such teaching comes from those who are already bound by chains of sin and the misery of carnality. We do well to measure all invitations we receive by whether they promote such worldly living or encourage us to avoid such action. The goodness of the Lord does not mean that He can or will excuse us in sin. He does not uphold any unrighteous behavior. Even the smallest infraction of divine law is something that prevents us from finding salvation unless and until we choose to repent and conform with holy standards.

Treacherous Dangers

There are many ways that the enemy of our souls uses to try to prevent us from growing up unto eternal exaltation. I consider some pertinent ones below in the hope that we can continue to watch and be aware so that we can always detect his subtle snares and prevent his captivating devices. Instead, we can overwhelm our enemy by shoring up our protective defenses.

The Insidious Snake

We know that there is an outcast rebel seeking to occupy the Lord's territory. He is an enemy, usurper, and destroyer. He seeks to grasp us with his awful chains. We need to avoid this type of snake as he is treacherous. The ongoing conflict between good and evil is one of words and ideas as well as attitudes, desires, and behaviors. It is a contest of testimony and faith as we are placed in a situation to decide in whom and in what we place our trust for eternal salvation. We need to know the distinction between the satanic snake that bites and the rescuing Savior that heals. The strait and narrow path of bounded discipline and godly grace gives us not only pleasure in appropriate measure, but also spiritual safety, real happiness, and everlasting joys.

Of course, it is not always easy to identify snakes by their appearance alone. For example, snakes eat rats and mice. While such snakes do not harm gardens, they do harm gardeners! Hence, we need to be mindful of those things that hurt other bad things in the guise of appearing good. We are to be watchful of wolves that wear the clothing of sheep but inwardly they are ravening wolves. It is not simply the appearance of something that counts—it is the inner nature, the true disposition that matters. It is crucial for us to see to the heart of issues, ideas, and philosophies that may appear benevolent but are in fact intended to lead us away from our perfect Gardener.

Ferocious Frost and Halting Heat

While both cold and heat are necessary for certain plants to grow, they must be kept in a sense of balanced limitation. Otherwise, excessive amounts will kill plants. Likewise, too much of certain types of influence, without countervailing influences, will cause us great trouble in the garden. Opposition from the adversary, if it is not resisted, will cause us to cave in spiritually.

The Wrangling Weed

We face competition in this wilderness garden. There are influences that would seek to undermine our strength and dilute our growth. We cannot always uproot the weeds that flourish around us, but we can ensure that we are not crowded out by their thirst to swallow up all the attention and to pursue all the nutrition in the garden. Weeds of negativity can be disastrous to us. They can take away our energy and leave us bereft of determination. Therefore, we must soak up the nourishing goodness that God places in our path. Hence, we need faith that God will give us all we need to grow to a fulness of stature.

Diversions and Distractions

What would we say of a gardener that persistently avoided working in the garden?

What would we think of a farmer that was lulled into laziness or a farm hand that spent all their time playing?

What would we observe about a gardening implement that was never used in a garden?

What about a personal assistant that was always late for meetings, or a lawyer that did not like to read contracts, or a doctor that could not remember where they left their equipment, or a pilot that struggled to focus on the task of safety, or a basketball player that was more interested in the after-game party?

These all have something in common—they are not focused on the task they are supposed to be performing. What is the point of being a sun that does not shine, or a teacher that does not teach or a book that is never read? Food is to be eaten, music is to be played and listened to, movies are to be watched and seeds are intended to grow into plants, bushes, trees!

Well, in a similar vein, we can sense when we are on target, on point, on purpose in our lives. We are on earth for a reason. Not simply to have fun, go sightseeing, make money, etc. These are all important and useful in their time and place of course. However, they can never represent the full and deep reason of our being. We need to give spiritual wings to our highest dreams and loftiest aspirations.

This requires that we learn our purpose and stick to our task. We need to aim high and not allow ourselves to be derailed from our fundamental purpose of growing spiritually.

Efforts to distract us are everywhere. Spiritual diversion is both sad and avoidable. It represents a loss of focus on the things that really matter and evidences a focus on things that are secondary. We are all prone to this sort of spiritual confusion and anyone can be derailed if they do not take the Holy Ghost as their companion. We need to be wise. This means maturing and becoming sensitive to the purpose of our soul. The path of purpose will keep us grounded as we consistently remind ourselves of the great "why" of our lives—to become all that the master Gardener intends for us to be!

Dreary Slumber and Blinding Darkness

Worldly numbing comes from such things as illegal drugs, alcohol, gambling, junk food, etc. These so easily draw us away from the higher things of life. Rather than being in a state of spiritual slumbering, we can be morally astute, awake, enlivened, and aware. The murky mist of darkness is a form of spiritual fog, a pollution of the spirit. It comes in the form of vulgarity, promiscuity, and immorality. Are our spiritual sensitivities dulled or heightened? The remedy is to cleanse ourselves from toxins, to endeavor to overcome addiction, to be alert to our opportunities, and to see the light of a higher way, a better path, a nobler journey.

Raucous Lasciviousness

This tends to come in the form of loud carnal music, a disposition toward excessive violence, aggressive atheism, and media that promotes debauched thinking, lewd words, and crass behaviors. These seductive enticements can lead us astray. In fact, they cannot lead us anywhere else! There is certainly a distinction between moral turpitude and celestial striving.

The promotion of either virtual or bodily wickedness is not God inspired. We can discern the purpose and point of all things by whether they lead us to clarity of thought and high moral behavior or to dilution of moral conscience and actions we would not perform in our best moral senses.

The Remedies

Does the Lord have a remedy for the work of the enemy in the garden? Yes. He provides guidance and warnings. He lights our way in the dark. He sends watchmen upon the tower. These visionary overseers see the strategies and tactics of the enemy before he can do his insidious work. Their warning voices represent a way for us to avoid being deceived and overcome by the devious tricks of our adversary. The Lord will one day remove temptation from our path. For now, we need to prove to Him that we are more interested in becoming good than we are in pursuing worldly enticements.

Deep Clean

The Garden requires frequent and deep cleansing. The time will come when God cleanses His entire garden with a great purging and complete refining. This is a powerful and comforting insight. We know that Christ is the great antidote to the poisoning adversary. He is the great moral guide, the ultimate spiritual compass, the true North Star. He is the advocate of our souls. He encourages our greatest good, our noblest moral action, our most sublime character. We know that He will wash away the minor blemishes of carnality and the most deep-rooted filth within our souls. He will purge our dirt with His cleanliness. When He comes again, He will judge the entire world and burn all corruption out of His kingdom (Isaiah 4:4). His friendship overpowers the enemy. His purpose is to save us from our worst inclinations, our most treacherous desires, our seemingly unyielding bad habits. Indeed, He offers us great purification such as we have never known. This washing of the world will cover all nations, kindreds, tongues, and people. It will include every dark corner, every hidden agenda, every stain of carnality. It will wash the world to make it new, clean, fresh, and beautiful!

13

By the Gardener's Hand

Isaiah speaks poetically of the great love that God has for His people Israel. He refers to our Lord having "a vineyard in a very fruitful hill" (Isaiah 5:1–4). He uses an allegory or symbol to teach us a great lesson. The symbolism is that of a place of opportunity for great productiveness—a vineyard which is poised to produce numerous great grapes. The meaning is that the Lord has a vineyard—the family of covenant people. He has sought to make it a fruitful people in the ways of the Lord. He placed it in a region of holiness so that the legacy of production would never be lost. He protected it from enemies, removed obstacles from its ground, used the best materials, gave prophetic overseers to watch over it, and placed grape production at the very center of it. It was reasonable to assume that He would find that it fulfilled the purpose for which it was created—the production of a multitude of high-quality grapes. This did not happen. He asks the Jews to make a judgment about whether the Lord of the vineyard could have possibly done anything different or better than what He did for His choice piece of land. It brought forth wild grapes instead of the delicious and nutritious grapes He sought for and worked for so tirelessly. Therefore the family of Israel was then scattered—in the hope that by the long-term intervention of the Lord the vineyard would eventually bring forth the kind and quantity of grapes originally designed for it to produce.

The Lord did intervene in His vineyard, and He is doing so today at an ever-hastening rate. Let us consider the allegory of the olive tree in Jacob 5 to explore this divine interface. The allegory of the olive tree in the vineyard can be understood on various levels. It is my sense that one of these ways relates to the Atonement of Christ. We are told that the Lord of the vineyard did everything He could possibly do to preserve the trees and fruit of the vineyard. I understand this to mean that the Atonement of the Lord is the offering of all offerings, it is the greatest service that could be rendered, the ultimate effort which can never be surpassed, the mightiest act of divine love. The Father is the Lord/Master of the Vineyard, who gives His all to save it.

The servant represents the Messiah. The servants/laborers are the prophets, leaders, missionaries, and members of the Church. The vineyard is the world. The choice spot of ground refers to those places of promise where the righteous are sent. The fruit of the trees is the salvation of souls. Good fruit is pleasing to the Lord as it represents how individuals and families have become productive in the work of salvation. God employs the Law of the Harvest in His garden. Obedience always brings forth the blessings of heaven. As we follow God's Law, the results are assured. We will be blessed, prosper, and grow. We need to learn the specific laws upon which certain blessings are predicated and then follow them.

Of course, the Garden is also a place of great divine mercy. Only divine love and mercy can save a dying garden. When men might give up and "throw down the pruning shears," when hope seems lost, when discouragement mounts, when victory looks impossible, then God shows His greatest influence. He can save that which is lost. He can recover that which man thinks is forever gone. God has a long-term vantage point—temporary failures and setbacks do not cause Him to lose perspective. As we search and ponder Jacob 5, it is evident that the desired outcome takes a long time and is in many ways counterintuitive. It often appears to be a fool's errand. God tries much grafting and pruning to get the vineyard to produce fruit on a lasting basis.

The Generous Gardener

The prophet Jacob recounts the allegory of Zenos in which the family of Israel is compared to a tame olive tree nourished to growth in a vineyard. At one point the tree starts to die. The Master says, "I will prune it, and dig about it, and nourish it, that perhaps it may shoot forth young and tender branches, and it perish not" (Jacob 5:4). He practices what He promises. Of course, God is the cultivator of this tree and vineyard. The goodness of our God is manifest through His works in the Garden. His works are mighty and majestic, tough and tender, and small and simple. He is willing to give us every good thing as we prepare ourselves to receive His offerings. We can see that God, as the generous gardener, labors in the garden for the benefit of all the seeds—and trees—of His garden (Jacob 5:15, 72).

His multitude of mercies is abundantly evident. He can and will help us to have both some small successes and many mighty miracles as we come to know Him and His way of being in the garden (Alma 26:12, 26). His miracles include the creation of our spirits, the creation of the earth, and the creation of our bodies. They also include the redemption of our spirits, bodies, and of the earth. He is the active, gentle, caring, hardworking, patient, persistent, concerned, and powerful gardener. He endeavors to cultivate each seed one by one (Jacob 5:22). Indeed, what more could He do for us than He Has done, is doing, and will yet do? (Jacob 5:41, 47). Nobody works harder, wiser, or longer for us than Almighty God. This is difficult work requiring great patience, long-suffering, and temperance. He is the great pruner of our souls. Christ is the servant gardener for all seasons of our lives. Whether we are in the rejoicing light and warm heat of summer, the sickness and pain of autumn, the renewal of life in spring, or the darkness and cold of winter, we have a Savior to bring us the needed portion of aid and help. In sin, sadness, sorrow, fear, disease, disappointment, or death, He will give needed comfort and consolation. He will mourn with us in our grief and rejoice with us in our joys. In times of decay or rebirth, we are not left unassisted.

The Loyal Servant

The Lord of the Garden does not work alone in His nourishing of the seeds of His garden. Rather He calls servants to labor with Him and under His masterful guidance (Jacob 5:61, 70). These servants are to watch the tree and nourish it according to divine instruction—they are to look at it, observe it, tend it, protect it, help it, feed it, and do all things to ensure it has every opportunity to bring forth fruit in the fulness of the stature that it is capable of (Jacob 5:12). Although those servants are few when compared with the size of the garden they tend, yet they are devoted, hardworking, obedient, diligent, and blessed (Jacob 5:71–72, 75). Those servants are honored with a great trust, and they are loyal in their service. Those called as laborers in the Lord's Vineyard are to do their divine duty. This is how they gain the trust of God and the confidence of others. When we observe these steadfast servants, we can see the vivid contrast between faithfully persisting toward heavenly destinations (1 Nephi 8:21, 24, 30) and fumbling in confusion toward iniquitous places, people, and priorities (1 Nephi 8:31). These servants submissively soar to great spiritual heights by obtaining soft hearts and firm minds.

Foremost among those called to serve in the vineyard for the salvation of the souls of men (Doctrine and Covenants 138:56) are prophets and apostles. They are specifically called to help the Lord and Master of the Garden in His work of helping seeds to grow to maturity. Apostles—who have taken upon themselves the name of Christ with full purpose of heart—are earthly examples of their Redeemer.

They are *called* by the spirit of prophecy and revelation.
They are *sustained* by the prayers of the Saints.
They are given *authority* by the laying on of hands.
They have *power* by linking with the power of God through righteous living.
Their character is *refined* through fiery affliction.
They become *chosen* through faithful lifelong obedience, love, and service in following their Savior.

They are worthy of emulation, close to perfection, and evidence consecration of will (Mosiah 23:10–11, 14–15, 17–18). They show untiring devotion to their Leader and are bound to him (Helaman

10:4–7). Blessed are those who are prophet-led! We are wisely led as Latter-day Saints, for we are promised power, protection, and peace as we follow these chosen servants who are sure and solid types and symbols of the great Servant.

I have long thought that it is deeply interesting that Joseph Smith received his first vision in a sacred grove. This was a forest of spiritual fortitude. This was a naturally organic place of beauty and life. What grows in a forest? Well, for one thing, trees do. What grows into a tree? Well, a seed does. For me, the analogy is this: Joseph was a good seed in God's green garden (forest). This was where he would be instructed in those principles that would allow him to grow from being a seed into a mighty tree of goodness. He received a new understanding of God and the plans and purposes of the Almighty. He also obtained a new perspective of his own life and destiny. In a similar manner, each of us are specifically called to grow and develop in Godly ways.

In modern scripture, Joseph and Hyrum Smith are referred to as "green trees" (Doctrine and Covenants 135:6). It was worth it to the Lord that Joseph and Hyrum died as martyrs for the cause of the restored covenant. Their loss was tremendous, but the salvation of a ruined world requires whole-souled devotion and sacrifice. It comes with a deep cost. It is important to remember that if "green trees" like Joseph and Hyrum died to help save the world, then surely unfruitful trees who oppose the work of God will need to be cleared from the vineyard so that the world can be made new. This is strong doctrine. Our Lord would gladly save every tree of His garden, but He cannot force this. Each seed, each tree, must choose either the fire of purification or the fire of destruction. It is the choice we make that determines our place within the vineyard.

In Process of Time

This allegory takes place over a long period of time—thousands of years. Consider how the Lord is intimately involved with the work of saving the Olive tree:

The servant asks the Master why he planted a tree, or a branch of the tree in the "poorest spot in all the land of thy vineyard" (Jacob 5:21–22). Here we see that the servant was surprised that the Master was cultivating a poor piece of ground. The Lord said He knew the quality of that garden spot. Nevertheless, He made efforts over a long period of time and even the poor spot brought forth much fruit due to the efforts. There is a message in that for all of us.

We are told that both Lord and servant "did *nourish all the fruit* of the vineyard" (Jacob 5:28, emphasis added). So it is that both the Lord (Father) and servant (Son) paid attention to all the fruit—none was forgotten, overlooked, or neglected. Each was given the needed resources to survive and thrive.

Later, although there was much fruit, it was all bad. The bad fruit was also of different kinds, which suggests that every possible type of bad fruit was growing there. The Lord saw that there was no benefit in this regardless of all the work performed. He expressed deep concern about losing His tree (Jacob 5:32). Then the servant pointed out to the Lord that because of the grafting performed by the Lord the roots were good and there was still some potential for good fruit. The Lord responded by saying that this was not beneficial to Him unless the fruit being produced was good (Jacob 5:34–35).

The Lord and His servant saw that the bad fruit was stronger than the part producing good fruit—hence the good had died. The Lord responded with personal tears and a plea that He had done all that could be done to save the vineyard. (Jacob 5:40–41). The servant recognized that loftiness was the source of the trouble. The overreach of the branches overcame the goodness of the roots. Therefore, the branches took too much strength from the roots too quickly and caused the fruit to become bad (Jacob 5:48).

The Lord agreed to give the process of cultivation a little longer because He did not want to lose any of His trees (Jacob 5:51). The Lord of the vineyard expressed His hope that the roots would acquire further strength because they were fundamentally good, that the branches would become less lofty and that therefore the good would prove stronger than the bad (Jacob 5:59).

In interpretation of these symbols, it is evident that pride (the loftiness of the branches) can disturb even good roots (a good heart and good beginnings). When pride is allowed to flourish, the results will always be decay, dissolution, and eventually death even if the initial outcomes appear to show otherwise. However, as pride is pruned, then strong roots that seek goodness can overcome even pronounced arrogance. The intervention of the Lord and His servants is one of reminding the trees of the vineyard who they belong to and what purpose they serve.

I am reminded of the great story from President Hugh B. Brown about an experience he had as a young man. He found a currant bush on his farm that showed no signs of being productive but was instead growing nearly as tall as the trees. So he pruned the bush significantly. He thought the bush was tearful and seemed to say to him that he was terribly cruel in cutting the bush down like that. He responded, "Look, little currant bush, I am the gardener here, and I know what I want you to be. If I let you go the way you want to go, you will never amount to anything. But someday, when you are laden with fruit, you are going to think back and say, 'Thank you, Mr. Gardener, for cutting me down, for loving me enough to hurt me.'" President Brown goes on to compare this incident with his own experience some years later where he expected to be promoted to the position of General in the army. However, he was greatly disappointed when the presiding officer called him to a meeting and told him he was qualified but that he could not promote him. Brother Brown saw the words "THIS MAN IS A MORMON" on the paperwork on the commanding officer's desk. He was angry with God for preventing his progress, especially because he was trying to live his faith.

President Brown went on to explain, "And then I heard a voice. It sounded like my own voice, and the voice said, "I am the gardener here. I know what I want you to be. If I let you go the way you want to go, you will never amount to anything. And someday, when you are ripened in life, you are going to shout back across the time and say, 'Thank you, Mr. Gardener, for cutting me down, for loving me enough to hurt me.' Those words . . . drove me to my knees, where I prayed for forgiveness for my arrogance and my ambition." He also recounted how if he had received that promotion, he and his children may never have had the opportunity to progress in the spiritual life the way they subsequently did. So, looking back, he was deeply thankful for the pruning he had received even though it had been bitter to him at the time (Hugh B. Brown, "God is the Gardener" [Brigham Young University Commencement, May 31, 1968], speeches.byu.edu).

What lessons can we learn from this account?

Each one of us require pruning in the process of becoming fruit bearers.

That pruning will inevitably breach our expectations.

It will be difficult for us personally.

Our perspective of what constitutes "success" and "growth" does not always correlate with the viewpoint of God. He knows where our ambitions will lead us. Our complacency, arrogance, and other negative traits need to be rooted out of us—usually through great difficulty.

There is a dear cost to discipleship—but there are also rich blessings that accrue.

Blessings and opportunities will arise for us which we had not anticipated through this process of cutting down.

This pruning will yield substantial dividends in due course for us and those we love, which could not possibly be foreseen by us in advance. We become so much more than we would ever have become without God's intervention.

In due course we will be profoundly grateful for the humbling we have received.

God is the wise, patient, loving gardener of our souls. Trust in Him is never ever misplaced. God views greatness in our development, rather than in our status.

Other Servants

The Lord of the vineyard assigns His servant to call other helpers to work hard to restore the natural fruit due to its unrivalled goodness and preciousness. This would be the last time of pruning for the vineyard and would require a mighty effort (Jacob 5:61–62). Many others beside Christ are also called to service in the Garden of the Lord. Those called to labor with their Master serve to make a valuable contribution. They are expected to work hard to prepare the world for a restoration to pristine truth. The message of redemption goes to the entire vineyard so the precious fruit of pure undiluted goodness will once again fill the world. The greatest contribution they can ever give to others is their personal knowledge, testimony, faith, and love of the restored gospel. In this process these fellow laborers learn two great overarching principles that thereafter guide their lives and ministry:

Each seed in the garden is capable of being good and growing to become tremendously beautiful. So each child of God is capable, under correct watch-care of doing more good (works), enduring more, accomplishing more, and being more than they ever thought they could. Each person only finds out what they are capable of by being tested and tried in difficult ways and by responding to difficult tasks. The Lord often honors us by letting us stand on our own two feet (Jacob 2:2–3).

Each seed has access to nourishment which is divinely placed and cultivated carefully. So each child of God has access to divine help (grace) far more than we sometimes realize. The Lord is ever willing and able to help us—not to take over and do the work for us as that would not serve us well—but to help where we are weak and He is strong. We never need to worry about being alone or forsaken. We are lost without Him but with Him we can do His holy work. We can become more than we used to be or presently are (2 Nephi 4:20; Mosiah 2:30). In this gradual but glorious transformation we each need Him daily, deeply, and desperately. There is no growth in the garden of the Lord for any seed except that which He as the Master Gardener makes possible and actively facilitates.

The Grief of the Lord

The Lord of the vineyard is deeply saddened by the potential loss of His trees. Therefore He instructs those working with Him to only clear away the bad trees as the good trees grow and thereby show their capacity to overcome the influence of bad. The bad trees will be burned in due course so that the entire ground can be reclaimed for good (Jacob 5:66). In like manner, it cannot be imagined that God rejoices in the loss of even one soul. He grieves for the loss of any. He is sad when our souls are stifled by poor choices, when we are stubborn and hard-hearted, when we fail to rise to the glory of our potential. He weeps when we do not grow in life-giving ways but rather decay and perish spiritually.

He wants the good to overcome the bad—both within us and around us. He wants a good people, a good world, a good and great life for each one of us. His desire is to sweep bad out of His vineyard—the badness of sin, corruption, violence, hatred, and indeed all that is destructive of the glory of the spiritual life. He only clears away bad as the good grows. We are therefore blessed when we incrementally and intentionally remove badness from our lives and our world and replace it with goodness. This is the process of growth, and it takes time, effort, and consistency. It requires faith that God can help us to make a better world. That goodness must start with us individually and then spread outward.

The Last Labor

The Lord and all His servants worked for the last time to save the vineyard with total devotion so that they could find joy in the good trees and good fruit produced. Although the number of helpers was few, they were united with the Lord and therefore could accomplish His purposes (Jacob 5:70–74). This refers to the day in which we are living. The time is drawing nigh when the Savior will return to reclaim Father's vineyard. So the servants must labor diligently to ensure all preparations are put in place and the warning voice is raised. The work of salvation is the work of cleansing souls from the pollutions that would destroy the fruit. God wants a great harvest of souls. He wants each person to be part of the natural fruit, to be part of the covenant family. He wants us to be united in righteousness, bonded in Christ, equal in understanding and fruitfulness. The preciousness of this fruit can only be fully appreciated by considering that the Son of God gave His life to save the fruit. In other words, He valued each soul similarly. He regarded us with the same importance He saw in Himself!

Prior to the day of burning, which is fast approaching, the world is awash with evil fruit—doctrines, ideas, practices, and values—which mock God, foster carnality, denigrate family, and dismiss faith in the Lord. The gathering is happening to all types and kinds of fruit—good is gathered to good, bad is gathered to bad. That which is holy gravitates toward that which is righteous. That which is profane is attracted to that which is wicked. All things move toward that which they most resemble and long for. Therefore, it is critical that we gravitate toward the Lord and His good work (Jacob 5:77).

Twelve Olive Trees

I love the revelation to the Prophet Joseph Smith concerning the allegory of Zion in our day (Doctrine and Covenants 101:44–62). This is a revelation for our time. We learn in this how the Son of God sees His vineyard, His land, His chosen Zion, His covenant people, His house of Israel. He wanted His servants (the prophets) to protect His 12 Olive Trees (12 Tribes of Israel or 12 Apostles) from the enemy that seeks to destroy. It is critical to remember that the Savior's watchmen upon the tower—prophets, seers, and revelators—are the ones that give us needed and timely instruction. These brethren are wise advisers. They are both giant trees and prudent overseers (Doctrine and Covenants 124:61).

His instruction to place watchmen upon the tower is a pertinent message. The servants could not see the reasoning for this and contended among themselves. While they slept, the enemy came and did exactly what the nobleman had forewarned would happen if the servants were slothful. The nobleman chastened them and said tragedy like this is only prevented by high tower visionary leadership. He then told them to redeem His vineyard with all the strength they could gather. This was to be done immediately. The servants wanted to know when the nobleman would return. He said that the timing was His business and that the servants simply needed to act on instruction. The nobleman then blessed the servants with power to be wise and loyal in the commission. The servants did as commanded and after a long time, the nobleman returned as promised.

We live in a day of spiritual slumber. We need to be awake and aware and not be distracted by means of rationalizing and dissension internally. We do not need to worry excessively about when the Savior will redeem His vineyard. Rather, our focus is to be watching and ready to safeguard the fruit against the enemy. The Savior wants His vineyard to be productive. He has bought it with His precious blood. No price that we are called to pay could ever be too high, no labor too much, no inconvenience too great for our Savior to ask of us. The kingdom is to be one of fruitful disciples. The Savior redeemed His vineyard in a garden of olive trees and a hill of lifeless trees, through His infinite Atonement. We must never fall asleep to that abiding truth. The House of Israel—the people of covenant—cannot be saved outside of Christ's Atonement. This is the great truth we must always remember and never forget. We cannot afford to allow complacency or discord to displace our focus on building the kingdom of Zion.

14

Growing Tall

The nature that Christ desires for us mirrors His own. He is a God of united spirit, body, heart, and mind. He is also a being of perfect qualities. God is the whole union of all aspects of the divine nature. In us, He sees the potential for partaking of His grand and glorious nature. Let us first consider His nature and then how we can rise from potential to actuality in acquiring the elements of His divine nature.

The Nature of Christ

Happy, Beautiful, Joyful, and Radiant

Christ is described as an endless light that can never be darkened and an endless life that cannot die. He is therefore both the present and endless light and life of our world (Mosiah 16:9). The Christ we love blesses us and smiles upon us. In truth, His shining countenance gives us radiant light which illuminates us in amazing ways (3 Nephi 19:25).

Eager to Embrace

If we are willing, our Lord brings us out from everlasting darkness and destruction into His everlasting light and salvation. Indeed, we can be "encircled about eternally in the arms of His love" (2 Nephi 1:15) and be “encircled about with the matchless bounty of his love” (Alma 26:15). The repentant are “clasped in the arms of Jesus” (Mormon 5:11). He stands “with open arms to receive you!” (Mormon 6:17). Where else would He rather be? Where else would He want us to be?

Merciful

Ammon, the great missionary, explains that we glory in, rejoice in, and praise God eternally. We cannot overestimate His triumphant goodness because He shows power, mercy, wisdom, comprehension, and long-suffering toward His children in saving them from the polluted condition of sin through repentance. We cannot articulate in words alone our deep feelings of gratitude for how wonderful God is in rescuing us from darkness and death through the great joy of eternal salvation (Alma 26:16–17, 20). Indeed, we know that “God is mindful of every people” and “his bowels of mercy are over all the earth” (Alma 26:36–37). He is mindful of you in your small portion of garden! He is also aware of your brothers and sisters wherever they are.

Compassionate

I love the Book of Mormon description of how the resurrected Lord intentionally watched the people and noticed their sorrow (3 Nephi 17:5). They were sad that He was about to depart. So He stayed to give more attention to them! Their sadness then gave way to gladness!

Emotional and Personal

Christ is the perfect man. He is not afraid to show His deep love for others and His great concern for each person. Consider the touching encounter at the temple. He taught the people, then cried, the people noticed He cried, then He blessed each child one by one and prayed to His Father for each child (and probably each adult too!), then he shed tears again! (3 Nephi 17:21–22). What a conference this was! Full of doctrine, tears, blessings, and prayers!

Generous

Our Lord instructs His people to come to Him, to see, to touch, to hear, and to know Him (3 Nephi 18:25). He draws us close to Him! He also promises to give us a life which is eternal if we abide with Him! (3 Nephi 15:9).

Pure

Not only is our Lord pure Himself, but He has the power to purify us from stain. He can cleanse us better than any soap. He can purge us with more effectiveness that any other cleansing agent. His spiritual fire can burn all desires for carnality from our souls. He purifies all those who are willing, including those who are already good. We need to be refined and purified so we can abide His glorious presence (3 Nephi 24:2–3).

Partakers of the Divine Nature

It is one of the great purposes of mortality for us to acquire complete mastery over all things. We are to school our feelings, master our appetites, control our desires, and channel our thoughts. When the spirit body is combined with a temporal tabernacle, we are confronted with challenges not faced when we were only spirits. We experience life with all the senses. In truth, the spiritual life is to be heard, seen, felt, and sensed. Our bodies are to become eternal. Hence, our relationships in the eternities are to be tangible ones. We are to have eternal glory, which indicates never-ending light, truth, intelligence, and joy.

True religion is connective, experiential, and relational. It is to be practiced in the body. It is a journey of action that covers all our faculties, capacities, and capabilities. In this regard, laws, ordinances, and covenants are all received through participative action using thoughts, feelings, touch, sounds, and tastes. The gospel involves all elements of our nature—heart, mind, body, and spirit. It intrinsically concerns our innermost feelings, most noble thoughts, most honorable actions, and deepest desires. Our broken hearts are bound up by our kind Lord

(Doctrine and Covenants 138:42). Indeed, our minds, hearts and doings are to be centered on God's powerful Son for salvation (Alma 37:36).

Temple Tabernacle

The everlasting gospel gives us a remarkable viewpoint on the physical body. There is great beauty in the temporal body—not simply physical attraction but also spiritual meaning. We can enjoy the healthy happiness that comes from knowing that the mortal body is divine and precious. We are all born to resemble God in how we look—both spiritually and physically (Ether 3). The temporal body in its miraculous splendor reflects something of the transcendent glory of God. What it can do and how it looks are representations on a smaller scale of the powers of God and the grandeur of His presence. While the body is not inherently bad, it is naturally inclined to moral temptation and weakness (Mosiah 3:19), but we know our spirits can learn to control our bodies in righteous ways. Treating our bodies with a deep respect and sacred sanctity makes a marked difference on our perspectives, the choices we make, and the outcomes we see in our lives. Becoming holy necessarily involves learning to treat the physical body as the vital and eternally ransomed gift of God.

The temporal body is a temple (house) for our eternal spirit. It is intended to be a divine tabernacle of holiness. As we live righteously in our physical bodies, our spirits are touched by the Holy Ghost who communicates with our spirits. This is one of the most noble desires we can have in this life (3 Nephi 19:9). The Savior loves our eternal spirits and saves the penitent from the everlasting destructive effects of scarring sin. There is a great light and eternal beauty inherent in a physical body that is consecrated to the will of God. Also, a body that is plain, non-symmetric, or flawed in many ways is no less of a divine gift than a body that is more perfect in appearance and workings. God is the true source of all real beauty, both physical and spiritual, whether temporary or eternal. Doctrine like this makes a tremendous positive difference in how we see our physical selves.

Of course, we are not judged by God based on our physical appearances (2 Nephi 9:15). The Lord specifically teaches us that He looks beyond the physical into our hearts (3 Nephi 13:16–18). However, we are judged by Him both now and eternally based on the extent to which we desire to have closeness to God as part of our character (Mosiah 27:31; Alma 42:10, 23). We are to have the radiant image of God both in, and engraven upon, our smiling and glowing countenances. What better image could we ever have? (Alma 5:14, 19; 3 Nephi 19:25). As we become more like the Savior, we also become more beautiful to behold and eventually become as truly beautiful as He is to look upon. The beauty of holiness shines in our faces.

The Lord teaches us that we need to master our bodies and train them in ways that will make us more able to serve Him. Thus, exercise is important from both a physical and spiritual point of view. Being physically active has been a source of strength and renewal to me throughout my entire life. At various times in my life, I have participated in cycling, basketball, dancing, karate, tennis, squash, soccer, rounders (like baseball), British bulldog, volleyball, badminton, table tennis, running, break-dancing, and, of course, walking! When I was 39 years of age, I decided I wanted to cycle outside rather than just using a gym stationary bike all the time. One day, I completed an exhausting 24-kilometer (almost 15-mile) journey. It was wonderful to be out in the real weather doing such a difficult exercise. It made me feel alive. There is something about an uphill physical struggle that is really demanding yet also triumphant!

We can lessen physical and spiritual disease through embracing the vitality that comes from bodily motion. We are counseled to be exceedingly valiant for strength and activity because:

- it can assist us in spiritual warfare (Alma 53:20)
- it builds a bounteous spirit of determined purpose and spiritual resolve in standing against wickedness (Alma 46:21)
- it helps us to shoulder our relentless spiritual responsibilities (Alma 19:17)
- it helps us to guard against temporal and spiritual danger (Alma 58:21)
- it allows us to have sufficient reservoirs to deal with the inevitable ups and downs of everyday life and be constant in endurance (Mosiah 4:27)

This is no small matter, especially because we live in a day and age when giving in to physical appetites and passions for physical ease, gluttony, and excessive comfort are paraded as virtues by many. Although exercise is difficult, it is not regret inducing! More importantly, we know that righteous control over the body produces the benefits promised by the Lord.

While we are to seek to take the greatest care of our physical tabernacles, we are wisely instructed not to place undue emphasis on the physical at the expense of the spiritual. This is good doctrine with the power to give us spiritual balance and to help us to be at peace with our physical limitations. We do not need to be physically perfect in this life to please God and we certainly do not need to be better than someone else or wish we were more than ourselves to find real happiness. This doctrine gives us relief from unnecessary worldly burdens. Although I know personally that I need to remind myself of this truth because the tendency to bemoan physical limitations is a strong feature of our fallen mortal nature. As we mature spiritually the lesser things in life become less important to us and we make more time for things of real and enduring value. Of course, in the eternal scheme of things we are to care more for our eternal spirits and eternal souls (the resurrected body and spirit eternally joined together) than we are to care for the temporary things of this world (including the mortal body) (Alma 34, 40, and 42). To suffer and die physically is not a final tragedy if we keep our faith in Christ vibrant during our struggles. He will compensate us for our troubles!

We may transcend the boundaries of our usual mortal thinking to see that the Savior loves the temporal body. He heals and enhances our physical bodies through the power of faith in Him. The mortal body is to be appreciated, valued, loved, and honored by us. We are then more spiritually mindful about what we do with our bodies, how we dress them, what we put into them, and how we talk about them. The Son of God delights in this glorification for others as He knows through His own experience that an immortal tangible body is truly an eternally precious blessing. This all stands in direct contrast to the hateful viewpoint that the enemy of our souls has about both our now temporal and eventually resurrected body (Moroni 9:6). It is so wonderful when we hear and believe these teachings and come to apply them because then our lives change essentially and lastingly (Alma 32). We never regret becoming living temples of our God.

Humor and Play

We learn in the revealed word that our God is a kind, wise, and generous leader and He sees our need for fun, humor, and pleasure in life. He wants us to have the deep and healing kind which always benefits our true well-being. Good-natured laughter is healing medicine. Wholesome play helps us to release stress and is good for our bodies (2 Nephi 21:8; 3 Nephi 28:22; 4 Nephi 1:33). It is very important to allow our temporal bodies to receive the renewing refreshment and rejuvenating repair they need. God provides us with a spiritual and temporal oasis in the desert, a covert from the storm, and a refuge from the world along the exciting and treacherous journey to eternal life. My mission president invited us to "work hard and play hard." He was right. Play is a great method of reducing our stresses and tensions. Christ wants us to be both conscientious and joyful! We are permitted to have many times of happiness enjoying walking in the snow, dancing to music, and thinking happy thoughts!

Qualities of Godliness

In the process of growing spiritually, our perspective is altered for the better. This leads us to change our behavior. We become polished. Our views are elevated in fundamental ways. We start to seek intently and consistently for the true, holy, lasting, and beautiful things in life. We are to be edified in excellence of thought, word, and deed. We are to become sacred edifices in the hands of the Lord. We are destined to become fully divine. We are intended to acquire all the attributes, qualities, and characteristics of God. The Gardens of God in premortality, mortality, and post-mortality are purposefully structured in such a way that we can obtain every divine nature attribute. The full degree of divinity is available to us.

God encourages development of character. I am certain the gospel is true. I feel that living it properly requires my all. The Savior wants my heart, my soul, my everything. I would not want a salvation that was forced upon me or that I had done nothing substantial to qualify for myself. I am deeply grateful for repentance as I know that I must grow into perfection gradually with the merciful help of my Savior. This helps me to be conscientious while also being hopeful that all is not lost when I mess up. Latter-day Saints know well that we believe in salvation by grace after all we can do. I believe without hesitation in His power to transform us. The Lord will assist us in developing a celestial character comfortable enough to reside in the presence of God on a permanent basis (Ether 12:6, 27). Imagine that!

The full scale, scope, and magnificent grandeur of the endless glory and eternal opportunities given to the faithful will only become apparent in the life to come. We can begin now to cultivate all Christlike attributes within ourselves. Let us consider some of these. Many of the descriptors show us the different types and levels of God's qualities. We see the holistic nature of His qualities. He works with us according to our circumstances and needs. He also has the capacity to help us develop these qualities over time, as they are not static and final but rather develop as we improve. Our divine attributes grow over time through experience.

Faith

This is very necessary for us to acquire in this world of secular cynicism about spiritual realities. We can be filled with faith and that belief can make us complete. I love that Enos is told "thy faith hath made thee whole" (Enos 1:8). God is informing Enos that He knows him and his standing before the Almighty. He tells Enos that his sin is washed away because Enos has faith in the Messiah. God sees the faith that Enos possesses! God also tells Enos that he had never heard or seen Christ before this event. God knew Enos's past, his experiences with the divine and his opportunities. He knew and told him that he had now been made whole through faith. In essence, Enos had his standing before God revealed to him and learned how such a standing was reached.

Revelation so often tells us what is apparent to God but not yet clear to us, even when we are the one involved in getting the revelation! It takes divine revelation to know of our standing before God.

This is an individual encounter. I am convinced that God loves to have these personal interchanges with His people. Christ sees us when we are striving, stretching, seeking, and searching. He is watching our efforts and applauds our intentional work to draw close to Him.

God can bless us with the kind of faith that is:

- **Sufficient**, meaning enough for the need of the moment (Mosiah 4:11)
- **True**, meaning verified (Mosiah 4:3; 26:15–16)
- **Firm**, meaning grounded (Mosiah 27:14, 33)
- **Steady**, meaning resolute (Alma 32:29–30)
- **Steadfast**, meaning lodged, fixed, permanent (Enos 1:14, 20)
- **Unshaken**, meaning not dislodged (Alma 44:4)
- **Visionary**, meaning forward looking (3 Nephi 6:14)
- **Much**, meaning more than a little (Jarom 1:7)
- **Strong**, meaning capable (Alma 13:18)
- **Great**, meaning beyond basic, significant (Alma 27:27)
- **Confirmed**, meaning validated, vindicated (Helaman 3:35; 6:1; 15:9)
- **Increasing**, meaning growing (Moroni 7:30)
- **Strengthened**, meaning developing (2 Nephi 3:24)
- **Mighty**, meaning powerful (Jacob 3:1)
- **Exceeding**, meaning greater than the usual (2 Nephi 9:23)
- **Exceedingly great and strong**, meaning beyond elemental, surpassing even the good (2 Nephi 31:19)
- **Enduring**, meaning durable, lasting (Jacob 4:6)
- **Finished**, meaning complete (Alma 1:25)
- **Saving**, meaning transformative (Alma 5:15; 32:40)
- **Everlasting**, meaning eternal (Ether 12:19)
- **Perfect**, meaning whole, finished (Alma 7:6)

We can fuel our faith. The people of Christ are those who believe in His name, meaning the totality of His authority, power, and character (Alma 11:40). Having humble faith in the Savior gives us healing of many kinds in this mortal life whether spiritual, emotional, mental, physical, or social (Helaman 8:15). The Savior is ready and willing to save His people. Those who believe in the name of the Son of God will be spiritually reborn of Him (Ether 3:14). We need a developing and lasting faith in Jesus Christ throughout mortality (2 Nephi 31:18–20). Our faith is not yet final or finished!

Hope

I reflect often on the deep need for hope in our lives. We all face sadness, disappointments, setbacks, losses, anxieties, and even times of despair. These are part of the human experience. At times, they may be especially pronounced due to internal struggles, relationship difficulties, severe illness, challenging financial circumstances, and faith tests. In such situations it can be easy to feel lost, dazed, and unsure of how to proceed. We thus have a great need for the hope of a new day, of spring, of resolutions, of health, of happiness, of healing, of forgiveness, of reconciliation, and the hope of salvation.

God has not left us alone to wander in the dark. He has prepared a means for us to have a lively hope in Him. To give us reassurance, solace, and comfort a miracle happened in a grove of light in 1820, as a young and sincere man found answers to his questions, solutions to his problems, guidance for his confusion, and peace for his troubles. Light kept the enveloping darkness at bay, and he found a new hope, a beautiful light, a determined resolve to keep going. This young man was the Prophet Joseph Smith, who sought divine direction on the state of his soul. God the Father and His Son give us hope when all seems lost. They do so with great eagerness, for they love to fill our world with light. As they did so lovingly and clearly with the young Joseph, so they will shower down tender mercies upon us. In them we will find a hope that is both for now and for eternity.

We are wisely instructed that we can defy despair through the acquiring and maintenance of hope in God. God offers us a hope that is:

- Perfectly bright (2 Nephi 31:20)
- Good (Jacob 4:11)
- Great (Alma 7:3)
- Firm (Alma 34:41)
- Sure (Ether 12:4)
- More excellent (Ether 12:32)

- Sufficient (Moroni 7:3)
- Pervasive and all encompassing (Moroni 7:45)
- Able to fill us completely (Moroni 8:26)

This is thus fully comprehensive hope that covers every possible situation imaginable. This hope is an assurance that the restored gospel is the antidote to worldly pessimism. Let us be helped up and sustained by hope and not overcome by dreariness, despair, and discouragement.

Love and Charity: The More Excellent Way

We are instructed that we can come to receive the gift of the pure and enduring love of Christ that fills us completely through sincere prayer and devotion. We are promised that "when he shall appear we shall be like him, for we shall see him as he is" (Moroni 7:47–48). We will not see a caricature of Him, but His actual face. He will not be hidden from our view. We will see the real person of Christ—in His living splendor! In addition, we will resemble Him. How inspiring is that! In this day when love is often counterfeited, temporary, or absent and when excessive selfishness, stifling criticism, crushing sarcasm, and sour cynicism are so widespread, the Book of Mormon shows that there is a better way—indeed a more excellent way. We can come instead to cultivate charity. We are to have love for God always (Alma 13:29). This divine love is to be a personal possession on the journey of discipleship, not simply an inspiring ideal. Charity is a state of being that we grow into as we live all gospel principles not simply a once-off event or a once-off experience. The following principles are revealed for our heavenly help.

Charity is the standard of our Heavenly Father. It is how the Savior lives and how He shows His disciples to live. It is the pure love that Christ has for us and that we can have for Him. It is conditional in that it is only given to true followers of Christ. Those who genuinely and consistently follow the Savior obtain it. Charity is a spiritual gift in that it is acquired from God based on our personal prayers and desires to be true disciples of the Son of God. (Moroni 7:47–48)

Such divine love is deep and active. It does not wait to be loved but rather seeks to love first. It is concerned with substance not simply form. It is stronger and more potent than lesser forms of feeling in degree and kind, such as those like concern or kindness. It is inextricably linked with humility, faith, and hope. It never fails. This surely means that any endeavor motivated by charity is always inherently successful. Further, it endures forever meaning that it persists through difficulties of all types, and it lasts throughout time and eternity. It is the greatest of all as it is the supreme pinnacle of all personal attributes. (Moroni 7:43–48)

Charity allows us to accomplish eternally meaningful things with our lives. It is concerned with the lasting and significant things of life such as our reason for being and doing what we do (Moroni 7:45). We are to be clothed with it which suggests it is to become part of us and is to protect us and represent who and what we are to the world (Moroni 7:48). We are to possess it for all people, including those we dislike. Charity is bounteous and outward looking and flows from us to include all people regardless of their circumstances or backgrounds. It seeks to bless, lift, and help everyone it touches (Moroni 7:47).

This pure love is essential for exaltation. It is a qualifying requirement for godhood, not an optional extra (Moroni 7:46–47). Consequently, we are commanded to obtain it as opposed to invited to or suggested to (Moroni 7:46, 48). We are to cleave to it meaning to tie ourselves to it with a deep and abiding connection (Moroni 7:46). As we come to experience the blessings of obedience and repentance, we can come to be filled with pure charitable love (Alma 38:12; Moroni 8:17). As we seek to obey God, our hearts are overrun with deep and abiding love for others. Oh, how great is the correcting, directing, and comforting goodness of our God!

We are given to know that we can overcome defeat by choosing to cultivate the charity of Christ. As we become sure and solid in our works of faith, the Savior through His godly wisdom, power, justice, and mercy seals us as His true disciples. He takes us to the celestial heaven, there to have salvation in the form of eternal life (Mosiah 5:15). Those who gain eternal life through Christ are those who have come to know their Lord by personal experience when they had the opportunity to do so (Mosiah 15:23–25). Those who come to the Savior are mercifully, graciously, and tenderly received by Him (3 Nephi 9:14). The Savior is our continuous beacon and our ideal standard. We need to strive to follow Him in all things for the entirety of our lives (3 Nephi 15:9).

God both possesses and shares with His children a matchless bounty of love (Alma 26:15). God can help us to discover redeeming love on recognizing our release from the confining bands of death and the entangling chains of hell (Alma 5:9, 26). He enables us to develop strong, esteeming, and exceeding love for our spiritual leaders (Jacob 1:10; Mosiah 29:40). As we come to sense the love of God in our lives, we can grow ever closer to Him and indeed be filled with divine love (Mosiah 4:12; Alma 38:12). Indeed, we can in due course acquire the kind of pure love that Christ possesses (Moroni 7:47). This love is described as perfect, everlasting (Moroni 8:16–17), and enduring (Moroni 8:26). I have never heard of a better love story than that. Indeed, there is no love deeper, truer, more lasting, or more powerful than that!

Virtue

This is one of the most demanding doctrines of the restored gospel. I don't think I have ever met anyone who has sailed through life and found the law of virtue to be completely easy to live always. We all know what it is to be tempted in this area. It is most definitely through the grace of Christ that we can come to righteous and realistic terms with this commandment. Repentance is ever available to us if we are truly desirous of it. Nonetheless, the value of moral purity simply cannot be overstated. Given the deluge of immorality in our world the need for personal chastity has never been more important. We can radiate purity to the world only as we seek it ourselves. Let us consider some helpful insights into this theme.

The Lord loves morality as it blesses His beloved children (Moroni 9:9). I am assured that we can vanquish vice through the power of virtue. The Savior, who is described as a refiner's fire and like fuller's soap, can cleanse us from impurity. What better feeling can we have than to be made clean? (3 Nephi 24:2–3). Striving to be pure in heart gives us a powerful sense of well-being (2 Nephi 6:3; Enos 1:9–12;

Mosiah 28:3). The Lord helps us to be chaste in our thoughts, words, and deeds—this is a protective and holistic approach (Mosiah 4:30).

This spiritual law of purity applies to every accountable person everywhere, in every time and age of the world (Alma 42). Positive consequences always follow obedience, so it is wise to remember that we want to be blessed with good things (Alma 29:4). We draw close to God, others, and our own true selves as we base our choices on holy purity (1 Nephi 15:36; Alma 5:57). We want to rest comfortably in the presence of God, and as He is a holy being, we must become holy beings to be able to abide the glory of holy heaven (Alma 5:22–25; Helaman 13:27). God loves the lovely light of moral law (Jacob 3:3). As we seek moral holiness, the Holy Spirit dwells in us as living holy temples—meaning holy persons or places (Helaman 4:24).

Moral purity blesses us in that we are made free to truly feel real love (Moroni 7:47). Of course, striving to live with a pure heart and clean hands during an entire lifetime is not easy for any of us (2 Nephi 4:17–19). It requires real faith and courage to be chaste, especially when confronted with major unexpected challenges. It is often a daily battle that requires the best of us. We can choose to believe that the Lord's divine standard of virtue is possible and profitable for us to live by. When we fall, we can repent—how necessary and wonderful is the cleansing balm of repentance! (Mormon 9:6). As we learn to control and direct all our passions, we will be filled with joy (Alma 13:12). We will live lives of lasting goodness, great love, hopeful peace, and powerful happiness (Alma 33:23).

Remembering that we are literal spirit children of God empowers us to raise our sights to a higher level of seeing and behaving than we would without that understanding. We are independent spiritual agents with personal power to act righteously (2 Nephi 2:26). When we are tempted to be impure it is helpful to imagine ourselves and everyone else dressed in white and living up to their true potential. I have tried to envision others in the temple dressed in white. This will help us to view them with pure eyes. We will then be more inclined to be holy ourselves and to invite others to be holy also. It is extremely unlikely that we will sin with or against another person when we view both ourselves and them in a heavenly light (2 Nephi 9:49; Alma 23:3; Alma 27:28).

As we strive to be virtuous, we develop freedom from sorrowful regret (1 Nephi 13:8; Jacob 1:15). We obtain:

- pure desires and spirits (1 Nephi 8:10–12; Alma 41:5)
- pure thoughts and minds (2 Nephi 9:47)
- pure feelings and hearts (2 Nephi 25:16; Jacob 2:10; 3:1–2; Alma 5:19)
- pure actions and bodies (Mosiah 4:30)

This allows us to develop a clean character consisting of moral trustworthiness and integrity (2 Nephi 9:14; 30:6; Alma 13:12; 32:42).

Knowledge

When we are feeling that we lack understanding or guidance we can overthrow confusion by engendering resolute confidence in the knowledge and wisdom of God. God can give us a knowledge that is:

- Small (Jacob 4:2)
- Great (1 Nephi 1:1; 2 Nephi 10:20; Mosiah 5:4; Alma 24:36)
- Perfect (2 Nephi 9:13–14; 32:7; Alma 32:21, 26, 29; Jacob 4:12; 7:4; Moroni 7:15–17)
- True (2 Nephi 10:2; Helaman 15:13)
- Much (Mosiah 28:18; Alma 9:19; 3 Nephi 5:20)
- Exceeding (Helaman 6:34)
- Greater (Ether 4:13)

Indeed, God is full of truth (2 Nephi 2:6) and has all wisdom (Alma 26:35). And He loves to teach us of His ways!

Temperance, Diligence, and Patience

Alma encouraged the people he was teaching to be temperate in all things—moderate, controlled, disciplined (Alma 7:23). Likening this verse to ourselves, we are to be diligent in obedience always—meaning conscientious, responsible, careful—including when it is difficult to do so. We are to be fully patient, meaning not partially or inconsistently. These are particularly needful qualities to have when we face multifaceted setbacks, unexpected difficulties, and long-term challenges.

However, that is precisely what these attributes are designed for—they are at their best when the journey is long, when the trek is arduous, and when the temptation to give up is readily apparent. God will not call us to go through persistent growth without also facilitating us with the needed personal characteristics to proceed successfully. After all, God is involved in our long-term enhancement which stretches over a very long period. He takes a view which obviously requires a deep sense of longevity. Mighty trees take a long time to become such. We ought not to be confused that our growth takes a considerably enormous length of time, stretching from premortal life through mortality and into the eternities that lie before us.

Brotherly and Sisterly Kindness

The kindness that God possesses is described as loving (1 Nephi 19:9) and everlasting (3 Nephi 22:8). He enjoins us to become likewise kind on a deep and continual basis.

Humility

When we are disturbed by the haughtiness of pride, we can reduce the conflict within us by focusing on serene humility. We can strive to emulate deeply in our own lives the meek characteristics of our Savior in our lifelong quest for the spiritual life. Christ is believing and humble and we can be likewise. The starting point for our journey home is our desire to want to believe the gospel (Alma 32). Becoming humble is a key prerequisite to being ready to meet God and we can attend to this personal matter promptly and genuinely (Alma 5:28). This means having a soft heart willing to be divinely led, having a visionary mind, and being protected from evil both now and always, both in the body and in the spirit (1 Nephi 14:7). God speaks in plain humility (Ether 12:39) and with His help we can become:

- humble (Alma 13:28)
- truly humble (Alma 32:6, 14–15)
- more humble (Helaman 3:34)
- increasingly stronger in our humility (Helaman 3:35)

- able to obtain the deepest depths of humility (Helaman 6:5)
- exceedingly humble (3 Nephi 6:13)
- sufficiently humble (Ether 9:35)

Thus, genuine benevolence replaces the arrogance of bragging. Humility is quiet but powerful inner strength.

Work

The cultivation of our souls involves actual work. The Lord is not going to do our work for us. He will help us, but this still requires effort that can often be physically strenuous, emotionally uncomfortable, mentally difficult, socially exhausting, and spiritually demanding. It is spiritually focused work that makes people spiritually great. As expected, the restored gospel propounds the virtues of work. There is great worth in sincere, diligent, honest work.

We have a scriptural mandate to work for temporal survival and spiritual development. Worthy work has the power to bless lives and make us a godly person:

> Spiritually focused temporal work is a symbol of our spiritual journey home to the promised presence of God (1 Nephi 18:1).
>
> We are to work after all manner of temporal works and the Lord blesses us richly both temporally and spiritually for doing so (2 Nephi 5:15; Ether 10:22–28).
>
> We must work for our own support and to provide for those in need (Mosiah 27:4–5).
>
> Farming and making clothing are naturally productive and healing works (Mosiah 10:4–5).
>
> In terms of avoiding excessive materialism and indulgent luxurious vanity we are instructed to work with our hands but not to worship the objects we make as idols (2 Nephi 12:8).
>
> We need to work to defend ourselves, families, and property against spiritual and temporal attack from enemies (Alma 50:2).

We can obtain a bolstered resolve to work hard temporally and spiritually through internal and external challenges:

To do the work of salvation well the Lord helps us to believe in ourselves (Moroni 8:2) by teaching us that we are the great, marvelous, and wonderful work of His hands (1 Nephi 1:14; 2 Nephi 4:17; 27:34; Jacob 4:8).

We can work with the resources we have even when they are different to what we hope for or expect or are used to (Helaman 3:7).

We can work with success amidst sorrow (Alma 26:27), have much success (Alma 17:4), great success (Alma 23:4), and exceeding success with Godly help (Alma 59:1).

We can allow the Holy Ghost to work within us for our instruction and guidance by inviting us to do holy things (Jacob 4:15; Words of Mormon 1:7; Moroni 6:9) and thus come closer to God (Alma 19:36).

We can work a good work by serving God with divine power (Moroni 10:25) and by possessing good attributes within us (Alma 5:41; 7:24).

We can work many mighty miracles with divine help (4 Nephi 1:13; Mormon 9:16) while also humbly guarding against the self-inflicted poison of pride (Helaman 10:5).

We can engage in lifelong good works of righteousness (Alma 5:16; Mosiah 5:15) thus working in a way that will stand us in good stead at the final judgment (1 Nephi 15:32; Alma 11:41).

We can eternally rejoice in the ongoing work of salvation when we enter the kingdom of God (Alma 41:12–15).

The Bravery of Courage

When I was a young boy, I was extremely afraid of public speaking. When invited to speak in sacrament meeting at the age of 10, I was petrified. I did not realize at the time that people sometimes say no to such requests. The idea of refusing simply did not occur to me, so I said yes. I was nervous for the entire week or two prior to speaking. When I got up to speak that Sunday morning I was shaking like a small tree in a large storm. I had to hold tight to the pulpit as I thought my knees would buckle. My hands were perspiring heavily due to worry. I struggled to speak as I was filled with stage fright as it were. My mouth was dry beyond belief. However, I trusted in God and I got through the ordeal. I raced through the 150 seconds of my talk and then sat down.

My relief on concluding this time of trepidation was phenomenal. I admit that many times after that I faced and had to overcome a similar sense of trepidation. After having spoken literally hundreds of times in talks, classes, firesides, and other settings, I still sometimes have some initial fear in presenting. However, the fear is greatly reduced. In addition, I have learned to love speaking and teaching about the gospel. Some people might view it as terrible to put a child through this kind of ordeal. On the surface it might seem wrong and even abusive, but I disagree. I never would have learned to overcome this fear if I had not been asked to do it at such a young age and so frequently afterwards.

This incident reminds me of the charge to be "anxiously engaged in a good cause" (Doctrine & Covenants 58:27–28). This is simply to say that we are to be initiators in the work of the Lord. We are to be problem solvers, solution providers, creative actors. We are to work hard and smart at doing many good things without being compelled, nagged, cajoled, assigned, or reminded. Our power is to do good, not simply to act after we have been instructed continually and reminded regularly. Sometimes people say that the anxiously engaged in these verses does not mean anxious, worried, or stressed but rather means diligent, conscientious, concerned, interested, etc. I agree with that. However, I would also point out that I was fearful, afraid, nervous, frightened—yes, even anxious—at the thought of speaking in front of more than one hundred people when I was a child. However, I still acted. Hence, I was in fact anxiously engaged! I was actively involved even though I was terrified. This is the kind of thing that makes living the gospel such a joy because it requires hard things from us. Greatness is born from serious difficulty.

I have learned that spiritual light dispels spiritual darkness (Alma 26:3). Now the light of God within me gives me courage to face whatever fear confronts me (2 Nephi 19:2). I now see this message repeatedly (Mormon 8:14–16). Hence, when we are confronted by mental cyclones, psychological mountains, physical landslides, social tsunamis, spiritual earthquakes, financial shock waves, and emotional famines, the marvelous messages of revealed truth, comfort, and beauty can help us tremendously.

Fear is a barrier to our doing the work of the Lord. Cheerful and confident spiritual courage comes from the conviction that we are on the Lord's errand, and that He is mightier than all the earth (1 Nephi 4:1–3). We can be more concerned with pleasing God and really helping people than anything else. Consider the great examples of those who lived righteously and preached repentance continually:

Samuel the Lamanite—even when he was verbally and physically threatened (Helaman 13–15).

Alma the Elder—even when faced with being cast out and killed (Mosiah 17).

Lehi (1 Nephi 1), Abinadi (Mosiah 11, 18), and Nephi (Helaman 10:4)—even when threatened with unpopularity or death.

The young stripling warriors—who showed great valor in the face of war and gave the honor to God and their mothers (Alma 53:20).

Both Moroni and Joseph Smith—who safeguarded the Book of Mormon plates and preached its divine message despite threats of robbery, persecution, and death (Moroni 1 and Joseph Smith—History).

As we deliberately confront our foreboding and fears we can:

- learn to be bold but not overbearing (Alma 38:12)
- develop great courage (Alma 56:45)
- manifest exceedingly great courage (Alma 62:19)
- show exceedingly valiant courage (Alma 53:20) in doing the work of the Lord

With resolute bravery we can choose to develop mastery over our desires, control over our appetites, and discipline over our passions. Our character will be firm, solid, and strong. We will come to resemble our Lord, God, and King (Moroni 7:48). Our relationship with God will be one of seeing and being close to Him (3 Nephi 12:8). Our relationship with ourselves will be one of contentment due to our peace of conscience (Alma 38:12). We will then be well prepared to have never-ending comfort and happiness in the literal presence of God (Mosiah 2:41).

15

Becoming Majestic

In the scriptures, we are invited to ask of God, to knock on the door to heaven, to seek every good thing. Indeed, we are both to seek and find those things which are "virtuous, lovely, or of good report or praiseworthy" (Articles of Faith 1:13). The doctrine involved is that we believe not just in thinking about goodness, or learning about righteousness, or teaching about truth. We believe in doing good! We believe in good action, in holy practice. We believe in holistic goodness that covers every facet of life and every type of virtue. We seek after those things that are good. In other words, we desire everything and anything that is good, holy, beautiful, and righteous. The aim of discipleship is to help us to become eventually as good as God already is. God is:

- Immediately good—meaning in present circumstances (Mosiah 25:10)
- Supremely good—indicating there is no goodness He does not possess (Alma 12:32)
- Exceedingly good—revealing goodness far beyond the basic (Alma 60:11)
- Greatly good—showing His goodness is qualitatively superb (3 Nephi 4:33)

- Infinitely good—displaying His goodness as irrevocable, unchanging, and eternal (Helaman 12:1; Moroni 8:3)

Through Him we can partake of much good (2 Nephi 3:24) and every good (Moroni 7:20–22, 25, 28). Indeed, we are to become good in the godly sense!

Holiness

In the revealed word, holiness is associated with sanctification, blamelessness, purity, and righteousness (3 Nephi 28:39). It is one of the characteristics of Christ (Mormon 9:5; 3 Nephi 26:5). Holiness is therefore connected with uprightness. It is contrasted with misery by Lehi which means it is associated with happiness and joy (2 Nephi 2:10–11). We can develop holy hearts (Mosiah 18:12) as we partake of holy thoughts, dispositions, and actions. It is a blessing bestowed upon those redeemed by Christ (2 Nephi 8:11). Indeed, it is very much the attribute of being without spot, blameless, cleansed from all sin and iniquity through the cleansing grace of our Lord. We only become both perfect and sanctified in Christ by God's grace (Moroni 10:33). Our holy sanctity is therefore a Christlike one, it is to have all our sins washed away so that they cannot he held against us. We become without blemish through His cleansing blood. How remarkable is that?

Mercy

We can rejoice that God is truly merciful, genuinely compassionate, and rejoices in being generous (Alma 26:16–17, 20, 35–37). God has:

- Much mercy (2 Nephi 4:26)
- Great mercy (Jacob 4:10; 3 Nephi 22:7)
- Exceeding mercy (Jarom 1:3)
- Infinite mercy (Mosiah 28:4)
- Abundant mercy (Alma 18:41)
- Many mercies (Alma 34:38)
- A soul filled with mercy (3 Nephi 17:5–7)
- Tender mercy (Ether 6:12)
- Pure mercy (Moroni 8:19)

Thankfully, this mercy does not rob justice but can overpower justice when it comes to the penitent, so that God is both just and merciful (Alma 42:25).

Ability to Persist

In this process of character polishing, we become more substantial persons in that we can deal with difficulty, surmount tragedy, and continue through great challenge. Our inclination becomes one of hope rather than pessimism. We are actively looking for light, seeking for improvement, believing in progress. All these things are manifest in the goals we set, the agendas we pursue, the principles we value, the time we spend on certain pursuits, the outcomes we focus on, and the relationships we foster. Our interests become more aligned with what is worthy of our time and attention.

This upward reach is pleasing to the Lord. He is interested in our striving for a higher level, reaching a loftier life and seeking greater integrity. The music we gravitate toward, the books we incline to, the entertainment that draws us in, the lifestyle we cleave to—all these things are essentially shaped by the process of coming to see how the Savior sees us. He has the great vision of what we can become. This is not a small, limited vision. It is not injurious or controlling. It is good for us to catch the vision of what the Lord thinks can happen in our lives. The elevation of our souls is what He desires. As we move toward this newness of life, we become aware of the richness of this developmental experience. Our character is reformed, and we are brought to a great sense of personal wholeness and peace.

Consecration

We activate our divine growth through the process of submission and obedience. We know that we can submit ourselves to the invitations of the Holy Ghost by deliberately subjugating the carnal tendencies we all face (Mosiah 3:19). This is how we become an eternally better version of ourselves. The Savior can fully redeem us if we pursue a life of spiritual submissiveness and consecration (Mosiah 15:7). Our conversion can eventually become fully complete when we lose desire for all types, kinds, and degrees of sins. Our true, deep, overriding, and persistent desires are known to God and the actual living of our lives reveals our true beliefs and makes known to ourselves and others the desires of our hearts.

We can, with great personal effort and astounding divine intercession, gradually reach the point in this life where we are fully devoted to God (3 Nephi 28). The three Nephites fully repented of sin, were sanctified, and were immortalized by God (Ether 12:27). Then they spent all their time and effort without worldly distractions in the ministry of singing redeeming love (Alma 5). There is no higher life than this as we then find divine rest (heaven) on earth. To qualify for this divine life within we need to live according to our testimony even when it is uncomfortable, lonely, and dangerous to do so. We come to value God more than we value this life, this world, and all the opportunities of the world.

His Image in Your Countenance

Whose image do you see when you look in the mirror? Do you see a Christlike person looking back at you? Do you see the image of Christ?

Whose image does Christ see when He looks in a mirror? He sees His Father's, and His own. In similar manner, He sees others who appear like Him—in other words, His children.

In a brilliant teaching device of asking introspective questions, Alma asks members of the church, those who were already covenant disciples, if they had yet experienced a spiritual newness of life. He wanted to know if the likeness of the Savior was now reflected in *their* countenances. Were their inner natures, desires, and wishes transformed from worldly to divine? (Alma 5:14). Alma was interested in knowing if these church members could envision themselves at judgment day being approved of by the Savior because their mortal works were righteous (Alma 5:16).

Alma was enquiring if these members of the Lord's church could introspectively say of themselves that their interior life was unpolluted by carnal things. They needed to have both behavior that was upright and desires that were good. He essentially asked if the image of God was more than superficially upon them. The word he used was "engraven"—meaning recognizably and permanently etched—upon their image. This suggests a deep transformation in that the Savior becomes a visible and eternal influence upon our very thoughts, feelings, spirits, and bodies (Alma 5:19).

Alma instructs the people that the good shepherd calls the sheep. He says, "in his own name he doth call you, which is the name of Christ" (Alma 5:38). Moses was called "my son" by God, as was Joseph Smith. Think about that! We might therefore say that Moses was the son of Jehovah or Joseph was the son of Christ. Hence, if we were discussing family names and surnames, we might address Joseph by the full name of Joseph Smith Christ or Joseph Christ. This might appear shocking or even blasphemous to us, but it is in fact the promise of spiritual rebirth! Hence, the scriptures urge us to take His name upon us. This is not simply metaphorical. We are to receive a new name, a saving name, a godly name—His name. Do we define ourselves as spirit children of the Father and spiritually reborn children of Christ in the body? If we sense that we are His children and He is our Father, it becomes apparent that He acts in a fatherly way toward us. I have sensed His wonderful fatherly regard in my interactions with Him. His instruction has been timely, His training has been pertinent, His discipline needful, His attention helpful, His sacrifice vital, His watching reassuring, His investment encouraging, and His protection necessary.

We can consider the name we have taken upon ourselves. It has become our family name, our surname if you will. The doctrine is not simply that the name of Christ is placed upon us but also that the beauty of Christ infuses our souls. His character shapes us, His qualities mold us, His attributes become ours. He gives us infusion, not confusion! His love pervades us. As you and I follow Him, we are transformed from the inside out. Our hearts and minds are changed. Our countenances are even shaped and altered. We start to take on the characteristics of Christ, His divine nature, His perfect attributes. He sees us as worthy of His perfect name!

Let us consider the meaning of "El" in Hebrew. It means God. Consequently, we have these holy persons/places and the meaning of their names:

- **El**ohim—God
- Emmanu**el** (Jesus the Christ)—God is with us
- Micha**el** (Adam)—Who is like God?
- Ab**el** (Son of Adam and Eve)—Breath
- Gabri**el** (Noah)—Rest or repose
- Rapha**el—**God has healed
- Isra**el** (Jacob the son of Isaac)—Triumphant with God
- Rach**el** (wife of Jacob)—Ewe
- Ishma**el** (Son of Abraham)—God listens
- **El**ijah—Yahweh is my God
- Ezeki**el**—Strength of God
- Dani**el**—God is my judge
- Nathani**el—**Gift of God
- Samu**el**—God has heard
- Lemu**el**—Devoted to God
- Jo**el**—The Lord is God
- Ang**el**—Messenger of God
- Beth**el**—House of God
- Peni**el—**Face of God
- Hall**el**ujah—God be praised
- We also have the names ending in "**iah**", which perform a similar function in Hebrew:
- Azar**iah**—Helped by God
- Hezek**iah**—God gives strength
- Isa**iah**—God is salvation
- Jerem**iah**—Appointed by God
- Jedid**iah—**Beloved of the Lord
- Jos**iah**—God supports and heals
- Mos**iah**—Savior
- Nehem**iah**—God has comforted
- Sar**iah**—Princess of the Lord
- Zachar**iah**—God has remembered

It is wonderfully apparent that these people, places, and expressions have literally been given the name of God. As we follow Him, we become far more godlike in so many ways than we may realize. Even if our name does not contain "el" or "iah" in it, we will find that when God intervenes in our lives, He pours His name, power, love, and blessings into us. I invite you to consider how God has placed His marvelous goodness within you. You will find some precious insights as you do so.

I also note the following words. Although they are not related to Hebrew, they nevertheless teach us something important:

- Sentin**el**—a soldier or guard who keeps watch
- **El**evation—the action or fact of raising or being raised to a higher or more important level, state, or position.
- Tw**el**ve—as in 12 tribes of Israel, 12 apostles etc.
- He**l**d—grasp, carry, or support with one's hands
- Fid**el**ity—faithfulness to a person, cause, or belief, demonstrated by continuing loyalty and support

This is just a tiny sample. I am struck by the fact that God is written into the very nature of our language, our speech, our challenges, our relationships, our protections, our rejoicings, our sorrows, and our deepest hopes. Our very lives are embedded in the reality of the Supreme Being. His nature and character are consistently reflected in our lives.

As we learn to live righteously, we come to resemble God in our personal spiritual qualities. Then, we see the divine within us and in others. The divine mandate to become like God in every way then becomes our inspired destiny (3 Nephi 12:48). Achieving this is a gradual and monumental work and is accomplished with the enabling help of God at every stage of the journey. In this stretching and enlightening trek, we really discover through comprehensive understanding that the pure, undiluted work of God is truly beautifully desirable. In our upward climb toward God, we are stunned by beauty, educated by truth, polished through repentance, and enhanced through discipleship. Some things are simply beyond the capacity of mortal beings to fully comprehend (Mosiah 4:30). The eternally glorious blessings that await those who remain loyal to God's word are far greater than the blessings we have already experienced. As we learn to obey all the spiritual laws of God, we come to love ourselves with pure charitable love. How good, merciful, generous, kind, forgiving, and loving is our God! (Mosiah 23:15). The work of becoming perfectly good is the work of the master sculptor—we are His masterpiece in the making.

He loves the holiness He sees developing within you. He acknowledges your growth. He always sustains your efforts to elevate your life. He values the friend in you. He perceives an overcomer in you. He encourages the protector in you. He has tremendous hope in you.

16

The Refiner's Fire

God tells Israel that He has refined and chosen us "in the furnace of affliction" (1 Nephi 20:10). This scripture is a firm reminder that the children of God have a noble capacity for greatness. All expressing a willingness to come to the covenant of the House of Israel, have not been selected to face continual ease, luxury, and tranquility. Rather, they are picked to face great obstacles and surmount deep difficulty. They are both elected to confront trouble and made stronger in the very process of polishing that comes with the heat of trial, tears, and tribulations. They can be made like unto their fashioner as they personally experience the refining fires of all types, kinds, and degrees of testing.

The everlasting gospel helps us to gain important understanding about how to successfully persist through difficulties of all kinds and degrees. We learn that we should not be surprised that opposition in all things is a necessary feature of mortality (2 Nephi 2:10–15). This fallen world is the perfect testing ground for each of us in that we face the very things that we are reluctant to face. The most important lesson I have learned is to put my trust in God, especially when the circumstances are difficult. I have been divinely supported in every difficulty I have faced. We truly have the divine promise of eternal redemption (Alma 36:3, 27). The Prophet Joseph Smith had a remarkable and sustained capacity to rise above oppressive opposition; this stemmed to a great degree from the revelatory messages that imbued his thoughts, feelings, and actions (Mormon 8:22). Knowing that we each have a designated unique work to do on the earth and will be enabled to do it all as we serve the Lord provides power to endure anything and everything the world can throw at us (Alma 14:13).

I have come to believe that opposition is to be comprehended, meaning both understood and risen above. The restored gospel teaches us to face, transcend, and learn from these difficulties. There is no latter-day recession in the power of the Atonement of Christ to save us (3 Nephi 9:14). The mighty power of the priesthood protects and saves us. Many sacred and wonderful experiences happen as we ascend spiritual mountains and feel inspired. The Spirit comforts us, God strengthens us, and divine promises sustain us through intense sorrow, deep pain, pronounced disappointment, and mournful loss (Alma 60:13, 36). Through all these experiences we can find the most abundant life possible.

Difficulty can be our friend and benefactor. It allows our ascent to eternal glory. It may act as a blessing to us in mind, body, heart, and spirit. This refiner's fire challenges us and makes us great. Goodness can increase because of trouble. To be tried and tested is to have the opportunity to have our souls stretched. The daily walk of true discipleship is not an easy matter. Over a lifetime it is a spectacular achievement. It takes effort, courage, and persistence to endure in faith one day at a time. Over a lifetime this work amounts to a life of devotion, wisdom, and significant growth. To endure in righteousness each day is to achieve and accomplish something remarkable.

Facing each type of opposition, which comes often with deep intensity, and surmounting it, is admirable, commendable, and praiseworthy. It may seem a small or unimportant achievement at the time but daily discipleship—especially when it is conducted in the arena of serious challenge—represents slow but sure, steady, and real progress up the spiritual mountain that leads to God's actual presence. We can overcome all the danger, disease, and death that confronts us in this garden of testing called mortality.

Consoled by the Comforter

The Holy Ghost is both a powerful truth teller (Moroni 10:5) and a comforting peace giver (Doctrine & Covenants 6:23). I love the Holy Ghost. He is a real personage. He is a lovely Spirit. He is a "He" rather than an "it." I do not think of Him as simply a force, but rather a messenger of goodness, a true friend, a wise associate. He is our constant guide and our sure help if we will let Him be. He will bless, lift, and direct us. He warns us, brings us peace, and soothes our souls. He is loyal to His Father, true to Christ, and reliable to us. With His aid we become determined and assured. We gain lasting confidence and calm resolution through His influence. What a treasure! He truly is a constant companion if we will invite Him to travel with us. If we cultivate an environment in which He would be glad to dwell, He will be close to us each day of our lives. We need the *Holy* Ghost to be with us to become *holy* people.

As I have reflected on the Holy Ghost and His influence in our lives, I have been struck—at times gently and at times powerfully—by the following roles of this holy personage:

Prompter—It was He who moved upon the young Joseph Smith to ask of God in prayer in a manner that caused Joseph to act.

Revelator—It is He who inspires, uplifts, and cleanses us.

Testifier—It is He who impels sacred words and ideas into our very souls so that we are blessed to know, feel, and understand divine truth. He does this with varying degrees of intensity depending on our need, but always in a way that reaches us deeply if we allow it.

Leader—It is He who directs individuals, families, wards, stakes, the entire Church, and the whole world to come unto Christ through service, obedience, and instruction. The people who need the restored gospel are often the people in our sphere of influence. Do we need to find them or just see them anew through the eyes of the Holy Ghost?

Comforter—It is He who consoles us in our afflictions, large and small, daily and always, deeply and generously.

Gift—It is He who brings spiritual gifts into our lives. As we remember and repent, these remarkable endowments change us and thereby bless others.

Guide—It is He who seeks not to dominate or control us but to lovingly help us to make major decisions. He is trustworthy, honest, and reliable.

Teacher—It is He who speaks to our minds and hearts with words of peace, doctrinal insights, and messages of hopeful encouragement.

Protector—It is He who warns us of all types of danger and keeps us safe from spiritual deception as we faithfully and humbly listen and obey.

I am so thankful that the Holy Ghost leads us onward, forward, upward, and heavenward. He does not encourage us simply to stay as we already are but rather to become better "line upon line, precept upon precept" (2 Nephi 28:30). This is incremental, almost imperceptible, advancement. However, it is sure and steady.

Thus, when we feel turmoil within, we can remember that God is peaceful. He will surely help us to quiet our internal battles through His ministry of peace. God can bless us with:

- Continual peace (Mosiah 1:1)
- An undisturbed peace (Mosiah 27:4)
- Much peace (Alma 1:33)
- A state of peace (Alma 40:12)
- An entire peace (Alma 51:2)
- Peace spoken to our very souls (Alma 58:11)
- An exceedingly great peace (Helaman 11:21)
- An enjoyable peace (3 Nephi 6:16)
- Some degree of peace (3 Nephi 7:14)
- A constant covenant of peace (3 Nephi 22:10)
- A walk of peace (Moroni 7:4)

I know something about ailments. A quarter of a century ago I developed a peptic ulcer. This was my first serious experience with physical and emotional pain that was not caused by another person. I was very stressed and confused by it. Feeling like someone is digging your insides out with a screwdriver is not heaven on earth. I had lots of medical tests and finally got triple therapy treatment. What a relief it was for me to get that help! But pain has been a friend in disguise—it has taught me so much. Seven years later my ulcer recurred.

More pain, sorrow, and triple therapy! The treatment did not seem quite so effective this time but still helped somewhat. I have also experienced firsthand the severe pain of food poisoning—that was no garden picnic. This refiners fire was a prelude in the process of preparing me for a newness of life.

I have only had two bone fractures in my entire life. Both occurred at church activities. The first was when I was playing basketball at the stake center. I collided with another person in the air and then ended up on the floor. The pain was great. I did not sleep well that night and went to the hospital the next morning. It took at least six weeks for my elbow to recover, so I was at home for that time. I pondered much on cause and effect, as it was impacting me personally! The second event was playing dodge ball with the youth in a cultural hall. I was too competitive and wearing the incorrect footwear for the task did not help. I tripped and fractured the very same elbow as before. I hope I have learned to be wiser now but only time will tell! My elbow still clicks years later as a reminder that life happens in ways we cannot possibly always anticipate! God allows us to experience outcomes from our choices—how else can we learn to be wiser? If He were to step in and prevent every undesirable outcome, this shielding from pain would keep us in the role of children forever.

About 20 years ago I started to experience much pain which was different from the ulcer. I needed much medical testing and faced much stress. I felt deep and regular pain. Before and after the diagnosis of Irritable Bowel Syndrome, it seemed like a never-ending stream of problems. I took medication which worked initially, but gradually I had to change to other medications that worked for a time but eventually stopped working. I was desperately sore many times and alternated between constant visits to the bathroom and being in bed exhausted for many days. There is a great education in experience. I have learned lessons from this suffering that I could never have understood before, such as empathy for those who suffer. I am grateful that my faith is still intact. In fact, it is stronger than it has ever been. Difficulty does not have to diminish our faith and instead can truly strengthen and refine it.

My sickness eventually culminated in very serious, major medical surgery. I often asked myself if there was a root emotional problem that I was unaware of or was refusing to look at. I have learned that there was, and I am now much better at detecting these problems at the root and dealing with them before they become almost insurmountable. It is my conviction that the emotional and spiritual difficulties we face can manifest themselves in the physical. I am convinced that is what happened to me. Fifteen years of intense stresses and strains led to physical burnout of an extreme kind. I have had a similar thing happen to me emotionally where for a time I literally could not function normally because of the intense stresses and strains that had completely overcome my physical, emotional, and even spiritual well-being for a time. I was forced to rest and that was the only way I could recuperate.

What was the Lord trying to teach me? I know He was educating me in gaining a new perspective, a greater sense that choices have consequences sometimes foreseen and sometimes not, an improved capacity to love, a better view of the importance of the preciousness of the life we have. I have also endured persistent joint pain, emotional lows, concentration challenges, memory lapses, skin troubles, nose bleeds, and headaches—to name just some. The joint pain has been especially frustrating as I have had to limit my exercise which is not my preferred option. I had very much enjoyed running, dancing, stair climbing, trampolining, skipping, etc. but find now that they can put too much strain on me unless I am wise. Wear and tear from many years of use combined with a chronic medical condition means that I have had to lessen my efforts quite dramatically.

Of course, I did not give it up altogether as I enjoy the feeling of aliveness and health that come from exercising. I walk much and try to appreciate the gift that is to me. We can always find something to be grateful for if we look hard enough. Each of these experiences has been difficult to endure. However, each has softened my heart, mellowed my nature, calmed my rush to judgment, expanded my sympathy, enlarged my empathy, deepened my patience, turned me to God, and helped me to be thankful in heightened ways that would not be possible otherwise. My three medical surgeries, time spent in hospital, and literally hundreds of medical visits and tests over the years have taught me much about compassion for those who suffer. I have also come to understand that we need to find healthy outlets for the deep stress we face lest we become overcome by it. I have known that God is much closer to us than we sometimes suppose.

I also know much about other types of trials including car and house trouble, false allegations from others including close friends, losing my father and stepfather to death, failing to get some job opportunities, facing the sickness and other extreme troubles of family members, navigating the world of interpersonal conflict in various settings, feeling downhearted when seeing the hostilities of this fallen world constantly, feeling the pinch of coming under fire from opposition of diverse kinds, witnessing the suffering of people and animals throughout the world, and sometimes feeling like a complete failure in my efforts to do and be good. All of this is a necessary part of my mortal journey. It is expedient that I become acquainted with all these things so that my mortality can mean something truly precious to me. I have become much more attuned to God's refining power in my life.

Endurance

Of course, we each face challenging troubles of every kind and degree in a real crucible of affliction. These are stark realities in a world of real choice, genuine trouble, and contrasting alternatives. God faithfully provides the way through (not out of) all difficulties, even if sometimes that takes more time and patience than we wish it did. As we come to understand spiritual truth, we come to see God, others, and ourselves in a very hopeful light. The restored gospel is a joyful way of life, a way of thinking, seeing, acting, and being that can transform everyone and anyone from being a gross sinner to a most humble saint (Alma 26).

Study of Scriptural Doctrine

I have learned to love the word of God with great rejoicing. There is potent power in God's word. It is an intensely optimistic message of gratitude and joy amidst our difficulties. There is nothing more motivating. The pure word can:

- **touch** us deeply, **nourish** our hungry and thirsty spirits, and **stay** in our memories always (Enos 1:3)
- **console** us in our afflictions (Jacob 3:1)
- **please us and heal** our wounded souls (Jacob 2:8)
- **enable** us to experience the mighty change of heart (Alma 5:12).
- **more powerfully impact** us than anything and everything else in life including suffering through violence and experiencing life trials of all kinds (Alma 31:5)
- **allow** us to work out our individual salvation (Alma 34:37).

We can find respite from loneliness through the power in the word of God. Instead of being forever down in the dumps, we can be quickly and regularly immersed in inspiration. The desire to believe in the gospel can work within our hearts so that we can give the glorious gospel a fair chance to really take root inside ourselves (Alma 32:27–28). The restored gospel is the highest truth, the greatest good, the best possible reality and the most wonderful life. However, we only come to see this gradually through a process of faith, time, and experience. Spiritual truth is both fundamentally simple and deeply profound. It provides for spiritual signs and generous gifts and is the perfect vehicle for personal development.

Our own conversion inexorably inspires us to want to share the good news of the gospel with others. For example, even many of the very hard-hearted Lamanites who were hardened by anger were converted on hearing the soul softening word of God (Mosiah 28:7). The word of God is a constant companion on the road of life, even when no other mortals travel with us. Scriptural doctrine lodges itself within our souls and unlocks strength to persevere. For me, the scriptures and the words of prophets and saints across the world have been a constant bulwark to my soul. I have learned so many wonderful and precious truths from the revealed word that have shaped my life in marvelous ways.

For a Wise Purpose

It is such a powerful education to us to see both beauty and ugliness, health and sickness, success and failure, freedom and bondage, harmony and conflict, rejoicing and disappointment, happiness and sadness, loneliness and belonging, friendship and betrayal, excellence and mediocrity. Only this can help us to become what we are destined to become. The stronger the opposition against us, the more important it is that we are true to our principles (Alma 56:56). Great blessings both precede and come after great opposition, when we remain true and faithful to God. If we trust in God, the painful joy of mortality helps us to become spiritually mature vessels of love and light (Alma 26:35).

Each person has unique tests and trials to face and the background context impacts on every important choice we make, but sin has no inevitable hold over us as we are free at the core despite powerful temptation. It is good to resist giving in to passions, appetites, or desires. It is also a miracle to repent and be forgiven as it heals our spirits and restores our faith (Jacob 6:5). We can embrace heavenly uplifting forces and with self-control we are free to become masters of righteousness. If we are humble, the difficulties we face refine and perfect us.

Our Father in Heaven allows us to experience inclinations opposed to His plan of salvation in mortality for the purpose of helping us to see that we need Him. It is also vital for us to learn the difference between true chaste love which promotes the plan and physical lust which denigrates it. The physical wants of the natural man can be replaced by the spiritually righteous desires of the saints of God (Mosiah 3:19).

We can succeed spiritually in the arena of life. We can have power over our impulses. Sinful desires can be surmounted through personal agency, combined with the strong power of the infinite Atonement of the Lord. Instead of being submerged by sin, we can feel sunlight in our soul. We can become a spiritually minded person who is a friend to God. Godly persons can and do possess the power of God in a degree, as heaven is inhabited and ruled by those who have learned to govern their passions through righteous principles. The beautiful powers of heaven reside within us as we become more spiritually enlightened (Alma 40:12).

All sin can eventually be overcome including actual behavior and even the very desire to sin. And even if some thorns in the flesh remain to the end of our mortal lives it must surely be the case that such are removed in the resurrection. This is divine, uplifting, empowering, wonderful, and eternally liberating doctrine! The wisest use of this life is to follow the perfect guidance of our Heavenly Father in all important matters. The Spirit lets us know with deep spiritual certainty that we can rely for our redemption on God totally, completely, and without reservation (2 Nephi 7:2). Eventually we will know what is mysterious or unknown to us now. The scriptures are books of faith and the doctrinal lessons they teach us are vitally important.

Enter the Rest of the Lord

There is such a thing as entering into the rest of the Lord in this life. We can actively undermine doubt through the fortitude that comes from fueling our faith. Our faith is to be focused on the Son of God. This genuine belief and reassuring trust allows us to look forward to a time of incomparable, everlasting rest in Jesus Christ. This rest will be a precious reward to those who have wrestled against the great difficulties of this world. Thankfully, the scriptures teach us that we can have a great portion of spiritual rest in this life. This holy rest connotes a sense of relief, contentment, and respite. Divine rest indicates an enjoyment of the fruits of our sincere labors and endurance. Indeed, our Lord has promised that when He comes to the earth in glory in the last days that He will bring a marvelous rest to the faithful House of Israel from sorrow, fear, and bondage (2 Nephi 24:3).

We are taught in the revelations about three types of rest—of the body, of the spirit, and of the soul:

> Regarding the body, we learn that difficult spiritual and temporal journeys require that we rest our bodies (1 Nephi 16:7), that the Lord gives us rest from sorrow, fear, and hard bondage (2 Nephi 24:3), and that there are times when we need to rest from our labors and recover from our sufferings (Mosiah 7:16; Alma 8:1).

Regarding the spirit, we learn that trusting in the certain promises of God allows our souls to rest (Enos 1:17) and to rest spiritually is to always do good works in a spirit of meek submissiveness (Alma 37:34).

Regarding the soul, we are taught that drawing close to God is described as entering into His rest (Jacob 1:7; Alma 12:34; 13:12–13); that through faith, repentance, and lifelong faithful endurance we are made clean before God and made ready to enter into His rest (3 Nephi 27:19); that as we labor in righteousness consistently we conquer the adversary and eventually find rest in the kingdom of God (Moroni 9:6); and that the peaceable followers of Christ's church have a hopeful rest in Him in this mortal life and a rest with Him in heaven also (Moroni 7:3).

With a spirit of rejoicing, anticipation, and excitement we learn to see our mortal challenges in a very different light. Whatever circumstance we encounter in this life can work for our temporary blessing and everlasting joy. Because of our faith in the promises of the Lord made certain through His Atonement and resurrection, we can hope to be lifted to eternal life (Moroni 7:41). Our true confidence is in the righteous redeemer who gives us hope of eternal life, which rests in our minds forever (Moroni 9:25). What better, higher, and holier thoughts could we have than these?

The restored gospel promises that one day the righteous will rest from all their mortal afflictions (Alma 34:41). In the spirit world the righteous go to a peaceful place called paradise where they rest from their worldly sorrows, cares, and troubles—what a relief that will be! (Alma 40:12; Moroni 10:34). The spiritual rest of the righteous during the Millennium will be consolingly glorious (2 Nephi 21:10). Being with the Savior means being in a place and condition of rest as we will be at personal peace with Him (Enos 1:27; 3 Nephi 28:3). Entering the presence of God forever means living in His rest eternally (Alma 13:29; 60:13). We sense His aid along the mortal journey. However, only when we reach the blissful destination of His eternal presence will we fully understand the need for the educational hardships we have passed through. Only then will we appreciate fully the great, joyful, and peaceful rest that has been bestowed upon us. Heaven is not simply a place for us to go to, it is also a condition of being. I believe that passing through sorrow is a necessary preparation for jubilant joy. For this to occur, we need to be softened by difficulty, polished by trouble, and refined by hardship. We need to become like gems of love in the form of diamonds of compassion, rubies of empathy, emeralds of forgiveness, and sapphires of concern. Our tough tenderness will endure eternally.

Cleansing the Inner Vessel

I know what it is to be forgiven of my sins. I have felt cleansed from my willful rebellion, my stubborn pride, my resistant shortcomings, and my limiting weaknesses. I have felt my sins washed away. I have known the erasing of my burden. I have felt it deeply. What relief I have known! What gladness that my stupidity is no longer a barrier to my progress. What peace to know Christ has wiped my selfishness away. What joy to know that I am clean! I have felt the sorrow removed, the guilt swept away, the joy return. I have known how my past has been blotted out, my transgressions mentioned no more, my soul allowed to soar! I know that Christ is the Savior of my soul. I know this intimately, personally, deeply, everlastingly!

We can transcend discouragement through receiving holy aid. God is clean both physically and spiritually. Cleanliness helps us to feel closer to Him. Our physical bodies are the outer vessel, and we all feel better after getting our bodies cleaned. Our inner vessel is our spirit. The cleansing that the Lord has in mind concerns not only the temporal body but also the inner vessel of our spirits. This involves our inner thoughts, feelings, words, deeds, motives, desires, and attitudes. The Lord always warns against spiritual duplicity. Spiritual cleanliness is the best, most beautiful, and happy way to live. This requires facing the battle over good and evil that goes on within us and striving to come off conqueror against our own carnal weaknesses, faults, and failings. Our internal desires and attitudes can be purified, refined, and made holy (Moroni 7:48).

God our Father has made the principles of His gospel possible, albeit challenging, to live (Alma 37:13). Sin is not necessarily inevitable and certainly serious sin is not inevitable. Of course, all of us are liable to sin during our lifetimes. In our fallen state we are all subject to small and large temptations. And although we advocate obedience in the first instance, we all need the precious gift of repentance desperately. Mistakes are very common as part of the process of mortality for all of us and God teaches us how to transcend these also. So God does prepare a way for us to avoid sin, or having sinned, to be reclaimed. This way is through our full acceptance of the atoning sacrifice of Jesus Christ which allows for redemption from sin and His perfect example allows us to reach for that divine standard in our own lives (Alma 38:9).

Our Savior is like a refiner and purifier of both gold and silver, two of the most precious substances on the planet. These metals when purified are of great worth because of what they symbolize—the value people place on them because of their rarity and meaning. They represent a special love. Spiritually, we are of far more worth to our Redeemer than any metals. He shows the value He places on us by His efforts to sanctify and save us. He can do this because He has the tremendous ability to clean our souls from the effects of sin. He can clean us in ways we cannot clean ourselves. He makes us qualified to stand in His holy presence. He literally purifies our souls just as fire purifies metals to make them more precious or as soap gets strong stains out of clothing (3 Nephi 24:2–3). His love has a cleansing impact upon us!

We can nullify the impacts arising from sin by immersing ourselves experientially in the doctrines of salvation. The adversary employs bodily temptation to achieve his desired ends of capturing us (3 Nephi 18:18). It is therefore important to use bodily resistance against his efforts. We are richly blessed to have wise prophets who warn against immorality in all forms, including pornography (Jacob 2:3). It is good in our quest for a life of virtue that we strive to avoid addictive entanglement (2 Nephi 13:9). The prophet Jacob warned his people against even starting to go down the road of thinking about unchastity because it leads to the conduct of unchastity (Jacob 2:5, 22–23).

Shunning, resisting, or moving away from immorality is a spiritually beneficial choice. We can desire to live by a much higher and happier standard than appeals to our sense of nature or duty alone (Alma 41:10). Both the desire (temporary drive) to do good continually and the disposition (more permanent inclination) toward righteousness are to become part of our very nature (Mosiah 5:2). The spiritual man is a friend to God because he is drawn to God and likes the same type of life that God does. He loves the doctrines God loves. He gravitates toward behavior that God rejoices in! Charity is the more excellent way of pure love that comes as we direct all our passions toward nobility (Moroni 7:47; Alma 38:12). The Lord's standard of chastity means wearing both modest clothing and the spiritual armor of God.

The Savior asks us to use our power of choice righteously or, having used our agency unwisely and having become caught in the relentless grip of addiction, He endeavors to persuade us to accept personal responsibility for our actions. He helps us to see the need to change and indeed helps us to change. He thereby uses both our agency and His Atonement to free us from sin. He helps us to see that we need to help ourselves and we also need to rely on our Redeemer (Alma 7:14; see also 2 Nephi 31:19; Alma 12:15; 34:18). Ultimately, we can overcome temptation altogether. We can reach a point where the adversary has no power over us because we lose the very desire to sin (2 Nephi 9:49). This is beyond even self-mastery. We receive the divine help of God so that our very natures are deeply changed. Such a change goes far beyond a change in perspective or even in behavior alone. Thus, our Savior suffered the affliction of addiction so that He could understand and help us to overcome it permanently (Mosiah 3:6–7; Alma 7:11–12).

The Power of the Lord

We can avoid apathy through exciting experiences with the power of God. Repentance is readily available to all willing to receive it. Virtue can propel us along the path to happiness and God can turn our red sins into pure, white, and clean righteousness. Only the restored gospel of Christ can redeem us from sin and bring us entirely and everlastingly into His cleansing embrace. I love the words of Ammon, which are some of the most potently hope-inspiring in scripture, about the goodness of God and His ability to save us from sin (Alma 26:15–16). Through the Atonement of the Son of God all persons may be saved. All means all. Christ can heal us completely. Of course, this does not occur based on His grace alone because our submission to Him is needed too. This washing of our souls is possible through genuine discipleship. It may be a long, difficult journey, but His word is certain, and His promises are sure. His help is powerful and constant.

There is marvelous wonder attached to eternal life. As we learn, know, and remember the word of God it will instruct, uplift, comfort, and edify us all the days of our mortal lives. We need all the help we can get on this difficult mortal quest toward the greatest type of divine existence there is. We are to be elevated to a much higher plane of existence, a much more glorious and grand way of living. This is what we were designed for and prepared for in the beginning. This is beyond our present spiritual imagination. In this mortal world we may have great fame, fortune, status, degrees, talent, etc. These may indeed be very impressive and worthwhile. However, none of these can compare with the splendor of achieving the fulness of our divine gifts, talents, and abilities. There is no greater satisfaction than having arrived at this condition of perfect being and fulfilment, which is to achieve the supreme pinnacle of perfection and to help others do likewise eternally. Eternal life is truly the greatest of all the divine bestowals of God. This is a firsthand, witnessing, and experiential knowledge. Our everlasting treasure in heaven is the precious gift of eternal life (Helaman 5:8).

In God's Strength

While the Lord expects us to be up and doing, He does not expect us to labor alone. The word of God teaches that we can go forward in the work of God with His divine help to assist us. We need to remember this often, especially in this fallen world where it is so easy to forget the real source of our power. God helps us with refreshing change, wonderful life, illuminating light, true happiness, edifying love, glimpses of beauty, transforming joy, and profound meaning. In the strength of the Lord, we can go confidently forward, genuinely onward, and truly upward.

Although we all struggle to live an ideal gospel in an imperfect world, we can overcome our weaknesses through the might of God. And we can face weakness in a constructive way that is neither pride inducing nor discouragement promoting. Repentance is a loving and merciful divine doctrine of relief from self-imposed burdens. We have many prophetic witnesses pleading with us to repent genuinely in mortality because they really love us (Alma 34:32–34). Repentance joyfully leads to the reward of a sure eternal happiness (Alma 42:16).

For example:

> Nephi said, "Oh wretched man that I am" but he later said, "I know in whom I have trusted" (2 Nephi 4: 17–19).
>
> Alma said, "Oh that I could be extinct in both body and soul" but he later said, "Oh what joy I felt" (Alma 36:15, 20).
>
> Enos said "The wrestle I had" but he also said afterwards, "My soul did rest" (Enos 1:2, 17).
>
> Ammon was "the very vilest of sinners" but later "could not bear that any human soul should perish" (Mosiah 28:3–4).
>
> What a stark contrast! God can really replace our darkest nights with brightest days! He can change us in miraculous and lasting ways (Alma 7:13–14).

We can transcend the scarcity of an unsatisfying life of sin through the bounty of becoming more like God. The Lord gives us great opportunities and makes us responsible agents. These obligations are a privilege as they help us to learn judgment, wisdom, justice, and mercy. Revelatory messages equip us to cope well with pain, sorrow, and disappointment and to surmount error, sin, and unhappiness. Our enduring can be more than merely coping—it can mean rising to new spiritual heights (1 Nephi 11).

When we are feeling that life is unfair, that we are failing, and that happiness eludes us, we can be reminded that God is a being of justice and can bless us to be likewise (Mosiah 2:38; Alma 12:18). God is a victorious being and can bless us with great triumph (Alma 46:7; 57:22). Our God is happy, and He can make us happier than we currently are and we could otherwise ever be (4 Nephi 1:16); bring us to a state and nature of happiness (Alma 41:11; Mormon 7:7); and can bestow upon us endless eternal happiness (Mosiah 2:41; Alma 3:26; Mormon 8:38). We can trust these hopeful promises.

When we feel weak and powerless, our strong God can bless us with:

- much strength (Jacob 5:18)
- greater strength (Alma 56:18)
- full strength (Alma 52:31)
- miraculous strength (Alma 56:56)
- exceedingly great strength (3 Nephi 3:14)
- mighty strength (Ether 7:8)

We will need that strength to rise above every weakness in life, especially those ones that are a thorn in the flesh to us.

God is a Being who has:

- All power (Mosiah 4:9)
- Mighty power (Mosiah 23:24)
- Everlasting power (Alma 36:29)
- Miraculous, Marvelous, and Matchless power (Mosiah 1:13; Alma 9:11; 10:5; 57:26; Helaman 4:25)
- Almighty power (Mormon 9:26)

He can therefore:

- fill us with power (1 Nephi 17:48)
- enable us with exceedingly great power (Helaman 6:5)
- give us such power (Helaman 8:12)
- bestow upon us greater power (3 Nephi 7:18)
- bless us with convincing preaching power (3 Nephi 28:29)

What wonderful, generous, expanding, and magnificent help! We will need this power to overcome every serious enemy of our lives and to accomplish the phenomenally difficult tasks that confront us now and in the future.

When we feel uncared for or that a cloud of spiritual threat hangs over us, we can undermine apathy through the blessing of comfort. Our Savior cries over us, prays for us, blesses us, and will one day hug us literally (see Alma 26:15; 3 Nephi 17:21–22; Mormon 5:11; 6:17). We can be greatly strengthened by knowing the tough tenderness of Christ. We can know the splendid nature of His beaming qualities (3 Nephi 12:14). God is beautiful and He can help us to experience His saving love which is far beyond beauty (1 Nephi 11:8) and exceeding of all beauty (1 Nephi 11:8). He can help us to become most beautiful (1 Nephi 11:15). His creations can be very beautiful (Mosiah 23:4), reminding us of the loveliness of His glorious endeavors.

When we feel unfulfilled inside, we can be reminded of 4 key truths regarding joy:

1. It is **from God and is real**. God feels jubilant joy.
2. We can **feel** it. We can be joyful (Alma 13:25), feel most joyous (1 Nephi 11:23), and feel great joy (1 Nephi 13:37).
3. We can **increase** in it. We can be filled with joy (1 Nephi 5:1, 7), experience increased joy (2 Nephi 19:3), know exceedingly great joy (Mosiah 3;13), have much joy (Alma 2:8), be filled with great joy (Alma 4:14), gain added joy (Alma 17:2), know such joy (Alma 19:6), feel overpowering joy (Alma 19:14), be brim with joy (Alma 26:11), be carried away with joy (Alma 26:35), be swallowed up in joy (Alma 27:17), rejoice with incomprehensible joy (Alma 28:8), know more full joy (Alma 29:14), sense sweet and exquisite joy (Alma 36:21), delight in exceeding joy (Alma 36:24), and have hearts swollen with joy (3 Nephi 4:33).
4. It can **last forever**. We can taste everlasting joy (2 Nephi 8:11).

What great and needed promises these are! Great and glorious joy awaits us as we pursue these glad tidings.

It is possible to learn to resist temptation. We can learn to school our feelings, educate our motives, reign in our aspirations, refine our appetites, and control our thoughts. Captain Moroni was a man who yielded his heart to God willingly and genuinely. We are told that he got to the point of spiritual development where the adversary's attempts to entice him were futile. This is a powerful doctrine. It is both true and faith promoting to know that each of us can come off conqueror in the great battles of the soul that are waged inside of us. By doing this, the children of God can become renewed in stunning righteousness. By this submission of soul, we can gain all victory and prepare the earth for a day of majestic glory that is to come soon (see Alma 48:17).

Having mortal life is good, but having spiritual life is even better and having celestial life is best of all (2 Nephi 33:4). Repentance, baptism, and subsequent lifelong obedience leads certainly to this eternal life (Jacob 6:11). This life, which is beyond our present comprehension, is after all a gift of our beloved God. Endurance is a worthwhile necessity, a journey of discovery, and an enjoyable privilege. When we finally close our eyes for the last time as we pass on to the next life, imagine the peace and relief that we will feel knowing that we have been firm in the faith. This reassuring certainty gives us our needed spiritual daily bread and water along the long road leading to our anticipated eternal reward.

I wrote a poem in 2017 that reflects my deep desire to cleave to the Savior of my soul, notwithstanding all the fierce opposition I have experienced:

Battered Harshly
Beaten Down
Bloodied Mercilessly
Cursed Rage!
That Bespeaks my Strongest Weakness
My Unexpected Blight
O Dominion of Darkness
I am Not Thine
O Strange Enemy
Strangle not My Better Nature
My Feeble Wish
My Fainting Knowledge
Attack the Monstrous Foe
Awake, Arise, Uphold
The Near Forgotten Dream
The One Bright Ray of Hope
I Cannot Forget
It is Within Me Still
Majestic Meaning
Transcend Triumphant
The Ascending Staircase
The Pivotal Pronouncement

The Heavenly Expedition
This Journey of My Timid Soul
To a Land I Must Endeavor to Reach
And Why Not?
For Mercy's Sake
Unleash the Mighty Weapon
Forbid Me Not
Please, I Beg Thee
O Caring Light
O Home Amidst the Clouds
Welcome Me Yet
And Cast Thine Benevolent Eye
Upon My Captivated Fellow Travellers
Uphold Them Upon the Sands
Make Their Feet Stronger than Clay
Survey Their Great Introspection
They are Looking to Thee Still
They are Reaching Yet
O Captain of My Broken Soul
Be With me, Near Me
Hold Me
In Thy Mighty Arms
Thine Blessed Gaze
Let Me See
And Never Depart from Beauty!

Although I have failed many times in my quest for discipleship, I know that hope is ever available. I am still striving, wrestling, struggling, and trying. It is my earnest desire to look to Him, reach for Him, cleave to Him. I know that the Savior is stronger than my enemies. His success is greater than my deepest failure. His power is more than my weakness. His knowledge transcends my ignorance. His love buoys up my heart.

In like manner, consider how far you have come in the race of life. Think about the many trials you have passed through without giving up, the appealing temptations you have resisted, the love you have shown in the face of hatred, the forgiveness you have offered when you were hurt, the service you offered when you felt too tired, the times you checked your words to protect others, the moments you calmed your angry feelings, the experiences where you overcame desires for retribution and instead extended peace. You have covered more miles than you know, overcome more obstacles than you realize, said many genuine prayers, read the word of God thousands of times, awoken many mornings with the resolve to keep going. You have triumphed more than you think. You have done far more good than you know, answered the prayers of many others, lifted the burdens of the weary, and inspired the faith of those hanging on for a word of consolation. Your suffering has sanctified your soul, mellowed your spirit, softened your heart, and quietened your tempest within. The Redeemer has purified your soul through the fire of difficulty, the pang of sorrow, and the challenge of tribulation. He is the great cleanser, healer, comforter, and redeemer of our souls!

By a similar token, we can look forward with an eye of faith (Alma 5; 32) to achieving the great potential within us. As we look back to see God's hand in our lives, we also need to look to the future with a sense of visionary expectation and believe that God will help us to achieve our possibilities. As we gain perspective about the fact that mighty trees take a long time and much effort to become magnificent, we come to see that the nature of our developmental growth toward the astonishing grandeur we can acquire is a long term one. It takes a considerable amount of time and effort. It requires a long view. It needs a premortality, a mortality, and a post-mortality before it can come to full fruition. It happens incrementally, in the context of difficulty, and takes patience to allow it to unfold adequately. Hence, why lifelong learning, reflection, perseverance, and perspective are so important. Each stage of life in our life cycle comes with its own needs, demands, opportunities, and challenges for very good reason!

And It Came to Pass

The phrase "and it came to pass" carries an important message when we are weighed down with affliction. All mortal opposition, including persecution, worry, and heartache, is temporary and will eventually end (Alma 34:41). This is not to make light of serious difficulties, but it may serve to minimize their potentially negative impact on us in the here and now. The consoling and reassuring doctrine is that all tests serve a useful spiritual purpose now and hereafter but also that there is no need for any eternal temptations. The heritage we receive from our genetics and upbringing is important, but of far greater importance is the crucial personal power of our God-given agency and the stunning greatness of Christ, "who is mighty to save and to cleanse from all unrighteousness" (Alma 7:14).

We can learn to view suffering through the impressive understanding that comes from knowing true doctrine about the purpose of mortal testing—not simply to try us but also to make us ready for the incomprehensible joy of salvation (2 Nephi 32:9). I know from my own personal and numerous experiences with tremendous physical pain and the corresponding emotional hurt that accompanies it, the mental exhaustion that pervades it, and the spiritual testing that goes with it, that suffering is a means to an end—the end is our development. How grateful I am for divine comfort, the loving kindness of family and friends and for wise and caring medical professionals. I have been supported in these trials as God promised.

Of course, some losses are very pronounced, deeply felt, and last for mortality in its entirety. Thankfully such losses are only temporary, and the best is yet to come for us. Trouble can help us to be less selfish and to exert ourselves more to reach out and help others—this benefits our everlasting souls (2 Nephi 2:2). In some ways the gospel is truly at its strongest when life is at its most difficult. We need the gospel to help us to come through so many trials as stronger and better people and ultimately as celestial souls. Sorrow may make us more pliable in the hands of God.

17

A Very Fruitful Tree

We have a perfect scriptural illustration of the distinction between good and evil trees and hence good and evil fruit (3 Nephi 14:16–20). The Lord tells us that trees are known by what they produce. As thorns do not offer sweet grapes and thistles do not produce tasty figs, so likewise bad trees do not give us beautiful and tasty fruit. Good trees bring forth lovely fruit. Corrupt trees offer fruit that is not worthy of consumption. In fact, a good tree not only will not, but cannot give bad fruit. Likewise, a bad tree simply cannot produce fruit that is good. It is not possible according to the law of the Lord. Bad trees and bad fruit are burned. Good trees and good fruit are preserved to bless.

So it is with the children of God. The production of that which is corrupt traces back to corruption within. The good yield of that which is precious stems from goodness within. We are all producing some type of fruit—either good or bad—and what we produce depends upon us. If we want to be a fruitful tree in the garden of the Lord, our focus must be on being good seeds, good trees, and hence, producers of good fruit. It is a simple formula which each of us can follow.

THE GARDEN OF NEPHI

I want to highlight a touching revelation to Nephi in his garden (Helaman 10:4). God tells him that he is blessed for his works. God reveals to him that He is aware that he has taught the gospel without allowing himself to be tired, distracted, or diverted. God sees the persistence of Nephi! God also tells him that Nephi did not allow fear or interest in self-preservation to prevent him from preaching to hostile crowds. He plainly informs Nephi that his interest has been in doing the divine will and keeping divine commandments. What a great insight Nephi receives into his own soul! Not only does God know what Nephi has physically done, but He also knows the internal desires of his heart. God knows the inner man. God knows his efforts and his inclinations. God therefore pronounces blessings upon Nephi based on his persistent efforts to be faithful. God welcomes the achievement of Nephi in continually seeking to do the right things.

I am moved by the truth that Nephi was pouring out his soul in prayer for the redemption of his straying people atop a garden tower (Helaman 7:10). This makes me think of the temple. There surely is no more sacred place on the earth than a high point for divine communion located in a garden setting. We need a place of revelatory convergence between heaven and earth to express our deepest desires to God. Our temples are usually in garden settings and are elevated above the earth. They are well kept, beautiful, holy, sacred, set apart places that are not contaminated by the vulgar. They represent a pinnacle point that is higher than the sordid, lifted above the carnal, and removed from the base concerns of lowly living. God heard the pure prayer of Nephi and blessed him to bless His people. God sees which way we face. He knows we are in a fallen world. However, He knows when we are looking upwards, reaching higher, striving toward the divine. Settings of natural beauty are sublime places in which we can commune with God without the petty distractions that so often surround us. I have several places of natural loveliness where I have spent many, many hours in thought, prayer, reflection, and genuine calm. In such places, my soul has soared in renewal and determination to put off worldliness and rise in righteousness.

The Fruit-Yielding Tree

As wonderful as seeds and seedlings are, it is intended that we each become trees in God's Garden. And we are to be mighty towering trees with strong trunks, outstretched branches, and numerous leaves. As the glorious visions of Lehi and Nephi show us, the trees of life in scripture are majestic trees of beauty, light, life, splendor, and radiance. Trees of life offer precious and tasty fruit which brings joy to the souls of those who partake of it. Trees are good for life, shade, and protection from the elements. Trees live a long time and produce other trees. The Tree of Life is a symbol of God and His marvelous radiating love, which is an attractive beacon to our souls—like a lighthouse guiding a storm-tossed vessel home to safe shores.

Likewise, we can become living trees of life. Hence, we, like the master tree of life, are to be real and powerful symbols of the love of God as displayed in our coming into the world to perform our sacred ministries. We are to reach our divine potential in becoming more than a divine offspring with great potential—we are to accomplish much good and achieve the realization of our promised potential (1 Nephi 8:10–12; 11:8–9, 21–23; John 15:5). "For I, the Lord, will cause them to bring forth as a *very fruitful tree* which is *planted in a goodly land, by a pure stream, that yieldeth much precious fruit*" (Doctrine and Covenants 97:9, emphasis added).

What lovely imagery! What encouraging promises! Our highest nature is to receive nourishment and to give nurturing to others. We are to reach upwards to the light. We are to make a conscious choice to be good and hence to grow upwards, outwards, forwards, and onwards. Each seed can make the full and complete transition to becoming a tree. Our purpose in doing so is to gain joy everlasting and spread that loving joy to other seeds/trees around us. We are made for growth—nothing else will satisfy the divine desire for up-reaching implanted within us. We are to grow even when it might seem that conditions around us are not optimal. We are to grow through all seasons of our lives, with exceptional growth coming "in the season thereof."

The summers of our lives see warmth, heat, and light, and we may rejoice in these although they will perhaps sometimes be too warm or not warm enough. Of course, fall always comes and the leaves fall from the trees. In like manner, we will see some aging, decay, and death in our lives. However, fall also brings some lovely colors with it! In the dark winters of my life, I have metaphorically walked with Christ, knelt with, sat with, learned from, cried with, fasted with, served with, labored with, suffered with, and rejoiced with Him. He has been a travelling companion along the highways and byways. He has been my light in the dark, my solace in the storm, and my friend in adversity. Winter will bring cold and dark, but also Christmas! Spring will bring change, renewal, and much rain! We may not always anticipate these seasons, nor may others discern them accurately. Nevertheless, the Gardener is watching, cultivating, planning, and orchestrating. He is awake, aware, and acutely attuned to his plans and purposes. This growth occurs through being nourished, by being invited upwards and by progressing through obstacles. The very seasons are a symbol of the undulating patterns of our lives. All seasons bring both challenges and blessings.

TREES OF RIGHTEOUSNESS

The Lord has specifically declared that He sees the potential for His Zion people to be called "trees of righteousness" (Isaiah 61:3; Doctrine & Covenants 55:5). The Lord is aware of those among His pure people who mourn, experience affliction, and are burdened. He has great blessings in store for them. He wants to give them beauty, joy, and relief. He will turn this difficulty to their good. They will be trees of righteousness, the harvest of the Lord, His crop, His fruit trees, the fruition of all His labor and love. The law of the harvest teaches us that there is such a thing as a time to prepare, a time to plant, a time to cultivate, a time to nurture, a time to be patient, a time to harvest, and a time to enjoy the fruits of that harvest. I want to focus in this chapter on the result of all our hard work, consistent patience, persistent discipline, enduring love, and multi-dimensional efforts. Hard work is not just labor. Patience is not just waiting. Education is not just memorizing. Trials are not without meaning. Trying—even in the face of persistent failure—is not without significance. That outcome is found in the marvelous soul growth that comes to us and those around us as we labor in love, cultivate strength, develop loyalty, build a future, and act intentionally day after day, year after year—for an entire lifetime.

Cocreators with God

God is a creator—He organizes chaotic matter into something useful, He makes plans and fulfils them, He institutes laws that make opportunity possible. Consider the beautiful colors of the rainbow, the rich pattern of every snowflake and yet the unique design of each one, the majestic sounds that comprise music, the capacity that comes with spoken and written language, and myriad other examples. We experience great growth in this life. This development is in many ways godlike. For example, we expand in our capacity to turn confusion to understanding and chaos to order. We make plans, we devise schedules, we aim for deadlines, we pursue goals, and we accomplish creative acts through vision and work. Whether we are involved in sculpting, composing, playing music, writing poetry, acting in plays, working with wood, performing dance, crafting metal, making art, or engaging in architecture or other creative enterprises, we are truly learning to be like the Great Creator of all things.

A Culture of Excellence

I see inspired art, beautiful music, superb literature, wonderful science, heavenly sculpting, academic prowess, and athletic accomplishment as indicators that God is opening our senses to greater ability and capacity. Of course, in the purest sense, only God can polish our capabilities in ways that represent the greatest good, the deepest marvels, and the most beneficial wonders—in both time and eternity. As we gravitate toward God, He improves all our faculties. Indeed, I sense that as we have our capacities opened by the power of God, that every aspect of our being is enlarged, refined, magnified, expanded, purified, and elevated. The celestial gospel is a culture of excellence. As we turn away from the petty, self-seeking, combative, arrogant stance of the natural person, we start to acquire an attitude of seeking for those things that are good, beautiful, and worthy of emulation. Our sincere quest becomes for improvement. Everything we aspire to then reflects God's marvelous excellence in all things. The tree we become is one of sublime loveliness. This may seem like an impossible objective, but with God, it is not.

Garden of Remembering

There are so many vital things that we need to retain in remembrance during this testing school of mortality. One of the most important things is our divine nature and destiny. It is very easy to lose our focus on who and what we are, including our essential purpose in this life. We are well advised to remember that we are created for glory—not in the sense of narcissistic self-aggrandizement—but surely in the sense of the glory of growth toward divinity, of progress toward becoming great trees in the garden of the Lord—much like mighty oaks grow tall and strong. We can remember that we are to be trees that are not removed from the garden of God: "Wherefore, stand ye in holy places, and be not moved" (Doctrine & Covenants 87:8). This is what trees do—they stand in the place they are planted! The trees we are talking about here are firm, steadfast, grounded, deep-rooted, strong, and do not get blown down by the wind, moved by the floods, or chopped down by enemies. They remember the purpose of their planting—to remain in their appointed place and to bear fruit. These trees endure so that they can witness the return of the Gardener!

Tower of Security

The man we call Captain Moroni was not a casual and careless commander. He actively prepared his people to defend themselves against inevitable encroachments from enemies. This required vision, planning, effort, and endurance. We are told that he created towers of security to protect his people (Alma 50:4). Hence, the towers needed to be higher than the pickets and the secure places needed to be upon the towers. This sense of elevation gave the Nephites a real advantage over the attacking Lamanites.

In like manner, our perspective as we tower in spiritual growth above the ground becomes much clearer. We are far less likely to be caught off guard by those who would seek to chop at our foundations to destroy our progress. We need to have that sense of lofty vision—not pride or arrogance—but a sense of reaching for heaven. That is the only type of vantage point that will keep us safe as we strive for character progress in the challenging circumstances of the last days.

The Deep Things of God

I believe in the deep potential that lies nested within each one of us. It is initially latent, untapped, and in embryonic form. However, God is calling it forth. He is speaking to you and me. He is whispering gently, but with determination. He is inviting us to look up, reach up, grow up, and stand up tall. He has some deep doctrines to share with us, some deep experiences for us to pass through, and some deep transformations for us to encounter. Is the growth He has in mind for us simple or complex? Is it superficial or deep? Is it easy or hard? I think the answer to those questions is that maturity allows us to grow beyond the simplicity of childhood to the complexity of adulthood. Real growth requires more than simply surface change—it demands profound internal alteration and magnification. True development is both challenging and majestic. I sense that He wants something for us far more grand than we may envision for ourselves. The natural man or woman is content with the easy carefree life, an existence without great difficulty, a path without struggle.

God is calling forth the deep glory within us, the sense of the majestic, the nobility of soul that can only come with growing through hardship. We are to stretch, increase, expand, and soar in the things of the spirit. We are to reach higher than we ever have before, to confront all foes, to dig deep within our souls, to become tremendous in understanding, comprehension, character, and wisdom. Thus, we need to face the complexity of every bittersweet adventure, to come to know the depths of sorrow, and to be propelled heavenward like a mighty oak. We are to come to know God through the full range of educational emotions, physical experiences, social interchanges, spiritual learnings, and intellectual strivings. This is to be an experiential education in the nature and character of God. Hence, we are to become intimately acquainted with the deep things of God.

The Thoughts, Language, and Behavior of the Lord

As we grow toward divinity, we come to see the holy in life. We move away from thinking thoughts based on carnality, sensuality, and depravity and develop thought patterns of virtue, selflessness, achievement, accomplishment, and hope. Our mindset shifts toward a higher order. We aspire to think on heavenly things. As we mature in the things of God, our speech changes. We move away from language that is crass, crude, vulgar, cynical, critical, sardonic, and brash. In its place we cultivate expressions of cleanliness, purity, optimism, praise, kindness, and love. With development in the things of God our actions transform from the dishonest, lowly, vengeful, and spiteful to the truthful, inspiring, gentle, respectful, decent, and striving for the good. Our works and deeds become grounded in spirituality, morality, and sanctity.

A World Reborn

I have had some wonderfully powerful, moving, and vivid dreams that I have never forgotten. I have sensed some ethereal, melodious, and touching words, music, and images beyond what I have ever sensed in normal life. I have envisaged being transported from a dull world to a new world of beauty, color, song, imagination, and miraculous realities. For me, these dreams have meant that the Son of God will yet transform the world from a dark and dreary wilderness to a land of glorious abundance. This applies to both my personal world within and the material world around me.

God is the creator of our earthly home (1 Nephi 17:36). The Lord wants the earth to be lived upon by His dear children. Thus, God is able and willing to save the entire earth. He can save not only seeds and trees (individuals) and forests (families), but also the entire Garden (world). He is in fact the Lord of the whole earth (Doctrine & Covenants 55:1). In the last days, the House (family) of Israel will flourish wherever they are located (including in deserts, wilderness areas, and mountains) and shall do so in unexpected ways (Doctrine and Covenants 49:24–25). Miraculous blossoming will occur (Doctrine and Covenants 117:6–7). God who made all things will bring growth and abundance to His entire garden. This will impact all forms of life and all things upon the earth in a positive way. All those who live in harmony with God's word will find that deserts will be no more, barrenness will yield to life, war will bow to peace, poverty will bend to riches, and despair will submit to hope. The Church and Kingdom of God on the earth has a critical role to play in preparing the earth and all nations and peoples for this transformation to a new world order based on spiritual blossoming. No other organization has the power to change the world in the grand ways that the earthly kingdom of Christ can and must.

Indeed, faithful individuals build strong families, and united families build a powerful Church. Callings, service, and community love benefit the Church and the world. One world in Christ—meaning one united planet Garden—comes through the consistent efforts to unite in the work of salvation in all aspects. As the Church of God becomes the Kingdom of God then the whole world is better prepared for the transition to a terrestrial paradise that commences with the Second Coming of Christ in magnificent glory. Christ created the earth, and He will save the whole earth at the end of the world. His power is one of creative redemption. In this sense, the Lord is both the author and finisher of the creative process for this planet.

The Millennial Garden

It is clear from holy writ that the earth and the skies will be made new at the Second Coming of Christ. The waste places will become productive, the wild will be tamed, the polluted will be cleansed, and the corrupted made pure. Places scorched and barren will become full of beautiful life. This process of renewal will be a blessing to the land, plants, animals, waters, and to the people who abide on the earth. This will be a time of great rejoicing, new gratitude, pronounced happiness, and powerful singing. The transition to terrestrial living will include all things on the earth. Then this earth will be even more beautiful and holy than it is now. It will be a day of new revelation, of uncovering of secrets, of dispensing mysteries, of learning hidden things. These will be plain and precious things of great importance, things worth knowing about. These will be days of increased light, magnified knowledge, expanded comprehension, of finding answers to questions we have not even considered yet (Ether 13:9; 2 Nephi 8:3; 3 Nephi 20:22; Isaiah 4:2; Doctrine and Covenants 101:30–34).

It is significant to note that the earth will be thoroughly cleansed in a baptism of fire when the Savior purifies it from all evil. The elements shall melt with fervent heat in a refining act of spiritual upgrading. Can anyone conceive of the impact of this cleansing? The scale and scope will be astounding and far-reaching. All vice removed, all iniquity banished, all crime vanished, all sickness revoked. There will be an initial upgrade to the earth and all things on the face of it from telestial to terrestrial living conditions—this will mean an immediate improvement in living conditions as so many worldly things will be removed. Envision this:

> No need for police, criminal lawyers, judges, or prisons!
> An internet devoid of dishonesty, immorality, contention!
> Fruit yielding trees and vegetable providing ground that never gave produce before!
> No natural disasters, no war, no famine, no financial crashes!
> Children born in health, plenteous food, honest and fulfilling work, refreshing recreation, opportunities to serve, joyous music, amazing art, wonderful drama, excellent architecture!
> Lands of promise, healed relationships, new friendships, association with resurrected beings, close-knit covenant communities, righteous government!

However, even this greatly refined earth will still only be a preparation for a greater world yet to come when the covenant faithful will "possess it again in eternity, no more to pass away" (Doctrine and Covenants 38:20). Thus, the new Garden of Eden that arrives with the Millennium is only a precursor to a more glorious world to come. That means the benefits and blessings of those one thousand years are temporary. However, the eternal possession of the earth for the faithful family of God will bring even greater bounties, treasures, and qualities. This pertains both to the earth itself and to our personal experience and family opportunities.

The Celestial Garden

We are instructed that the meek are blessed with an earthly inheritance (3 Nephi 12:5). This new earth will be transformed to a "sanctified, immortal, and eternal state" (Doctrine and Covenants 77:1). I cannot imagine a better home than that! We know that fully redeemed souls will inherit a completely righteous, celestial earth where the sanctified Father will abide in eternity (Doctrine and Covenants 88:14–20). What promises these are! The humble will receive the blessing, in due course, of abiding on the purified earth as a matter of family inheritance. What is an inheritance? It is what we receive from our loving parents. It is our legacy, our birthright. This earth will be our inheritance—our rightful home, our blessed abode, our sanctuary of love, our place of riches. The humble will see the full flowering of this earth to its great and grand destiny. It will be like unto a sea of transparent glass, a great Urim and Thummin of knowledge, light, understanding, and comprehension. It will then contain no noxious weeds, no distressing illness, no fractured relationships, no broken hearts, no destroyed dreams, and no repugnant evils. It will be glorified beyond what we can presently envision.

This will be more than a new Garden of Eden. This will be greater than any previous paradise. Why? Because we will then be different than we were before. We will be new—in mind, heart, spirit, and body. We will have knowledge, comprehension, gratitude, and capacity we never knew until we have been changed in the ultimate way. We are refined through experience, edified by excellence, made better through struggle. It will be a new world of additional opportunities, healed relationships, tender love, pure priesthood power, and endless life. This will be the ultimate place of heavenly peace, of eternal rest, of ebullient joy, of everlasting glory. My belief is that our resurrected bodies will be composed of the sanctified elements of this ultra-purified earth and hence they will not be subject to the carnality that our flesh is presently subject to (Doctrine & Covenants 88:29). This gives me great hope that our goodness will be expanded and increased in the Resurrection beyond what it is capable of now. That is comforting doctrine. This celestial earth will be purified, beautiful, and holy to a degree never seen before on this planet. I imagine that the sights, sounds, tastes, smells, and touch will be elevated beyond anything we can presently conceive of. The bounteous beauty will be spectacular.

Clearly, the full meaning of becoming a Tree of Life lies in the eternities. We will continue to grow and develop after this mortal life. In eternal lives we will find new children belonging to us. The resurrection glory will be far beyond mortal privilege. We will be radiant, glorious, and full of love forever. In eternity, we will never cease to know love, joy, happiness, and knowledge. We will be beings of light, vessels of love, and persons of power. Indeed, we will know a fulness of joy, life, creative capacity, and light.

18

Garden of Beauty

I HAD A DREAM AS A YOUNG MISSIONARY THAT I HAVE NEVER FORGOTTEN. In my dream, I was covered with strong chains in a dark and depressing dungeon. There was no way I could escape to freedom without help. Then, I saw a large vat of hot acid. I immediately knew it was the kind that burns. Suddenly, my branch president from my home branch was there. I sensed that he had the opportunity to free me from my prison if he was just willing to put his arm into the container of acid. He looked at me with concern, then looked at the acid. Then he said sorry to me and went away (incidentally he was a good man in real life and a real people person but there were some things he could just never do for me). It was evident he would not do what it took to save me.

Then another man entered. I recognized Him immediately. It was my Lord. He looked at me and then at the vat of acid. He then smiled at me with the most beautiful smile of love I had ever witnessed either in a dream or reality up to that time in my life. He proceeded to put His entire arm in the vat and screamed terribly. I was immediately released from my chains. I woke up with fright and intense sorrow. I had tears in my eyes. However, I also felt greater relief than I could ever explain.

I have never forgotten that dream, which was thirty years ago. My understanding of the Atonement of Christ took on new meaning for me on that night. I have taught it differently since then. I know with all my soul that Christ has a love for me that surpasses the love of even great mortal men. I know that He is the loving shepherd of my soul. I see differently because of being able to see, in some small measure, my life through His eyes. I likewise know that He feels this way for you also. His love for you surpasses understanding.

I believe it is vital for each of us to catch the mighty vision of our lives. I see the rich beauty of us being like a seed in God's Garden. We can be a good seed—able to grow, capable of development, destined to produce after our kind in the likeness of divinity. We can only grow to our full potential in a garden setting. Although we all must pass through the veil of tears, the mist of darkness, and the lone and dreary world, it is vital to remember that this mortal life is not our ultimate destination. All of us spend some time in the depths of despair, in the gutter of difficulty, in the land of loneliness.

But then we catch a glimpse of a higher place. We see a high mountain, a forest of fortitude, an altar of supplication, a Temple of Holiness. God calls to us and we feel a stirring within. We recognize a voice, albeit a whisper. It is a voice we know. It is a message we trust. It is a love we remember. The Father and the Son beckon to us with outstretched arms. We ascend to some pinnacle points—sacred places where God touches our hearts, opens our eyes, whispers in our ears, and unveils our understanding. We sense something special. It is a new view, a different vantage point, a revelatory hope. This new view of ourselves will inspire, encourage, and motivate us powerfully and lastingly. We can thereby transcend the limiting beliefs that occupy this telestial world. We can rise to a Christlike view of ourselves.

I would like to give some practical examples of the principles I have been sharing. No doubt you will see many examples I do not mention. This book has been an attempt to jump-start a very personal dialogue within you. It is a conversation you will have with yourself. As you reflect on the way you presently see yourself and the way God sees you, I believe this will spark within you a voyage of discovery to a new place. A place of greater contentment, peace, and hope for you personally. A destination and way of traveling inspired by a sense of revelatory vision.

God's School

This world is like the school of the Lord. We are each a student in God's school. We start as an infant in kindergarten and can eventually be a teacher/professor in God's University. We can learn and teach. We can be a good student in God's school—focused, interested, engaged, and empowered. We obtain the treasure of knowledge as we learn and teach in God's school. We are surrounded by the classrooms and the curriculum of the Lord. Now is the time to gain great education through our perception and diligence.

God's Fold

The people of this world are invited into the fold of the Lord. He is the great shepherd. We are his sheep. We can be guided, led, and protected. We can each be a good sheep in God's fold. More than this, we can learn to guide and protect the flock and become true under-shepherds. We are followers who can become leaders. We are ministered to and learn to minister to others.

God's Business

We can be a good employee in God's business. With training and experience, we can become trusted to be an executive, then a partner. We start out stocking shelves and sweeping floors (there is no dishonor in this). As we mature in our apprenticeship, we see ourselves as potential decision makers and collaborators in the business. We gain confidence and competence and invest in the business. We are not just being provided for, but we learn to provide for others.

God's Mountain

We are a climber on God's Mountain. We start as a nervous climber and eventually become a trained guide who can safely lead others as they climb the mountains of life toward great achievement themselves.

God's Police Force/Fire Department/ Army/Navy/Air Force

We start out as an officer and gain experience so that we can obtain more dependability and eventually become a chief with responsibility to manage others in their efforts. A good soldier can become a candidate to be a general. Thus, we increase our capacity to protect those under our stewardship.

God's Airline

We begin as a passenger. Then we become part of cabin crew. Then we get our pilot training. We can graduate from copilot to captain after appropriate apprenticeship. In this role, we can bring others safely to where they need to go—the Kingdom of Heaven.

God's Hospital

We commence as a good patient and receive the healing we need. Then we turn our attention to wanting to heal others. We get our medical training and become a doctor. Eventually, we become a consultant surgeon who can help numerous people to heal and heal others. We become a doctor of healing.

God's Courtroom

This world is the Lord's Courtroom. Each of us is a witness in the courtroom of life. We need to learn to discern the courtroom drama for what it really is and distinguish good from evil, heroes from villains, truth from lies. As we learn from the Master judge, we can become qualified to discern darkness from light. We can become lawyers and judges ourselves. We can separate reality and illusion. We can each be a good witness/lawyer. We can help others detect truth and error. We can advise others in wise ways. We can in due course become a good judge ourselves.

God's Workshop

A good apprentice can become a good blacksmith, carpenter, or mason. As such, they can learn to cleanse, purify, refine, strengthen, and mold metal, wood, or stone into the shape it needs to take to be useful and constructive. A master craftsperson can bless others through the gifts, skills, and abilities they have acquired through observation and careful practice.

God's Book

This world is like a book in the hands of the Almighty. We are each a character in the unfolding plot. We can become a good character, contributing to the victorious success of a difficult story. We can in due course become a writer, crafting stories that inspire, encourage, and ennoble others.

God's Drama

We are involved in an emerging divine drama. We are both actors and spectators in the play of life. What will our role be? What legacy will we leave? Will we be a hero or villain? Only we can determine whether our acting (actions) will be based on duplicity or undergirded by honesty. If we learn the lessons well, we will become not simply a side-line spectator, or even an active actor—we will become a creative director, giving power to words and life to plots.

God's Choir/Orchestra

We each have a role to play in the Choir of the Lord. We can be a serious singer that brings our commitment to the project. It is good to not hold back and yet to avoid trying to upstage everyone else. We sing for God's glory. Or perhaps we may be an instrumentalist in the Orchestra of the Lord. We may play our instrument well or poorly. We may turn up for practice or neglect our studies. We may daydream or direct our attention conscientiously. As we seek to play a productive role as a performer in the production of the Lord, then we will know the great joy of effort and contribution. Our gift will shine. Our light will motivate others. The beauty of the performance will be world class. Eventually, we will become the choir/orchestra director. Then, we will give voice in joyful harmony to an audience eager to witness musical gifts expressed in perfect collaboration.

God's Government

The universe is governed by God. He presides over it in perfect righteousness. As a servant in God's benign empire, we have a vital work to do, a core role to play. Our service is unique. This is not a lowly station but a mighty privilege. To serve is to save. We are also learning how to be leaders in God's administration. We are destined to become ministers in a cabinet of selfless service. Goodness is central to our function. Righteous leadership is powerful, influential, and worthy.

God's Temple

The Garden of the Lord is a temple sanctuary. We are like a stone in that temple. We are not unimportant, irrelevant, or invisible to God. We are needed to hold the structure together. We play a part in contributing to the building of that sacred structure. As we seek to be a strength to the overall building, then we can become an architect and builder of temples. As Christ is the Rock, the Stone of Israel, we can likewise be one who supports and sustains the work of constructing, edifying, and maintaining holy places.

God's Kingdom

This earth is in truth the Kingdom of our Lord. He is the perfect King. He is the great Sovereign, whose primary concern is the true well-being of His subjects. His Kingdom is intended to be one of great glory. We are like subjects who serve in the royal garden or like knights in royal armor protecting the land. We are also His apprentice princes and princesses. We can learn to be trained by Him. We are dignitaries, royalty, chosen for a work of grandeur now and eternally.

Gradually, we can learn to rule and reign as Kings and Queens. We can each become a person of good nobility in God's Kingdom.

I love to ponder the core concept of Hymn No. 284, "If You could Hie to Kolob." There is no end to:

- worlds, matter, space, light
- spirit, race, priesthood, being, life
- wisdom, might, virtue, love, union, truth, glory
- work, improvement, progression, youth

What a revelation! My spirit senses the truth of these words. I cannot conceive of ceasing to exist. For mortals that is not always a pleasant thought. I believe this is because we often think in human ways. We do not think entirely like God does. He is not bored with the realities of eternity. In some way incomprehensible to us presently, God lives in a state of perpetual glory. He lives life to the full. He treasures eternity. It is not an interminable pain to Him to be alive forever. He lives in a state of blissful glory. There is no finality to His existence. This is not solemn gloom for Him. He wants to live. He loves to bless. He relishes creation. He rejoices to help us become amazing vessels of every good attribute and noble power He already possesses. This is the core doctrine and marvelous truth that inspired this hymn that focuses us on eternal powers and principles. This is what awaits us as we come to terms with the never-ending nature of celestial brilliance!

See Yourself through the Eyes of Your King

See yourself through divine eyes. Envision yourself as someone who matters to God, for you truly do. Picture yourself as precious in His view, as notable in His perspective, as special in His considerations. This is not hyperbole, arrogance, delusion of grandeur, or misplaced conceit. This is humbling doctrine. It is transformative. God's loving concern for you and for me is astounding while also being understandable. Who else would be the focus of His affection, the object of His interest, the reason for His plans?

The Lord told His apostles in Jerusalem that "*I am the vine, ye are the branches*: He that abideth in me, and I in him, the *same bringeth forth much fruit*: for without me ye can do nothing" (John 15:5, emphasis added). In other words, His life gives life to those who follow Him. His love flows through us, His thoughts become ours, His joys are mirrored in our rejoicings. We are not separate and distinct from Him. We are connected at the roots and united in the fruits! You and I are part of Him and He is part of us. We are of the same family. We are to be one—finding nourishment from the same life-giving truths, powers, and blessings! I am therefore assured by the everlasting truth that the Savior Jesus Christ:

- loves your soul
- sees your goodness
- cultivates your opportunities
- recognizes your possibilities
- applauds your efforts
- values your promises
- rejoices in your growth
- respects your discernment
- encourages your character
- admires your victories
- honors your influence
- appreciates your refinements
- welcomes your achievements
- connects your family
- preserves your righteousness
- sees you in glorious grandeur

Thus, imagine yourself a million years from now. See yourself in robes of light, with a countenance of love, with a forever family, in a place of peaceful abundance. Envision yourself in a glory beyond words. Recognize the deep divinity within you. See yourself with the shackles of sin removed, the limitations of disease taken away, the barrier of ignorance broken, the sorrows of your life put into eternal perspective. Behold yourself in a kingdom of creative opportunity exploring all your talents, exercising all your gifts, pursuing all your interests, utilizing all your powers. Know yourself as being one with others you love, those you admire, those you relate to, those that you have come to resemble. Sense yourself as obtaining the fulness of character, the richness of eternal knowledge, the substance of all that is available in time and eternity. Picture yourself as a vessel of joy, a being of light, a person of love, a man or woman of Christ. This is how He sees you.

Truly, we can be richly cultivated by and in Christ. We can reach perfection in Him. We can find peace in Him. We can know hope, love, and joy through Him. Indeed, all good, true, and beautiful things find fulfilment in and through Him. You and I are to be clothed in the same all-encompassing robes of righteousness as He is (see 2 Nephi 4:33). He hopes that you will see yourself as He sees you—as someone of deep importance who is worth loving and worth investing in on a long-term basis. You matter to Him, and your life is significant. Know that you are loved. You really are. You are a sublime seed in God's magnificent Garden. His vision is for you to become a towering mighty living tree in His presence, to be part of a fruitful forest in His eternal home, to abide eternally in the exalted Eden that never ends. His view of you is glorious. May you see yourself through the eyes of Christ's perfect love, now and always. You are loved by Him—forever!

Notes

Notes

Notes

About the Author

THOMAS HOLTON LIVES IN IRELAND.

He has graduated from three universities and completed two years toward a professional diploma in financial planning.

He has taught English, mathematics, and taxation. He has worked in insurance, tax advice, and financial and legal management.

His Church service includes a mission to England, temple ordinance worker, adult Sunday School teacher four times, ward mission leader twice, Sunday School president three times, elders quorum president twice, branch Young Men president, a member of branch presidencies/bishoprics for fourteen years, stake high councilor, and Church history specialist for the island of Ireland.

He credits the Lord for helping him endure health challenges for twenty-five years.

He is also the author of *Alive in Christ.*

He and his wife, Veronica, are the thankful parents of one son.